MAJOR McKINLEY

Major McKinley

WILLIAM McKINLEY
& THE CIVIL WAR

WILLIAM H. ARMSTRONG

THE KENT STATE
UNIVERSITY PRESS
Kent, Ohio, & London

© 2000 by
The Kent State University Press,
Kent, Ohio 44242
All rights reserved
Library of Congress Catalog Card
Number 99-048531
ISBN 0-87338-657-4
Manufactured in the United States of
America

07 06 05 04 03 02 01 00
5 4 3 2 1

Frontispiece: Private William McKinley
Jr. *Courtesy of the Stark County Historical
Society, Canton, Ohio.*

Library of Congress Cataloging-in-
Publication Data
Armstrong, William H.
(William Howard), 1932–
Major McKinley : William McKinley
and the Civil War / William H.
Armstrong.
p.   cm.
Includes bibliographical references
and index.
ISBN 0-87338-657-4 (pbk.: alk. paper) ∞
1. McKinley, William, 1843–1901.
2. McKinley, William, 1843–1901—
Military leadership.   3. Soldiers—
United States—Biography.   4. United
States. Army—Biography.
5. Presidents—United States—
Biography.   6. Ohio—History—Civil
War, 1861–1865.   I. Title.
E711.6.A76   2000
973.8'8'092—dc21
[B]   99-048531

British Library Cataloging-in-
Publication data are available.

TO *Gloria* WITH LOVE

The one thing which [McKinley] cherishes most in

his heart is that in his youth he was a soldier . . . of the

Grand Army of the Republic.

—John D. Long

CONTENTS

ILLUSTRATIONS AND MAPS

MAPS

PREFACE

William Allen White, the editor of the *Emporia (Kansas) Gazette*, could not fathom William McKinley. He found him "a handsome man, with a matinee idol's virility," but try as he might, he could see only the surface of the man, and he questioned whether there was anything significant underneath. Observing McKinley on a campaign swing through Kansas, White found him "too polite, too meticulous. . . . His Prince Albert coat was never wrinkled, his white vest front never broken." He was "gentle but always, it seemed to me, carefully calculated. . . . He was unreal."[1]

Some years later, after meeting McKinley at his Canton, Ohio, home and in the White House, White still could not find what he called "the real man back of that plaster cast which was his public mask." He was convinced that McKinley was "destined for a statue in a park, and was practicing the pose for it. . . . He had somewhere back in his youth or young manhood, possibly as a soldier in the war, buttoned himself up, and had become almost unconsciously the figure that stands now in Canton not far from his front door—William McKinley in bronze."[2]

If only White could have known McKinley thirty years earlier, when he was a soldier in the war, before he "buttoned himself up." He would have found a very different man: a carefree young private on sentry duty who allowed a tall, thin officer to pass and then called out to a friend—in the officer's hearing—"Say Jake did you ever see such a clothes pin of an officer as that fellow?"; a staff officer who, caught up in the excitement of a nearby cavalry charge, left the side of his commanding officer to join the charge and had to be reprimanded for his courageous but unauthorized conduct; a youth so captivated by a young and beautiful "damsel" in Maryland that some of his friends were "seriously alarmed" about his state of mind. If White had known McKinley then, he would have realized that, whatever the truth about the later politician, the McKinley of the Civil War years was "real." It is that McKinley, the gallant, high-spirited soldier— "as hot-headed as the average man when young," as he put it—rather than the cautious, self-controlled politician of later years whose story is told here.[3]

This is the story of an eighteen-year-old youth who enlisted as a private and marched in the ranks but whose abilities soon caught the attention of his officers and then of his commander, Rutherford B. Hayes, who obtained a commission for him and added him to his military staff. McKinley later served on the staffs of four other general officers and ended his service as adjutant of a division and a brevet major. He was the last of the Civil War veterans to reach the White House and the only one who had served in the ranks.

It is the story, too, of the war as he knew it: hard mountain marches and ruthless guerrilla warfare in West Virginia; crowded train rides and long marches back and forth between West Virginia and the battlefields in the East; long processions of the mule-drawn supply wagons he oversaw as a commissary sergeant and quartermaster; and bloody battles at Carnifex Ferry, South Mountain, Antietam, Cloyd's Mountain, Lynchburg, Kernstown, Berryville, Opequon, Fisher's Hill, and Cedar Creek. By the war's end, only 131 of the more than 2,000 Union regiments had more men killed in action or dead of wounds than McKinley's regiment, the 23d Ohio Volunteer Infantry.[4]

To understand the young soldier and his war is to understand better the mature man, for McKinley's military service colored his entire career. Service in the same army as those he called "black allies," who "must neither be deserted nor forsaken," led him to champion the civil rights of the freed slaves long after they had been abandoned by others. At the same time, his service as a Union soldier gave him the credibility to grasp the hands of the former Confederate soldiers and promote reconciliation between North and South. And his firsthand observations of such men as George Crook, Winfield Scott Hancock, and Philip Sheridan gave him the experience and confidence he exhibited as commander in chief in the war with Spain. Those who knew him well recognized the significance of his military career by calling him always—whether he was county prosecutor, member of Congress, governor, or president—"Major McKinley."[5]

Growing up as I did in Stark County, Ohio—where McKinley settled after the war—meant that William McKinley has been a part of my life as long as I can remember. The McKinley Monument in Canton was only a few miles

The author at the McKinley Monument in Canton, Ohio, in the summer of 1937.

away, and the park adjacent to it was a favorite place for family picnics. A small hospital stood where McKinley's home had once stood; our oldest son was born in that hospital. I was fascinated by the stories told by my mother's cousin C. L. Riley, a teacher at McKinley High School in Canton. When he was nine years old, his family had taken him to Canton frequently to witness the famous Front Porch Campaign of 1896. "The weeds grew high in our corn" that year, he said; events in Canton were too exciting to stay at home on the farm. After McKinley became president, Riley's great-uncle Washington Kelley (my great-great-uncle) took him to visit McKinley. During the Civil War, Kelley had been quartermaster of the 9th Indiana Volunteer Infantry—Ambrose Bierce's regiment—and had known McKinley from their service together in West Virginia. He renewed his friendship with the president at McKinley's home on North Market Street in Canton, while Riley, sitting on a little rocking chair McKinley had

thoughtfully brought out for him, watched and listened, captivated by
their conversation about the war. When McKinley died, my grandparents
took Riley with them to view the president's body at the Stark County
Courthouse. Later, they found a place across the street from the McKinley home, where they sat and watched the dignitaries come and go. Finally, they hurried to Westlawn Cemetery to see the president laid to rest.

My long-standing interest in McKinley was rekindled when I came
across the diary he kept during the first months of the Civil War. As I began
to investigate his early years, I discovered still other family ties to McKinley. My great-grandfather George Washington Henning had taught with
McKinley's sister Anna, and at least one of Henning's children had been her
student. Henning and McKinley, one a draft-resisting Democrat and the
other a Republican veteran, once put their differences aside and spoke from
the same platform, an event that plays a small part in the story that follows.
This study, then, has been a labor of love, giving me a glimpse of my own
heritage while visiting a part of McKinley's past.

I owe a debt of gratitude to McKinley biographer H. Wayne Morgan. I was
a stranger to him when I asked him about the feasibility of a study of Mc-
Kinley's military service, but he gladly offered his advice and gave me
his encouragement, for which I thank him. I am grateful also to the late
Hudson Hyatt—a descendant of McKinley's cousin Sarah Miller and her
husband, William K. Miller—and Hudson's wife, Helen, for sharing their
knowledge of McKinley with me. Many other people helped to make this
book possible, especially Henry Dirks and Kay Hollestelle, who offered
their hospitality while I was doing research in Washington, D.C.; Russell
Karcher, who kept me informed about current developments in McKinley's
hometown of Canton, Ohio; Dr. and Mrs. Richard Waters, who opened
their home to me as a place where I could read the Civil War letters of
Benjamin L. Askue Jr.; and all the helpful librarians and archivists who
cheerfully answered my many questions about McKinley and the Civil War
and helped make this a better book than it might otherwise have been.

ONE *Private*

I always look back with pleasure upon those fourteen months during which I served in the ranks. They taught me a great deal. I was but a schoolboy when I went into the army, and that first year was a formative period in my life, during which I learned much of men and facts. I have always been glad that I entered the service as a private, and served those months in that capacity.

—*William McKinley*

When Fort Sumter surrendered and President Abraham Lincoln called for seventy-five thousand volunteers to suppress the rebellion, an enormous wave of patriotism swept over the Northern states. In Ohio, which had been challenged to raise thirteen regiments of soldiers, Governor William Dennison telegraphed the War Department that "without seriously repressing the ardor of the people, I can hardly stop short of twenty." Military companies quickly formed in communities across the state, and within a few days troops began to arrive in Columbus, eager to go to war.[1]

In the small town of Poland, in Ohio's Western Reserve, a war meeting was held four days after Lincoln's call for volunteers. The meeting adopted unanimous resolutions expressing "eternal hostility to traitors and rebels" and pledging "our lives and sacred honor in defence of the Union and our country's flag." Three different military companies were organized, including the Poland Guards, composed of young men from Poland, nearby Lowellville, and the surrounding countryside, many of them students at the Poland academy. The Poland Guards, led by Capt. William Zimmerman, who had gained some military experience as a private in a militia company in Pennsylvania, were soon drilling on the church green

1

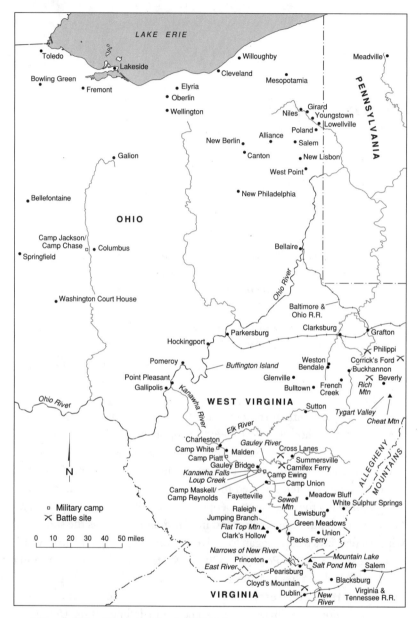

Ohio and West Virginia. *Map by Bill Nelson.*

and in the school yard, and the men and women of the town were busy making clothes for them.[2]

First Lt. William Rice was sent to Columbus to see if the company would be accepted by the state. When he was assured that it would be, he returned to Poland, and the men began to drill every day except Sunday in preparation for their departure for Columbus on June 6. On that day, the eighty-six members of the company, dressed in dark gray woolen shirts, gathered for religious exercises in the Presbyterian church and then marched to the Sparrow House, a local tavern, where Havelock caps and New Testaments were presented to the men, a Bible to the company's chaplain, and swords to Zimmerman and Rice. The swords were presented by Charles E. Glidden, a local attorney, during "an able and patriotic address" to the officers and men of the company. Then the Guards started off for nearby Youngstown to board a train to Cleveland and Columbus, accompanied by a brass band, a "beautiful flag," and some seven hundred citizens in a cavalcade of wagons and carriages stretching two miles along the road. At Youngstown, they were met by several military companies that led them to the depot, where they were sent off to loud cheers from the crowd.[3]

Among those who accompanied the Poland Guards to Youngstown were two cousins, William McKinley Jr. of Poland—known to family and friends as William or Will—and William McKinley Osborne of nearby Girard, who was living with McKinley's family and studying law and was also known as Will. The day's events and especially the speech of Charles Glidden at the Sparrow House had deeply impressed them. McKinley said later that Glidden's speech had been "full of patriotic sentiments, and I remember, too, that the speaker quoted some poetry that moved me, but what it was I do not recall, but I was thrilled by it." McKinley had thought about volunteering earlier but "decided to wait and study the situation a little more carefully first. I wanted to see how the boys lived in camp, and wished to understand myself so thoroughly that I would not regret any action I might decide to take." On their way back to Poland the two cousins decided it was their duty to enlist; they had also concluded that enlisting was the only way to keep the community's respect. McKinley told his mother about their decision and asked her permission to go to war. He said she put her arms around his neck and told him, sobbing: "William, I never shall see you again." But he assured her that he would come back to her "alive and well." In the end she gave her permission, as did Will Osborne's father.[4]

Will Osborne said that their enlistment was "in cold blood, and not through the enthusiasm of the moment. It was done as McKinley has done the most things of his life, as the logical offspring of careful conclusion." McKinley himself said, "I came to a deliberate conclusion, and have never been sorry for it." Deliberate as his actions were—and one of his later associates, Joseph Foraker, said that McKinley was the most deliberate man he ever knew—McKinley had volunteered out of a deep sense of patriotism. In a speech after the war, he attributed to all the volunteers the feelings that had motivated him. "They enlisted in the army," he said, "with no expectation of promotion; not for the paltry pittance of pay; not for fame or popular applause. . . . They entered the army moved by the highest and purest motives of patriotism, that no harm might befall the Republic."[5]

McKinley and Osborne left for Columbus on June 11, five days after the Poland Guards had gone. The next day, they arrived at Camp Jackson, four miles west of Columbus, where they found the Guards, McKinley said, "in the best of spirits, feeling glad that they had enlisted in so high and noble a warfare—the protection of the American government and the destruction of rebels and traitors." On June 13, the Poland Guards, including McKinley and Osborne, were mustered into the service of the United States.[6]

The mustering officer, John C. Robinson, a captain in the 5th United States Infantry, thought McKinley looked so young that he asked how old he was and whether he had the consent of his parents. At eighteen, McKinley was one of the youngest members of the Guards, and standing only five feet six and one-quarter inches and weighing only about 125 pounds, the pale youth looked even younger. But, one of McKinley's comrades said, "the answers of the recruit were so prompt and so decisive, and his desire so very modest, only asking to be enrolled as a private, that the officer without further hesitation administered the oath" to him. With their right hands upraised, the Poland Guards swore "true allegiance" to the United States and affirmed their willingness to obey the orders of the president and their officers—and then they returned to their quarters and cheered until they were hoarse. There was but one sentiment among them, McKinley said: "Our Country, it must and shall be preserved." To guarantee its preservation, the Poland Guards were committed to being soldiers for three years, "unless sooner discharged."[7]

There was little in Will McKinley's background to prepare him for war. One of his grandfathers had served in the War of 1812, two of his great-grandfathers in the Revolution, and McKinley was proud of their service. But apart from some youthful playing at soldier with paper caps and wooden swords after the Mexican War, his own life had taken a different course—quieter and more studious.[8]

His father, William McKinley Sr., who managed various iron furnaces, was also one of the directors of the school in Niles, Ohio, as well as treasurer and clerk of the school district. He was a lover of Shakespeare, Burns, and Walter Scott, and the McKinley home received some of the best periodicals of the time: the *Atlantic Monthly* (young Will McKinley's favorite), *Harper's Monthly*, and Horace Greeley's *New York Weekly Tribune*. Each evening the family gathered in the sitting room, where they spent an hour taking turns reading aloud. His father's work, however, often required long absences from home, and the care of the family's nine children was left to McKinley's mother, Nancy Allison McKinley. A strong person, she took on the task with assurance; her husband soon learned not to intrude on her "particular realm" in the upbringing of their children.[9]

Because of his parents' strong belief in education, they moved their family from Niles, where McKinley was born, to the nearby town of Poland—"the Athens of the Mahoning Valley"—when McKinley was eleven years old. McKinley described Poland as a "trim, neat little village on Yellow Creek, with its tasty white frame dwellings, its dear old academy, and the village stores, from which we got our political inspiration." It was the academy that attracted his parents, who wanted to provide a better education for the five of their children still at home. At the academy McKinley took a special interest in mathematics, poetry (Longfellow, Whittier, and Byron in particular), and Greek and Latin, proving himself "a close student, but not indifferent to athletics of all kinds"—and dancing as well. He also belonged to a literary society and demonstrated "oratorical powers and logical conclusions in debate" that were admired by his schoolmates.[10]

In the fall of 1859, McKinley entered Allegheny College in Meadville, Pennsylvania, making the trip with Will Osborne and Robert B. Murray of Youngstown. He was soon noted for his "winsome personality" and as a debater. The debates concerned the political issues of the day, and once when a zealous Virginia student cheered repeatedly for Jefferson Davis as the next president, McKinley "turned sharply upon him with a retort that before that came to pass Osborne and himself would fight the Southerner on his native soil."[11]

Illness, however, interfered with McKinley's studies. He became nervous and then depressed. "I felt so much discouraged," he said, "that it seemed I never would look forward to anything again. . . . I was discontented for many, many months. It seemed to me that my whole life was to be spoiled by my unfortunate nervousness." His illness forced McKinley to return home before the school year was over.[12]

With rest, McKinley's health returned, but financial difficulties in his family prevented his return to school. McKinley's brother-in-law, who had

William McKinley Jr. before he
enlisted in the Union army.
*Courtesy of the Stark County
Historical Society,
Canton, Ohio.*

a store in Poland, said in March 1860 that those were "the tightest times to get money" since he had been in business. Unable to resume his studies, McKinley turned instead to teaching. He taught in the Faukle School, three miles from his home, usually walking to the school rather than "boarding around" with the students' families as was the custom. He also served as assistant to Adam Case, the Democratic postmaster of Poland, who, despite their political differences, regarded McKinley as an industrious and conscientious worker. Along with his work, McKinley found time to court a sixteen-year-old girl in Poland, Lydia Wadsworth. Her parents, however, objected to the match and forbade her seeing him. He also continued his debating. Shortly before the war, he participated in a debate in Poland on the topic "Resolved, that it would be policy on the part of the Federal Union to evacuate Fort Sumpter." Three of the four students who took part in the debate were soon at war; one of them died of wounds he received at the Battle of Antietam.[13]

Religion played an important part in McKinley's life. His parents were charter members of the Methodist church in Niles, where "the Sunday morning procession of the McKinleys, big and little," going to church was a familiar sight. His mother and her sister were so involved that it was commonly said that they "ran the church, all but the preaching." When McKinley also showed an early interest in religion, his mother began to cherish hopes that he might one day become a Methodist bishop, the highest office, she thought, that he could ever aspire to. (On the morning before McKinley's inauguration as president, his brother Abner was heard to remark to their dubious mother, "Mother, this is better than a bishopric!")[14]

Camp meetings were a prominent feature of religious life then, emotional "protracted meetings" that challenged the conscience of everyone in the community. McKinley's sister Mary and her husband, Daniel May, once attended a local camp meeting and came back singing one of the songs they had heard there. May said that Mary "got real happy and g[o]t to shouting and praised God all night." The Reverend Aaron D. Morton, who arrived in Poland in 1855 to serve the town's Methodist church, took advantage of the community's interest in religion by holding a series of camp meetings, at which a good number of people were converted. One of them was Will McKinley, a youth Morton found "genial and pleasant, kind and obliging, his conversation was interesting, and interspersed with glows of unusual light." "One evening," Morton said, "without any excitement, or previous intimation," McKinley arose "and announced his intention of leading a christian life," saying, among other things, "God is the being above all to be loved, and served"; "Religion seems to me to be the best thing in all the world"; and "Here I take my stand for life." After McKinley decided that his baptism should be by immersion, Morton baptized him in a stream near Poland and accepted him as a probationary member of the church; he was received as a full member by Morton's successor, the Reverend William F. Day, who satisfied McKinley's religious interests by teaching him some biblical Hebrew.[15]

Morton said that McKinley "was not what you would call a 'shouting Methodist,' but rather one who was careful of his acts and words yet positive he was right. . . . He was always bright and was constantly saying things which attracted attention. . . . I often noticed him in church. He was the best listener I ever saw." "Many of us," Morton said, "thought he would become a minister."[16]

Morton was more than a pastor; he was also active in the Underground Railroad and was one of those who forcefully presented the antislavery message in Poland. Not only was Poland a Republican stronghold—the township gave Lincoln 336 of the 430 votes cast in 1860—but it was a place where antislavery speakers were given a sympathetic hearing. Morton had preached an antislavery sermon during the Frémont campaign; antislavery leaders Benjamin Wade, congressman from Ohio, and Professor James H. Fairchild of Oberlin College were among those who spoke in Poland during McKinley's youth; and Eliza Blakelee, one of McKinley's teachers at the academy, was a graduate of Oberlin College and "an ardent abolitionist." One of the men who joined the Poland Guards took pride in having a firsthand experience with the antislavery movement. Andrew J. Duncan, who married McKinley's sister Sarah after the war, had been in Kansas during the struggles between the slavery and antislavery factions there and had once volunteered as a bodyguard for John Brown.[17]

Those influences were reinforced by the beliefs of his own family. His mother said that "the McKinleys were stanch abolitionists, and William early imbibed very radical views regarding the enslavement of the colored race. As a mere boy, he used to go to a tannery kept by Joseph Smith and engage in warm controversies on the slavery question. Mr. Smith was a Democrat, and so were several of the workmen about the tannery. These disputes never seemed to have occasioned any ill feeling toward William, because he was always popular with the very men with whom he had the most controversy." *Uncle Tom's Cabin* helped shape his views on slavery. A theatrical version of the novel was presented in Poland when McKinley was thirteen, and the story was said to have made a deep impression on him.[18]

It was a young William McKinley, pale and slight in build, who enlisted with the Poland Guards, but he was also bright, inquisitive, fairly well educated, politically aware, averse to slavery, and absolutely committed to the Union he was now sworn to defend.

At the same time the Poland Guards left for Columbus, the other military companies that would be combined with the Guards in the same regiment were finding their way to Columbus from other parts of the state: the Zouave Light Guards from Cuyahoga County; Giddings's Zouaves from Ashtabula County, led by Capt. Grotius Giddings, the son of antislavery leader Joshua Giddings; the Galion Guards of Crawford County; the Cleveland Rifle Grenadiers with men from both Cleveland in Cuyahoga County and Wellington in Lorain County; the Bellefontaine Rifles from Logan County; the Ellsworth Guards from Ashland County; the Welker Guards from Holmes and Ashland Counties; the Ohio Union Savers from Lake County; and the Elyria Rifle Guards from Lorain County.[19]

As the companies traveled to Columbus, they were greeted by wildly enthusiastic crowds. A Michigan soldier who passed through the state at the same time said that his "journey through Ohio was a glorious one. Every hat & handkerchief & apron & bonnet along the road was thrown into the air. All manner of shouts & cheers of encouragement. . . . God bless you, farewell, give 'em h——l &c, greeted us at every step. . . . The whole country where we pass is in a blaze of patriotism." The only dissenting voice the Ohio men heard was from the "Red Apostle" at Elyria. Among the great crowd gathered at the depot cheering the Elyria Rifle Guards as they left for Camp Jackson was a man dressed in a red costume who boarded the train and "took occasion to admonish the crowd in loud tones, of the horrors consequent upon war." But his warning was unwelcome and unheeded. When he mentioned the Prophet Elijah, one of the listeners diverted the crowd by swinging his hat and shouting, "Three cheers for good old Elijah!" and the Red Apostle's message was lost in the uproar. Nevertheless, before the war's end, many in the crowd would come to understand what the man in the blood-red costume had been trying to say.[20]

A new regiment was formed from these ten companies, the 23d Ohio Volunteer Infantry. It was the first Ohio regiment to be formed for three years' service; previous regiments had served only three months. The companies' colorful names were lost in the assignment, the Poland Guards becoming simply Company E. The volunteers were surprised to learn that the regiment was also the first in Ohio in which the soldiers would not elect the field officers; the officers had already been appointed by Governor Dennison. One company that had originally been assigned to the regiment refused to serve under those conditions, and the captains of the other companies complained to the governor, but they eventually accepted what they were powerless to change. The governor's appointments were, in fact, exemplary: West Point graduate William S. Rosecrans as colonel and Cincinnati attorneys Stanley Matthews and Rutherford B. Hayes as lieutenant colonel and major. McKinley later said he recalled Rosecrans "with peculiar tenderness and respect. He was the first colonel of the regiment to which I belonged; my boyhood ideal of a great soldier." A few days later, however, Rosecrans was promoted and left the regiment. His replacement was another West Pointer, E. Parker Scammon, a strict disciplinarian who was not well received in the ranks. Major Hayes found Scammon personable but admitted that "he has not a happy way of hitting the humors of the men. . . . A good man, but impatient and fault-finding."[21]

Camp Jackson—soon renamed Camp Chase for Ohio's Salmon P. Chase—was laid out on a tract of 165 acres on the National Road west of

Columbus that included a racetrack and a cornfield, with some of the corn-
stalks and stubble still standing. Some barracks large enough for sixteen
men had been built, with kitchens attached. The men of Company E, however, were put into tents when they arrived and were told that they were
expected to construct their own barracks. A private of Company C engaged in building a barracks stole some hinges from an old door at headquarters and soon learned about discipline in the army. He was arrested and
"bucked"; "that is, while his wrists were closely tied together, [they]
brought them down over his knees, and then ran a stick through, so as to
bring his chin on his knees, at the same time throwing him backward, thus
rendering it impossible to move." When he was released, he was unable to
walk, his extremities were cold and his chest swollen, and he was bleeding
from his nose and mouth.[22]

Most of the recruits' time was spent in drilling (four hours a day), in
guard duty, and in studying military tactics. McKinley proved to be a good
student. His comrades said he "took to soldiering naturally and learned his
Hardee's Tactics with scarcely an effort." And he was learning to cook.
John Cracraft told how he and McKinley got up at half past four in the
morning because they "had to take turns at cooking. It went down pretty
hard. Smoked my eyes pretty near out while getting dinner." What free
time McKinley had he used in reading—he had brought a book of Byron's
poems along to camp—and in writing. He began a diary that he kept
for nearly five months. On one occasion he noted that he was writing in
the diary while on guard duty, "with my musket leaning against my right
shoulder." And as the Poland Guards' correspondent, he began to write
letters for publication in the *Mahoning Register*, a newspaper in Youngstown, Ohio, near Poland. In one of his letters to the *Register*, he assured his
readers that "our boys are all determined to stand by the stars and stripes,
and never give up until their lives are sacrificed, or the Government placed
on a firm and solid foundation."[23]

One of McKinley's first personal letters from camp was to his sister
Anna, explaining his reasons for enlisting. On patriotic stationery, showing a flag in color and the motto "The American States: One and Undi-
vided forever," he told his sister:

I volunteered to serve my country in this her perilous hour from a sense
of duty. I felt it was obligatory upon me, as a young man a citizen of this
highly favored land, to step forward at the call of my country, and assist
if possible in suppressing rebellion and putting down secession, what do
you think of it? . . . The Mess which I am in is composed principally of

the "Literati" of the company. . . . We have a good time, considering the cause in which we have enlisted, to protect the American Government, the Government under which we have lived so long—and enjoyed so many privileges, is it less than our duty to throw ourselves at the altar of our Common Country? Do we owe less to the United States of America? I think not. You will be astonished to hear that our Family gave their consent for me to enlist. . . . I know you will say I did a noble act.[24]

McKinley also told Anna about the frequent religious gatherings in his regiment, which came to be known as "the psalm-singers of the Western Reserve": "religious exercises in the company twice a day, prayer meeting twice a week, and preaching in the regiment once on sabbath." His diary entries show how heartfelt his own participation in the meetings was: "I found them precious to my soul—in fact, I felt more of the love of God in my heart at these meetings than I felt for some time before." Again he wrote: "[I] attended prayer meeting in the evening; I for one testified of the goodness of God. Many were the witnesses for Jesus. The spirit was at work in all of our hearts." When Gaylord Hawkins, the minister of the Methodist church in Poland, visited Camp Chase, McKinley listened to him preach and then wrote in his diary: "All day I felt the love of God in my heart and notwithstanding the surroundings there was an inward calmness and tranquility which belongs to the Christian alone."[25]

Independence Day held a special meaning for the men sworn to defend the Union. The regiment assembled in a hollow square on the parade ground, where Major Hayes read the Declaration of Independence, the regiment's brass band played "Hail, Columbia," and Lieutenant Colonel Matthews addressed the regiment—"most sublimely," McKinley thought. Matthews concluded by proposing three cheers for the Union, and then the troops were dismissed for the day. In the evening they were treated to a display of fireworks. Before the night was over, nearly fifty men who had celebrated too much were in the guardhouse. Other prisoners appeared in camp as well; twenty-three civilians from the Kanawha Valley in western Virginia arrived at Camp Chase. They had been taken hostage for Union men arrested by Confederate cavalry, and they remained in camp until the Union men were released.[26]

McKinley's company had been at Camp Chase for more than a month—some of the other companies had been there longer—and they still had not been furnished with uniforms or weapons. Many of the men had worn old clothes to camp, with the expectation of receiving uniforms quickly. Now some of them were in rags; men were seen on guard duty wearing only shirts, with blankets wrapped around them. When the first issue of clothing arrived, it contained nothing but undershirts and drawers, and to show their displeasure, the men turned out at evening parade wearing only what they had been issued. McKinley said that the regiment had been offered gray uniforms but their colonel had refused to accept them. "He will take none but 'blue.'" "Our eyes," McKinley said, "have already grown dim looking for our coats with the brass buttons."[27]

Ohio had been totally unprepared for war. George B. McClellan, the major general chosen to command the Ohio troops, found himself "a commander with nothing but men—neither arms nor supplies." Governor Dennison's private secretary said, with little exaggeration, "Ohio had no arms, no camp equippage, no commissary, or quartermaster department, with means to meet the sudden and large demand upon it." But with emergency appropriations from the legislature and through the efforts of Governor Dennison and Adj. Gen. C. P. Buckingham, the troops were eventually supplied.[28]

On July 16, the men finally received their fatigue dress—indigo blue coats, sky-blue pants, and caps—and two days later, they were issued knapsacks and canteens. Dennison had decided not to wait any longer for the federal government to clothe the troops and issued clothing from the state, superintending the issue himself and receiving "many a hearty cheer" from the recruits. Later, when the regiment was issued overcoats—large, heavy, blue coats, coming down below the knees, with capes covering the shoulders—McKinley pondered the men's appearance: "They give us the appearance of our Revolutionary fathers. May we be as bold soldiers as they were, and stand up for our God-given rights as they did. May we never forget that we owe to them the support of that Government they so nobly fought to establish. May we never become oblivious to the fact that it is ours to hand down to posterity this Government, as free, as pure, and as spotless as our sires transmitted it to us."[29]

On July 23, six weeks after they had been mustered into the service, the men were finally issued muskets, but they quickly stacked them and refused to accept them. They were, McKinley said, "of an old-fashioned sort, and the regiment—a proud one—insisted it should have the best arms then known to military science." Another soldier said, more bluntly, that the muskets were "of the make of 1825 passed over." McKinley admitted that "none of us knew how to use any kind of a musket at that time, but we thought we knew our rights and we were all conscious of our importance." The next morning the regiment was ordered to accept the muskets, but five companies, including McKinley's Company E, still refused them.

The members of Company E were then called forward, and each man was asked individually whether he would accept his musket. Only the officers and two or three privates answered "yes." Other companies were called out, reportedly with the intention of forcing the men to accept the arms, but as they were assembling, Captain Zimmerman informed the company that Governor Dennison and Maj. Gen. John C. Frémont were to review the regiment in one hour; he appealed to the men to accept the weapons for the review, which they did on being assured that they would not have to keep them.[30]

Frémont had recently been appointed a major general, and he and his wife were on their way from Washington to his command in St. Louis. Stopping in Columbus, he accepted an invitation to review the troops at Camp Chase with Governor Dennison, and the men were assembled in a hot sun for the review. Although more than four thousand soldiers were assembled, Frémont had time to review only the 23d Regiment. McKinley was one of the soldiers he examined, and the young recruit retained a vivid memory of the occasion: "General Frémont, I remember seemed a great man to me, a boy . . . whose mind had been thrilled with the story of his wonderful adventures in the West. I remember he pounded my chest and looked square into my eyes, and finally pronounced me fit for a soldier."[31]

When McKinley's company returned from the review, the men again stacked their arms in front of the barracks. Every other company had, as Andrew Duncan put it, been "frightened" into receiving the muskets, and the company was formed into ranks to be lectured by Lieutenant Colonel Matthews. He told them it was their duty to accept the arms and that "if you refuse[,] the last one of you will be shot[,] depend upon it." Finally, an agreement was reached in which ten of the best shots in the company were allowed to try the muskets and report on them. When they reported favorably, the men reluctantly accepted their weapons "but not without protesting against the appearance of them which was not very prepos[s]es[s]ing."[32]

McKinley was greatly impressed by Major Hayes's role in the dispute. Instead of threatening the men, as Matthews had done, Hayes went to their quarters and asked them to give him a hearing. Then he reasoned with them, with what McKinley thought "patriotic feeling" and "sound sense."

He said that many of the most decisive battles of history had been won with the rudest weapons. At Lexington and Bunker Hill and many other engagements of the Revolution our forefathers had triumphed over the well-equipped English armies with the very poorest firearms—and that even pikes and scythes had done good work in that glorious conflict. Should we be less patriotic than our brave ancestors? Should we hesitate at the very start of another struggle for liberty and union, for the best and freest Government on the face of the earth, because we were not pleased with the pattern of our muskets, or with the caliber of our rifles?

Hayes's appeal to the men confirmed the good opinion McKinley was already forming of him. Hayes's manner, McKinley said, "was so generous and his relations with the men were so kind, and yet always dignified, that he won my heart almost from the start." "From that moment our confidence in our leader never wavered."[33]

That same night the regiment was ordered to western Virginia. The men were up all night, noisily preparing three days' rations and packing their knapsacks. McKinley, who had spent a night earlier that week assisting the quartermaster prepare accoutrements for the regiment, took time the night before their departure to write to the *Register* that "the best of feeling pervades every soul, in prospect of approaching the enemy and having a hand in putting down the rebellion." Early the next morning the regiment of 1,020 men marched to Columbus; Hayes won their admiration by accompanying the troops on foot. At Columbus they boarded a train for Bellaire, on the Ohio River. Some of the men were drunk, and others amused themselves by shooting chickens, ducks, and hogs as the train took them across the state. After crossing the Ohio River, the regiment continued on by rail to Clarksburg in western Virginia. Almost everywhere in Virginia, the men were greeted with cheers and displays of loyalty; "At almost every house there was union flags aflying." The recent Union defeat at Bull Run and the departure of the three-month regiments had left the many citizens in western Virginia who were loyal to the Union feeling vulnerable. The 23d Ohio was received enthusiastically as the first of the three-year regiments sent to replace the troops who were leaving. The good reception by the people, coupled with the novel mountain scenery, aroused the troops; Hayes said they stood on the tops of the railroad cars "and danced and shouted with delight."[34]

At Clarksburg, the regiment was met by its old commander, William S. Rosecrans, now a brigadier general commanding the Army of Occupation of Western Virginia. At the beginning of the war, George McClellan, then in command, had sent Ohio troops into western Virginia to protect the Ohio border and especially the Baltimore and Ohio Railroad. The western counties of Virginia had opposed secession, and McClellan also wanted to protect the leaders of the movement to separate the western counties from

Maj. Rutherford B. Hayes of the 23d Ohio Volunteer Infantry. *Courtesy of the Rutherford B. Hayes Presidential Center, Fremont, Ohio.*

the rest of the state to keep them in the Union. After minor victories over Confederate troops at Philippi, Rich Mountain, and Corrick's Ford, McClellan was called to the East and was replaced by Rosecrans a few days before the arrival of the 23d Ohio.[35]

From Clarksburg, the regiment marched to Weston, a town occupied a month before by the 7th Ohio Infantry. This two-day march of twenty-three miles was the regiment's first long march. The men plodded through ankle-deep mud up and down one hill after another, each carrying a knapsack with his clothing, blanket, and personal belongings, a haversack full of rations, a canteen, cartridge and cap boxes, a musket and bayonet—weighing in all fifty or sixty pounds. Trying to keep up, they soon abandoned many of the supplies they had packed in their knapsacks. To their disgust, Colonel Scammon showed no sympathy but rather berated them for straggling: "The march of yesterday should be enough to demonstrate to every officer and man of this command the necessity of increased care in preserving discipline while on the route. The march of a Battalion must not be allowed to become the straggling journey of a mob." After the regiment's arrival at Weston, Scammon continued to criticize the men, finding fault with the "extreme laxity of discipline"; the camp's "foul odors" and "accumulating filth"; and the presence of gambling in camp. "Soldiers instead of employing themselves in making their tents and persons neat, & cleaning their arms & accoutrements . . . are seen sneaking around the banks of the river, or the rear of the tents, playing at cards or dice. . . . It makes men *bad,* and bad men cannot be good Soldiers."[36]

After the war, McKinley remembered how unpopular Scammon had been, but he acknowledged that the regiment learned to appreciate Scammon's discipline after they entered into combat. He was "not the most popular man in the regiment in its earlier days," McKinley said, "for we thought his discipline severe and his drill very hard, but after the battle of South Mountain, General Scammon was the most popular man in the regiment. We knew then for the first time what his discipline meant and what strength it gave to us on the battlefield."[37]

McKinley described Weston as a small town of about eight hundred inhabitants that looked "as if it might have once been a village of some stir and vitality, but since the war broke out it has buried all its vital parts in oblivion." At Weston, the regiment was divided: Lieutenant Colonel Matthews with five companies—the right wing of the regiment—was ordered to join the 7th Ohio farther to the south, while the other five companies, including McKinley's—the left wing—remained at Weston. The town's little brick Methodist church became the headquarters of McKinley's Company E.[38]

At Weston, McKinley began to experience the reality of the war: shortly after he arrived, an officer of the 10th Ohio Infantry was buried there; a sick soldier from the 7th Ohio died and was buried by men of the 23d; the first lieutenant of Company F was accidentally shot through the foot; one of the pickets was shot through the hand "by a concealed foe"; a drunken soldier who resisted arrest was shot and killed. Nevertheless, McKinley reported that "the 'Poland Guards' are well, and anxious to get into the fight." But instead of fighting they were disappointed by being assigned to guard duty. McKinley's first post was as a picket at Maxwell's Bridge, a covered bridge on the Buckhannon Road. Then he was stationed at Barnes Mill, at Bendale, south of Weston, where he served until the middle of August.[39]

Soon after his arrival in Weston, McKinley sent a letter to his mother by a courier who was going to Clarksburg. Later he wrote to his cousin's husband, William K. Miller, about the lighter side of army life. He said that while on duty two or three miles from camp, several men guarding a bridge heard strange noises and thought they had been caused by the enemy. The next night, McKinley and three others volunteered to

go out and catch the "seceshers" if possible. Accordingly we started out about dusk led by a certain lieutenant of our regiment. It would have done you good to have seen the above lieutenant prodding the thick bushes with his gilded sword, fancying to himself that he saw the hideous monster in the shape of a rebel. Ah,—the ambitious officer was disappointed; instead of sticking a secesh, he without doubt stuck a skunk. We came to this conclusion from the fact that a strong smell, a venomous smell, instantly issued from the bushes. We imagined a great many strange things to appear before us, but all proved to be shadows instead of realities. We at last arrived at the hitherto "scary" spot, stationed ourselves, and it was my lot to be placed in a cornfield by the roadside. I stayed there until morning, cocked my old musket, and was almost in the act of shooting a number of times, when the strange vision would disappear and on examination would discover a piece of fox-fire, an itinerant "hog," or a lost calf, which had undoubtedly wandered from its mother in its infantile days. We returned in the morning, sleepy, tired, and not as full of romance as the night before.[40]

Despite McKinley's light tone, life for the Union soldiers in western Virginia was often dangerous. They found the citizens divided in their loyalties, with Virginians serving in the Confederate as well as the Union army. In addition to the Confederate troops, the countryside harbored what the soldiers called "bushwhackers," guerrillas engaged in furtive attacks on the Northern troops and the civilians who sympathized with them. From the beginning of their service, the Ohio soldiers were subject to attack whenever they were outside their camps. Teamsters were shot on the road; water supplies were poisoned; soldiers on the march were shot at from concealed positions; messengers were shot—one was found dead under his horse's head, stripped of everything but his shirt and pants. Even band members were in danger; a member of the 8th Ohio Infantry's band was shot and killed on the road.[41]

Sometimes the soldiers retaliated in unauthorized ways. Members of the 23d were called on to bury a man killed by soldiers of the 10th Ohio Infantry. After guerrillas had wounded four of that regiment's men and killed another, one of the guerrillas had been captured and then shot "in trying to escape." Major Hayes thought the captive had been killed deliberately.[42]

Scouting parties were continually sent out to hunt down the guerrillas. On August 15, Company E was ordered to escort a train of twenty-five wagons carrying supplies for another regiment and to "clean out an infected neighborhood" on the way. The company halted at Glenville, where McKinley had heard that the "'seceshers' are thick. Nothing less than an attack from the enemy is expected." The company's overnight stay at Glenville gave McKinley time to ponder the danger he was in and to record his thoughts in his diary.

> Tomorrow's sun will undoubtedly find me on a march. It may be I will never see the light of another day. Should this be my fate I fall in a good cause and hope to fall in the arms of my blessed redeemer. This record I want left behind, that I not only fell as a soldier for my Country, but also a Soldier of Jesus. I may never be permitted to tread the pleasant soil of Ohio, or see and converse with my friends again. In this emergency let [. . .] my parents, brothers and sisters, and friends have their anxiety removed by the thought that I am in the discharge of my duty, that I am doing nothing but [that which] my revolutionary fathers before me have done, and also let them be consoled with the solacing thought that if we never meet again on earth, we will meet around God's throne in Heaven. Let my fate be what it may, I want to be ready and prepared.[43]

On the way from Glenville to Bulltown, the rear guard of the company was fired on from a hillside "by a concealed foe." Corp. Ferdinand Becker was shot in the back, Pvt. John Robinson in the neck, and Pvt. Andy Tiady through his right leg. They were the company's first casualties. Other soldiers climbed the hill where the shots came from but without finding the men McKinley called "assassins" and "skulking, blood-thirsty rebels." He said the company was "loth to give up the hunt until they had found and exterminated the cowardly wretches," and two scouting parties were sent out into the neighboring hills, but they captured only one man and his rifle.[44]

McKinley wrote to the *Mahoning Register* about his company's encounter with the guerrillas, but it was his last letter as the paper's correspondent. The soldiers had been ordered not to write letters for publication in newspapers. Colonel Scammon informed Captain Zimmerman that if any members of the company were writing for newspapers, they must stop. John Cracraft, who was the company's correspondent for the *Mahoning Sentinel,* continued to write for that newspaper, "bidding defiance to those who assume such dictatorial authority, as to proscribe the inalienable rights of men," and men in other companies wrote for other newspapers, but McKinley, obedient to authority, did not.[45]

When Company E returned to Weston, it and the four other companies of the regiment stationed at Weston were ordered east to Cheat Mountain to reinforce Brig. Gen. Joseph J. Reynolds, who was commanding troops assembled there to meet an expected Confederate attack. The order was well received. McKinley said that the men of Company E were "anxious to meet the enemy face to face, rather than continue this guerrilla mode of warfare." The march, however, did not start out well; about one mile out of Weston, one of the men was accidentally shot through the heel and thigh. As they hurried on toward Buckhannon and stragglers began to line the road, Colonel Scammon refused to let the men stop to fill their canteens. When some stopped anyway, Scammon pulled out his revolver to threaten them, but Andrew Duncan was convinced that if he had used his revolver "he would have been riddled through himself in two minutes." When they reached Buckhannon, Scammon ordered McMullin's Battery, which had accompanied the infantry, to pitch its tents inside the line of sentinels, but the men, thinking they would have to stand guard if they did, refused. Scammon threatened to shoot the lieutenant of the battery, but the lieutenant's men rallied around him and defied the colonel.[46]

As they continued on to Beverly, the men passed over Rich Mountain, the site, six weeks earlier, of one of the first battles of the war. Scammon again angered the men by not allowing them to look over the battleground.

But graves of both Union and Confederate soldiers were visible along the road. Passing the graves and marching closer to the enemy, McKinley had some "serious thoughts," which he recorded in a note to his family: "Soon, yes very soon, we may meet our once brothers, now aliens and enemies, face to face. It will be the fate of some of us to fall, fall at the cannon's mouth. If it be my lot to fall, I want to fall at my post and have it said that I fell in defense of my country in honor of the glorious stars and stripes. Not only do I want it said that I fell a valiant soldier of my country, but a soldier for my Redeemer."[47]

From Beverly, the men marched up the Tygart Valley, where they met General Reynolds. They expected to remain with him until they encountered the enemy under Gen. Robert E. Lee, who were "just over the mountain." But instead they were suddenly ordered to march back to French Creek, south of Buckhannon. Leaving their tents and knapsacks behind, they marched over Cheat Mountain on "a little foot path" in a pouring rain during the night, holding on to bushes on the steep sides of the mountain. On the way down, McKinley said, "in order to preserve our equilibrium and follow our leader we were compelled to lay hold on the backs of each other." Only about 150 men reached French Creek together; the rest straggled in for two days. They found French Creek to be "a warm-hearted Union settlement" founded by New Englanders, and with Lt. James Botsford and Corp. Augustus Heiliger, McKinley enjoyed the hospitality of a local doctor and his two "fine, modest daughters." He returned to the doctor's home a second day, "took tea there [and] had singing in the evening, a very pleasant time, and brought to mind the scenes of home." Not everyone had such a pleasant time there; several men in the regiment were found to have stolen overcoats and blankets and sold them, and they were drummed out of the camp "to the tune of the 'Rogues' march."[48]

The men had been called away from Cheat Mountain in the belief that the real threat to the Union troops was coming not from the east but from the south, and they soon moved south toward Sutton. Local tradition has it that while his company was in Braxton County, McKinley again enjoyed the hospitality of a doctor's home, in this case that of Dr. John L. Rhea.[49] McKinley's arrival at the town of Sutton caused him to "reflect on the devastation and misery caused by civil war. There are to be found but few civilians [and] all of the houses are occupied by soldiers." Lieutenant Colonel Matthews and his five companies joined the rest of the regiment at Sutton. When the reunited regiment left Sutton for Summersville, it was part of an army of eight thousand—eight infantry regiments, three mounted batteries, and three cavalry companies—under the command of Brig. Gen. William S. Rosecrans, with the 23d serving as Rosecrans's bodyguard.[50]

The threat was indeed from the south. Two separate armies were approaching, one under Henry A. Wise, the other under John B. Floyd. Floyd's troops had attacked and routed the 7th Ohio at Cross Lanes and then retired to a strongly fortified position on a hill high above the Gauley River at a place called Carnifex Ferry. Early on the morning of September 10, Rosecrans's army marched toward Carnifex Ferry, "every heart beating high with the expectation of meeting the enemy." McKinley's thoughts were on his feet; they were so sore from marching that someone took pity on him and let him ride part of the way on horseback.[51]

McKinley noted that the fighting at Carnifex Ferry began at precisely 3:24 in the afternoon, and for more than three hours "the booming of the cannon, the report of muskets could be distinctly heard, and the smoke could be seen rising to the Heavens." Rosecrans's forces were divided into three brigades, two of which assaulted the Confederates, while the third, Colonel Scammon's, which included the 23d Regiment, was held in reserve. But as the battle progressed, Rosecrans ordered an attempt to flank the Confederates to try to reach the ferry and cut off any possible Confederate retreat. Four companies of the 23d, under Major Hayes, were included in the flanking movement. McKinley, whose company was one of the four, said, "We went on quick time through meadows, corn fields and laurel thickets, over rocks [and] deep precipices. Part of our march was made on our knees, and to preserve a man's equilibrium was almost . . . [an] impossibility." They halted at the river, where they were under fire from the Confederate cannons, and then, finding they could not reach the ferry or cross the river, they began their way back. On their return, a rustling was heard in the bushes, and Hayes drew his revolver only to find to his surprise that the commotion was caused by his law partner from Cincinnati, Leopold Markbreit, who, despite his promise to Hayes to take care of their office, had left it, joined the 28th Ohio Infantry, and come to the war. McKinley said he would never forget the delight with which Hayes greeted him or Markbreit's pleasure in being forgiven "for having run away from the law office." Only two men in the companies commanded by Hayes had been wounded in the battle, but on their return Hayes and his men met the 10th Ohio Infantry, "with their dead and wounded. The sighs and groans," McKinley wrote, "were pitiable." It was dark before the companies returned, and by that time all firing had ceased.[52]

At nightfall, with his troops exhausted, General Rosecrans broke off the battle. During the night, Floyd, realizing that his army was in an untenable position, withdrew his men, crossed the Gauley River, destroyed the ferry and footbridge, and retreated to Big Sewell Mountain and, later, to Meadow Bluff. In the morning, when rumors suggested that the Confederates were gone, the 23d Regiment was marched to the battleground. The men found the area covered with abandoned supplies: cartridge boxes, tents, wagons, and trunks, including one belonging to General Floyd. They also saw the dead laid out together. One lieutenant "lay with his leg nearly torn of[f] with a cannon ball. Another was torn through the breast by the same misle[,] another was shot through the heart and lay weltering in his own lifes blood." Some of those wounded too badly to be moved were still on the battlefield. In later years, McKinley spoke of the Battle of Carnifex Ferry with a certain detachment: "This was our first real fight. . . . It gave us confidence in ourselves and faith in our commander. We learned that we could fight and whip the rebels on their own ground." But a few days after the battle, when the wounded were still dying, he and two other members of Company E, Albert B. Logan and Charles Long, sought out the chaplain and spent an hour in conversation with him. Perhaps some of them remembered enough Latin from their school days to reflect on the meaning of a battle fought at a place called Carnifex, Latin for a killer or an executioner.[53]

Three days after the battle, while the army was still camped near the battlefield, McKinley was detached to the brigade quartermaster's office as a clerk. Captain Zimmerman had earlier offered him the post of company clerk, but McKinley had refused it, saying he had enlisted to be a soldier and preferred to remain one. Still, when off duty, he had devoted a good many hours to doing clerical work for both Zimmerman and the quartermaster; he had been in the army only three days when he noted in his diary that he "wrote a number of letters for the Captain." Now he was detached from his company as a clerk to the quartermaster of the brigade made up of the 23d and 30th Ohio Infantry Regiments and, later, also the 26th Ohio Infantry. Rutherford Hayes may have played a part in his new assignment. Impressed by McKinley's "soldierly appearance," Hayes had advised Colonel Scammon to "keep your eye on that young man. There is something in him."[54]

As McKinley began his clerical work, one of the officers in his regiment, 2d Lt. James L. Botsford, originally of Company E but then serving as secretary to Colonel Scammon, gave him some friendly advice. Botsford was twenty-seven years old and had seen much more of the world than McKinley had. He was born in Poland, Ohio, but lived in California before the war, arriving back in New York City the day after the Confederates fired on Fort Sumter. Botsford had shared his California experiences with Major Hayes and others; he said his time there had been spent in "gambling, fiddling, spreeing, washing clothes, driving mules, keeping tavern, grocery, digging, clerking, etc., etc., rich and poor, in debt and working it out; all in two or three years." Botsford had taken a liking to McKinley and said to him:

Now, William, let me give you a word of advice. You can get along in your new place in such a way that it will be a bad rather than a good thing for you. On the other hand, you can easily make yourself so valuable to your superior that he cannot get along without you. Do little things not exactly under your supervision. Be conscientious in all your duties, and be faithful, and it will not be long until your superior officer will consider you an indispensible assistant.

It was advice McKinley took to heart and repeated to clerks the rest of his life.[55]

His clerical work took McKinley away from the soldiering he had come to expect. His duties seem to have been mostly in the commissary with its essential but unglamorous mission of supplying the brigade with rations. He told his sister Anna that it was "not a small job to assist in weighing, measuring etc. provisions for one thousand men, besides keeping a memorandum of the whole of it." But his new assignment did nothing to diminish his ardor for the Union cause. A month after he had gone to work in the commissary, seated among barrels and cracker boxes and surrounded by receipts and government forms, he was still able to assure his sister about his patriotism.

When I left home I thought my country needed my services. . . . Much as I love home and its blessed associations, my native country, the Government that gave me birth, freedom and education shall not be destroyed, if my services can assist to prevent it. What is home worth without a Government? What is life worth without freedom to enjoy it? Not once since I came into the service have I regretted that I ever volunteered, but rather been proud of it.[56]

Slowly, General Rosecrans moved his forces in pursuit of Floyd's army. At Sewell Mountain, they joined those of Gen. Jacob D. Cox, who had moved south from Gauley Bridge. From their camp, the Union soldiers could see the Confederates encamped on a nearby ridge. The Confederates were commanded by Gen. Robert E. Lee; Wise had been recalled, and Floyd was serving under Lee. The armies skirmished with each other, but heavy rains and impassable roads made it difficult to supply the armies, and neither would risk an advance. Finally, in early October, Rosecrans withdrew the Union troops to the safety of Camp Ewing, near Gauley Bridge.[57]

At Camp Ewing, Stanley Matthews left the regiment to accept command of the 51st Ohio Infantry. Rutherford Hayes was promoted to lieutenant colonel and, with Colonel Scammon commanding the brigade, assumed command of the regiment. Hayes was a man, one private said, "who has made himself universally beloved throughout the whole regiment, by his uniform kindness and respect to his subordinates." James M. Comly came to the regiment with an appointment from Governor Dennison as its major. Sickness also brought changes; among the many soldiers sent back to Ohio because of illness was Will Osborne, sick with a fever, who never returned to the war.[58]

In mid-November, after Floyd's army came close enough to fire its cannons from Cotton Mountain onto the Union camps and supply trains, the 23d Regiment and the rest of the Third Brigade left Camp Ewing and pursued the Confederates. They went as far as Fayetteville, but, with snow on the ground, they stopped there and went into winter camp. The Union forces were firmly in control, and President Lincoln could report to Congress that "after a somewhat bloody struggle of months, winter closes on the Union people of western Virginia, leaving them masters of their own country."[59]

Fayetteville consisted of a brick courthouse, a jail, some twelve or fifteen other public and commercial buildings, and about sixty houses. All but a few families—mostly women—had fled the town, and the brigade, impressed with the "fine houses, forage, [and] healthy location," occupied it, naming their camp "Camp Union." Soon, however, the fences, shrubbery, and shade trees had all been cut down for fuel and the streets trampled into a quagmire. The town had become what one soldier called "the muddy, dirty, God-forsaken village of Fayetteville." At least the countryside around Fayetteville was free of guerrillas, and the men could go where they chose without danger. They were, as Hayes put it, "undisturbed by the world." "Contrabands," too, fugitive slaves, frequently came into Fayetteville. Some of them were employed as cooks and servants by the officers, others went on to Ohio and freedom.[60]

McKinley and the other members of the Quartermaster's Department established their headquarters in a business block on Fayetteville's main street. Their supplies were brought by steamboat to Kanawha Falls, near the mouth of the Gauley River, where they were loaded onto mule-drawn wagons to be transported the thirteen or fourteen miles to Fayetteville. A visitor from Ohio described the scene: "steamboats unloading wagons, teams and stores, transportation wagons twisting in and out of piles of barrels, bags and bales, drivers yelling, mules braying, wagon masters scolding, and pretty much all hands swearing." Rains and the constant use of the already poor road to Fayetteville, however, soon rendered the road useless, and pack mules were substituted for the wagons. One of the soldiers stationed in Fayetteville said that "great droves, containing from fifty to one hundred pack mules each, arrived two or three times every week. Long before they came in sight, we could hear the voices of the drivers urging the brutes forward with cries and imprecations." The soldiers were also able to obtain food from the local people who came into town to trade pies, chickens, and butter for surplus rations.[61]

McKinley's work as a clerk and later his substituting for an ill commissary sergeant freed him from the building of fortifications, the repair of roads and bridges, and the inspections, reviews, and drills that occupied the other soldiers. What spare time he had he spent in reading and keeping abreast of the progress of the war; Cincinnati newspapers arrived only four to ten days old, and a telegraph line had been run to Fayetteville, bringing with it news of the war elsewhere. He also participated in the debates the men held in camp to amuse themselves. McKinley either stopped writing a diary or subsequent volumes of his diary have been lost; his last entry was on November 3, 1861. Some of the other men obtained furloughs, and some of the officers were sent to Ohio to obtain recruits for the regiment, which was depleted more by illness than by casualties. The recruiters often returned with packages from home, and civilian visitors sometimes appeared with welcome gifts.[62]

Late in December, Colonel Scammon sent Major Comly with six companies, two from each of the three regiments in the brigade, to occupy Raleigh (now Beckley), twenty-five miles to the south, to protect the Union citizens from the guerrillas there. Gradually other companies were sent until, by March, the entire regiment was at Raleigh, occupying the houses deserted by the town's inhabitants. The soldiers were involved in only a few skirmishes, most notably at the village of Jumping Branch, where the Union troops also burned eight houses, two churches, and several barns and stables—every building except two houses occupied by women and children—to prevent the Confederates from fortifying them again. Guerrillas were a constant concern, however, encouraged by a recent proclamation by Virginia's governor, John Letcher, asking Virginians to form guerrilla companies, and scouting parties were dispatched regularly to seek them out. When the guerrillas were found, the soldiers burned their homes as punishment for their attacks. The soldiers understood their orders to be to "burn, plunder and destroy all property belonging to the bush-whackers and those who aid and assist them." Company G of the 23d scouted on mules and was known as the "Jackass Rangers." On one occasion, when they captured some prisoners and brought them back to Raleigh, they were met on the streets by other soldiers who greeted them with "the oft repeated exclamation of 'Hurrah for Company G, why didn't you shoot the bushwhackers[?]'"[63]

The 36th Ohio Infantry, stationed at Summersville, had no reluctance about shooting them. Its colonel, George Crook, had been angered when captured guerrillas were paroled, and he made it clear to his men that they need take no more prisoners. He said that when his officers returned from a scout they would report that "they had caught so-and-so, but in bringing him in he slipped off a log while crossing a stream and broke his neck, or that he was killed by an accidental discharge of one of the men's guns, and many like reports. But they never brought back any more prisoners." One of Crook's men, who disapproved of such killings, told how one young prisoner, suspected of being a bushwhacker, was encouraged to try to escape and then was deliberately shot and, when he fell, shot again. He said "the boys described his *screams* after he was shot first as *heart-rendering*— they left him *unburied*. My God: has it come to this?" But another soldier in the 36th had no qualms about such killings: "If we ant out here to kill Bushwhackers what are we for?"[64]

The 36th Ohio was not alone. Members of the 11th Ohio Infantry found two men poisoning springs near their camp; their chaplain said that in twenty minutes the "would-be assassins were hanging on the nearest tree." Gen. Jacob Cox ordered two men hanged at Sutton for cutting off a Union soldier's head with a scythe; six months later the scaffold was still standing as a warning to others. The war in western Virginia was not measured in great battles but in numbing, everyday brutality on both sides.[65]

The 23d regularly received news about the rest of the war by telegraph. At Raleigh, Hayes posted the telegraphic dispatches so that not only the officers but all the men were aware of the news. "It is more than some officers would do," one of the men said, "but he is every inch a gentleman and treats his soldiers as such." They also continued to receive newspapers from home. The men of the regiment were angered when a Cleveland newspaper published a letter that referred to them as the "bloodless Twenty-third." One of them wrote to another newspaper, admitting that the 23d had not been in any great battles but arguing that it was simply their bad luck "never to be placed where we can share the honors that our troops are reaping everywhere but *here* in Western Virginia." He did not want the regiment's friends at home to think that "we are acting a cowardly part because we have never seen a fight, but that it is only one of the fortunes of war which we cannot help or account for." Another soldier in the 23d told his family that "I begin to think that we will never have the opportunity of being in a single battle although it is not our fault. Most of the boys are anxious to meet the Rebels at the point of the bayonet and try their skill with them and have a name as well as other Regiments." The soldiers need not have been concerned; their turn was coming.[66]

TWO Commissary Sergeant

The highest tribute that can be paid to a soldier is to say that he performed his full duty. The field of duty is determined by his government, and wherever that chances to be is the place of honor.
                                                    —*William McKinley*

*E*ach infantry regiment in the Union army had a commissary sergeant who was responsible for seeing that the regiment was supplied with rations. The commissary sergeant of the 23d Ohio, Arthur C. Humphrey, became ill in December 1861 and was unable to carry out his duties. In March 1862, one of the men in Company E, signing himself "Poland Guard," wrote to the *Mahoning Register* to report that a member of the company from Poland had taken over Humphrey's duties.

> Wm. McKinley, Jr., one of the youngest members of our Company, who joined us shortly after we went into camp at Columbus, was but a short time with the company when he was detailed as Clerk in the Quarter Master's Department. Some three months since, the Regiment Commissary Sergeant was taken sick, and was compelled to return to his home in Ohio, where he is still prostrate with illness. McKinley has been filling this laborious and trustworthy office ever since, to the entire satisfaction of the Department, winning many warm friends in the Regiment by his accommodating qualities and gentlemanly demeanor. He made a good and willing soldier, never shrinking from any duty, and fills the more responsible position he now holds, with great credit to himself and honor to his friends.[1]

On March 1, 1862, Humphrey, who realized that he could no longer do the work of commissary sergeant, was, at his own request, reduced to the ranks, and on April 15, McKinley was appointed commissary sergeant of the 23d Ohio. In his new rank, he was entitled to wear the large, sky-blue sergeant's chevrons above the elbows of his sleeves: three stripes in the shape of an open "V" with three cross bars at the top.[2]

McKinley's promotion reflected his abilities and diligence and the "accommodating qualities and gentlemanly demeanor" that "Poland Guard" recognized. Still, it could only have helped that he had friends in high places. John Cracraft, another member of the Poland Guards, had been appointed quartermaster sergeant of the regiment and, at the time of McKinley's promotion, was the regiment's acting quartermaster. McKinley's friend James Botsford had been promoted to first lieutenant, was the regiment's acting adjutant, and as such signed the order announcing McKinley's promotion.[3]

As commissary sergeant, McKinley worked closely with the officer who supervised the brigade commissary and was designated as "commissary of subsistence." The commissary sergeants went to the brigade commissary every day or every few days with details of soldiers to draw rations for their regiments. Then they took the rations back and issued them to the cooks. It was an unvarying task; as one soldier put it, "Storm or sunshine, weekday or Sabbath[,] when the time for rations comes rations must be drawn & dealt."[4]

At its maximum strength, a regiment consisted of 1,025 men, but that many were seldom on the rolls, and the officers were not supplied by the commissary sergeant but were required to purchase their food from the commissary. But supplying even half the full strength of a regiment still meant loading and unloading large quantities of food, all of which had to be weighed and accounted for as it was drawn and again as it was issued. If beef on the hoof was available at the brigade commissary, slaughtering and butchering were also necessary. One corporal who was assisting a commissary sergeant reported on a typical day's work.

I got my rations from the Brigade Comsy yesterday & dealt over 1100 loaves of bread & 4 barrels of potatoes & I am now waiting for it to stop raining & as soon as it does shall deal out 800 lbs of pork 150 lbs coffee 240 of sugar 5 bushels of beans 50 lbs of dessicated potato 500 lbs of crackers besides the soap candles, salt &c &c &c.

This will be supposed to be sufficient to last our little Regt 3 days if I give as I expect [to], 700 lbs of fresh beef & 550 loaves of fresh bread tomorrow.[5]

The supplies had to be transported from the brigade commissary on mule-drawn wagons or on the backs of mules, and a commissary sergeant became all too familiar with the ways of mules. They, too, had to be fed and, if not fed, could render a noisy protest. One veteran described the "hungry hallelujah" that woke him one night. "A mule had set up his hungry plaint, and then a line of two or three miles of his comrades were seemingly convulsed in an effort to surpass his performance. My first thought on awakening was that the roof of the sky had been kicked out." That was an everyday experience to those who worked in the commissary. The corporal who was assisting a commissary sergeant reported on his work to his parents at home by saying simply that he was "still 'among the mules.'" McKinley's field of duty, his "place of honor" in the army, was to be among the mules.[6]

The position of commissary sergeant was considered to be one of the desirable "bombproof" jobs, one performed behind the lines, free from fighting in battles and from drill and guard duty at other times. And the position had its privileges: often a horse to ride, wagons for carrying personal baggage, ample food, and membership in the military family of the regiment's commissioned and noncommissioned officers. But supplying soldiers in a battle or leaving a camp with foraging details to obtain food from the countryside sometimes placed even those in the "feeding department" in the way of danger.

McKinley was well suited to the position of commissary sergeant and well thought of by the men in his regiment. John Ellen, who served as a captain and quartermaster in the 23d Regiment, testified to the "very marked improvement and regularity of service" in the commissary under McKinley. He once said to veterans of the regiment in McKinley's presence: "If from any cause the coming of the supply trains were delayed and rations were short, 'Mack' did the next best thing and made requisition on the country round about. Whether in camp, on the march, or in the line of battle, it was your constant endeavor to bring to your comrades-in-arms the best that your department could secure."[7]

As peach blossoms and new grass signaled the coming of spring, the men were eager to move out of camp and resume the war. Colonel Scammon's brigade, which included the 23d Regiment, was now a part of Gen. Jacob

Cox's Kanawha Division. Cox was waiting until the rains stopped and the roads again became passable before starting on the next campaign, one devised by General Frémont, who had been placed in command of a new Mountain Department that included western Virginia. It was a movement farther south to disrupt the operations of the Virginia and Tennessee Railroad, a major link between those two states that allowed Confederate troops to be moved rapidly between the eastern and western fronts. Under Cox's overall direction, some of the Kanawha Division under George Crook would move toward Lewisburg. Others, including Scammon's brigade, under Cox, would advance to the railroad by way of Princeton.[8]

The movement began a few days after McKinley's promotion. It took the 23d Regiment through country already devastated by the war. "On every side," one soldier reported, "we see buildings destroyed, property taken or burned, fields turned to waste and rendered useless by intrenchments and camps." Lieutenant Botsford and the seventy men of Company C were sent ahead to scout for guerrillas. On May 1, at a place called Clark's Hollow, they found themselves surrounded by 50 to 100 guerrillas combined with a force of 350 Confederate soldiers. Botsford refused a demand to surrender, and the company took shelter in a log house and fought for two hours until Hayes and the rest of the regiment arrived. The Confederates then retreated, leaving four dead and eight wounded behind them. Company C had seven killed and sixteen wounded. Colonel Scammon at first accused Botsford and his men of negligence in being surprised by the enemy, but he eventually came to consider what Botsford had done at Clark's Hollow as heroic and later selected him as adjutant for his own military staff.[9]

Hayes and his men pursued the Confederates as they retreated the twenty-two miles to Princeton, engaging in a running fight that lasted for thirteen hours. As the 23d neared Princeton, the men saw smoke and soon realized that the town was burning. The officer in charge of the Confederate troops, Col. Walter H. Jenifer, had ordered the town burned to destroy the goods stored there, and at least one of the citizens cooperated by burning his own home. The men of the 23d, the first troops to enter the town, tried to put the fires out but saved only a few buildings. A soldier in Company B counted some fifty chimneys standing alone; the town, he said, was "mostly in ashes." One of the houses saved was owned by Dr. Robert B. McNutt. McKinley happened to ride up to the McNutt house and was accosted by the doctor's wife, Elizabeth, who was incensed that Union troops were looting her home. She asked McKinley "whether or not there are any gentlemen in the Yankee army?" McKinley politely raised his hat and replied, "Madam, I pass for one at my home in Ohio, and I shall see at once that these annoyances cease," and he had a guard placed at the house, who prevented any further trouble for the McNutts. Hayes subsequently made the McNutt house the headquarters of the 23d Regiment.[10]

A train of twenty wagons reached Princeton three days later with eight or ten thousand rations, and foragers brought in good quantities of bacon and fresh meat, which gave McKinley ample means of feeding the regiment. When the meat arrived, Hayes reported to Scammon that with the meat "and the new grass coming on" for the animals, "an enterprising army is not going to starve."[11]

Still, provisions were a constant concern in an area Cox said was "for subsistence purposes a desert," and when escaped slaves brought word that a large quantity of provisions was stored at Pearisburg, twenty-nine miles farther south, the regiment quickly moved there. The provisions were captured, including 600 bushels of corn, 250 barrels of flour, 9 barrels of cornmeal, and 6 barrels of salt. But they were soon lost. On May 10, when only ten miles from the railroad that was the campaign's objective, the regiment was attacked by a force of five thousand Confederates commanded by Henry Heth. During a fight of seven or eight hours, the Confederates drove the regiment back seven miles to the Narrows of the New River, where it was reinforced by the rest of Scammon's brigade. The Union troops then fell back three more miles to the mouth of the East River, where they went into camp. In its flight from Pearisburg, the regiment burned the church that contained the provisions taken from the enemy. Within a few days, McKinley had no bread to issue, and men were offering a dollar apiece for hardtack; the soldiers called the camp at East River "Camp Starvation" and "Camp Scarce of Crackers." Only the bacon they found in the countryside along the New River kept them fed. One company in the 30th Ohio Infantry sent out as foragers brought in a thousand pounds of bacon in addition to a boatload of oats for the animals.[12]

On May 17, the regiment was called back to Princeton, where the troops remaining there had been attacked by a superior Confederate force. With General Cox and the rest of his command, the regiment retreated to a camp on Flat Top Mountain, on the road between Princeton and Raleigh. The camp was in a beautiful location; from the mountaintop, the men could see the countryside fifty miles in every direction, "spread out like a map in full view." McKinley treasured his memories of "the expedition to Princeton, always in the advance; the burning of the village by the Confederate forces, the almost daily skirmishing with a retreating foe, the battle with General Heath, against fearful odds; the want of supplies, our beautiful camp at Flat Top mountain." But the ugliness of the war followed them to Flat Top. Soon after their arrival, a guerrilla poisoned a spring there, for which he was quickly hanged.[13]

Despite the failure of the campaign and the inconveniences of their new camp—the men lived in huts made of slabs of chestnut bark until new Sibley tents arrived—they benefited by being once again in a secure position, where McKinley could count on receiving the supplies the men needed. The regiment remained at Flat Top for nearly two months, engaged in occasional raids and skirmishes but mostly in drilling, reading, dancing, and practicing marksmanship; the regiment's smoothbore muskets had finally been replaced by rifled muskets. Then, in July, six companies moved fourteen miles away to Green Meadows and four companies went five miles farther to guard the crossing at Packs Ferry, on the New River, a vital connection between the troops at Flat Top and those at Lewisburg. Danger, though not pressing, was always a possibility; after the regiment left Flat Top Mountain, a soldier was found there, naked, tied to a tree, with five bullet holes in him.[14]

Telegraphic news from McClellan's army in the East convinced General Cox that his division was needed more there than in western Virginia. Because General Frémont had resigned and the Kanawha Division was now in Gen. John Pope's Army of Virginia, Cox appealed to Pope for permission to bring his division east, asserting that the Kanawha Division was "among the best-seasoned and oldest troops in the field, and for discipline and drill will compare favorably with any. . . . The army here is most eager in its desire to be transferred to a larger field, where they can be of more service." Pope sent permission for Cox to bring his best troops east, leaving five thousand men to guard western Virginia. Cox then asked permission to bring the troops by way of the Kanawha and Ohio Rivers and the Baltimore and Ohio Railroad rather than marching them overland. That, too, was approved, with orders to "hurry the movement. Troops are very much needed here."[15]

On August 15, the companies of the 23d that had been at Packs Ferry joined those at Green Meadows, where Hayes made a "short but spicy speech," congratulating the men on "the prospects now before you of your going where you will have something else to do besides guarding ferry boats." Over the next three and a half days, the Kanawha Division—5,000 infantrymen, two batteries of six guns each, 300 cavalrymen, 1,100 animals, and 270 wagons—marched back through Raleigh, Fayetteville, and Gauley Bridge and on to Camp Piatt near Charleston, "that famous march," McKinley called it, "averaging over thirty miles per day for three

days, to the boats that were waiting to transport us to our railroad con-
nections." The men were delighted with their change of fortune. They
cheered and laughed, and the regimental band played "We Are So Glad to
Get Out of the Wilderness." Union sympathizers and fugitive slaves followed the troops. A slave owner came to the boats to reclaim one of the
slaves, but soldiers in the 36th Infantry "made him leave in a hurry, some
kicked and some stoned him."[16]

At Camp Piatt, the infantry regiments boarded steamboats for the trip
down the Kanawha River and up the Ohio River to Parkersburg, while the
wagon trains, artillery, cavalry, and two companies of infantry continued
to Parkersburg on land. On the Kanawha, the boats passed large crowds,
mostly women and children, who were usually quiet, "without a single expression either in manner or voice, for or against us." But on the Ohio, the
men were greeted warmly by their fellow Ohioans. One of the soldiers said
that "we have been presented with everything the soldier could wish for to
eat; and the Stars and Stripes and handkerchiefs were waved at us from
every window, together with loud and hearty cheers, which seemed so
different from the greetings we had received in the enemy's country."
"This is God's country," the men would say. At Parkersburg, the entire division boarded the four hundred cars of the Baltimore and Ohio Railroad
that had been assembled to take them to Washington. The trip to the East
was attended by dangers of its own; one man drowned in the Ohio River,
and another was killed when he fell from a railroad car.[17]

The 23d reached Washington on August 24, where its train stopped
near the Smithsonian Institution. In the evening, the men marched to the
White House, "to see Uncle Abraham," one of them said. "He made us
quite a speech." Finding the Long Bridge that carried the railroad across
the Potomac broken, the men remained in the city for two days, fed by the
"patriotic ladies" of Washington. The delay gave the men time to see some
of the capital; it was McKinley's first glimpse of the city where he would
spend much of his adult life. Andrew Duncan visited the Smithsonian, the
Capitol, the Treasury, the Post Office, the White House, and various military fortifications, as McKinley probably did too. The city showed signs of
the war; Duncan said that ambulances were running all night to the city's
thirty hospitals. "This is a beautiful place, but the pall of war is spread over
it all."[18]

The bridge was soon repaired, and the regiment crossed to Alexandria,
Virginia, on August 26. Three days later, it marched eight miles to Mun-
son's Hill and the next day to nearby Upton's Hill, near Falls Church, to
guard Forts Ramsay and Buffalo, two of the chain of forts that protected

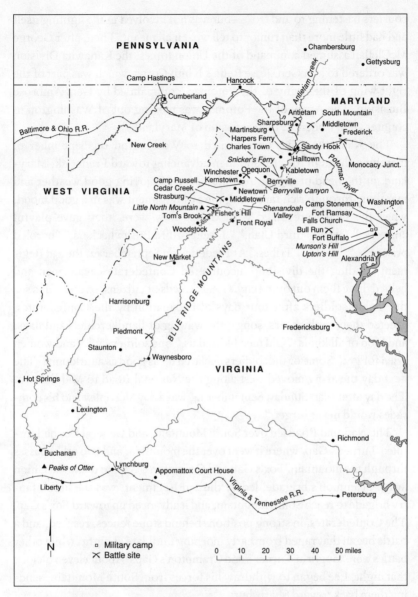

The Eastern Theater of the Civil War. *Map by Bill Nelson.*

Washington. The Second Battle of Bull Run had begun, and the "loud roar" of cannons from the battlefield could be heard.[19]

During its stay at Upton's Hill, the regiment was surrounded by the signs of war—"the roar of heavy artillery, the moving of army waggons, carriages, and ambulances with the wounded, marching troops, and couriers hastening to and fro"—but was not involved in the fighting itself and had little more than rumor to tell what it all meant. Then, after George McClellan assumed command of the Union forces, the Kanawha Division was ordered to join Gen. Jesse Reno's Ninth Corps, which was part of the right wing of the Army of the Potomac, commanded by Gen. Ambrose Burnside. The Army of the Potomac was moving out of Washington to counter Gen. Robert E. Lee's invasion of Maryland.[20]

The Kanawha Division returned to Washington on September 6, marching through the city and then advancing toward Frederick, Maryland, at the head of the entire Union army. Enjoying good weather and marching through rich farmland, the 23d Regiment was in a good mood; when the men were asked what troops they were, they gave playful answers: "Twenty-third Utah," "Twenty-third Bushwhackers," "paroled prisoners," "the Lost Tribes." At Frederick on September 12, the 23d Regiment, leading the division, encountered Confederate cavalrymen and helped drive them out of the city. Great crowds of citizens, overjoyed to see the Union soldiers after four days of occupation by the Confederates, greeted them with cheers, songs, the waving of handkerchiefs and flags, and food of all kinds. "Old men blessed us," one soldier said, "and women cried for joy." Some of the soldiers declared it "as good as a furlough." The next day the army moved west along the National Road to Middletown. The day after that, Sunday, September 14, was a day McKinley and his comrades would never forget.[21]

The National Road led over South Mountain, and General Lee had fortified Turner's Gap, where it went over the mountain, and two other passes through the mountain, Fox's Gap and Crampton's Gap, to delay the Union army. Scammon's brigade, led by the 23d Regiment, was the first infantry brigade to reach South Mountain, and it advanced up toward Fox's Gap. The Confederates, in strong positions behind stone fences, resisted, and a battle began that raged from early morning until late at night, while other battles were fought at Turner's and Crampton's Gaps. About eleven o'clock that night, Lee began to withdraw his forces from South Mountain, sending them back toward Sharpsburg.[22]

In 1893, after Rutherford Hayes's death, McKinley spoke about Hayes at Ohio Wesleyan University, giving his recollections of the Battle of South Mountain and Hayes's part in it.

It was a lovely September day—an ideal Sunday morning. McClellan's army, with Burnside's Corps in front, was passing up the mountain by the National road. General Cox's Ohio Division led Burnside's Corps, and the Twenty-third Ohio was in the lead of that division. Hayes was ordered to take one of the mountain paths and move to the right of the rebels. At nine o'clock the rebel picket was driven back, and on our pushing forward the rebels advanced upon us in strong force. Our regiment was quickly formed in the woods and charged over rocks and broken ground, through deep underbrush, under the heavy fire of the enemy at short range, and, after one of the hottest fights of the war, we drove them out of the woods and into an open field near the hilltop. Another charge was ordered by Hayes. No sooner had he given the word of command, than a minié ball from the enemy shattered his left arm above the elbow, crushing the bone to fragments. . . . The regiment made three successful charges in that fight, and lost nearly two hundred men—half of the effective force—in action.[23]

McKinley spared his audience by not describing the worst scenes of the battle. He did not mention the use of bayonets in the charges or the resulting slaughter. A member of his old company said that "our men bayonetted the enemy until hundreds of them fell and hundreds more surrendered." After the second charge, "the sight was fearful: Dead rebels lay actually piled upon each other; and I saw 17 laying on less than twenty feet square of ground." The lane the men had used to come up the mountain was "choked" with the dead; soldiers "threw them aside" to prevent their being crushed by the wheels when the artillery moved forward. Nor did McKinley describe the burial details. The Confederates had abandoned the field, so the Union soldiers had to bury all the dead. One of the soldiers in the 23d worked for three days burying twenty men from his own regiment and three to five hundred Confederates. He wrote home that "it was an awful job for the smell was horrible and the sight was what I hope never to see again."[24]

The 23d's losses, although not as great as McKinley thought, were heavier than at any other time during the war. Officially, thirty-two enlisted men were killed, eight officers and eighty-seven enlisted men were wounded, and three enlisted men were missing. South Mountain was, as McKinley said, "achieved at great cost"; nevertheless, he considered it "a splendid victory," and others agreed. One of the wounded officers, Capt. Abraham A. Hunter, had served in the British army for ten years. He said he had seen other charges by old soldiers, but nothing could surpass the "Ohio boys" in the charge in which he was wounded at South Mountain. "Neither at Inkerman or Balaklava or the storming of Sebastopol, in the Crimea, did he see nobler, braver, or more desperate fighting than he saw at South Mountain." General Scammon was particularly pleased with the men's performance in battle. He knew that the strict discipline he had enforced had produced "heart burnings and resentments," and he had agonized over his role as disciplinarian. "To be regarded as a mere martinet," he said, could be pleasing to no one. But all his efforts were rewarded at South Mountain. He said the cheer given by the soldiers before their charge there was the "sweetest music" he had heard since he first met the recruits at Camp Chase. The men had proved themselves soldiers.[25]

President Lincoln congratulated McClellan and his army for the victory at South Mountain: "God bless you, and all with you. Destroy the rebel army, if possible." The army Lincoln wanted destroyed had retired to a strong position on the heights between Antietam Creek and the village of Sharpsburg. After a cold night on the battlefield at South Mountain, the Kanawha Division spent the morning burying its dead and arranging to have the wounded and prisoners sent back to Middletown. Leaving a small detachment to complete those tasks, the division left the mountain to follow the Confederates. When the division arrived at Antietam Creek, it was placed on the Union left, near the bridge later known as the Burnside Bridge, with the 23d Regiment on the extreme left.[26]

The Battle of Antietam began on the morning of September 17, on the right, away from the Kanawha Division. During the morning, the division was ordered to attack to create a diversion. After two failed attempts, part of the division forced its way across the heavily defended Burnside Bridge; the 23d, with its brigade, crossed the Antietam at a ford downstream from the bridge and then remained near the bridge for two hours under heavy artillery fire while ammunition was brought up. Then, with the troops that had crossed the bridge, the men advanced toward Sharpsburg, "constantly and severely exposed," McKinley said, and charged Confederates positioned behind a stone wall. Soon, however, they were fired on from a cornfield on the left by newly arrived Confederate troops, A. P. Hill's division, returning from having captured Harpers Ferry. The brigade changed front to face them but was forced to retreat to a defensive position in front of the bridge and remained there the rest of the day.[27]

The supply train for the Ninth Corps had not come up before the battle began, and the men had gone to their battle positions at 2:00 A.M. without breakfast and with no rations in their haversacks. By 2:00 P.M., the men of the 23d Regiment, lying in a sheltered position across the Antietam awaiting orders to advance toward Sharpsburg, were exhausted and famished. McKinley, who was acting commissary officer for his brigade, was aware that his regiment was awaiting orders to move forward again and was determined to feed the men. Without consulting anyone, he went back to the wagon train and the commissary stores two miles behind the battlefield, gathered up the stragglers, and put them to work preparing rations. Then he loaded a wagon with cooked meat, pork and beans, crackers, and a barrel of ground coffee and asked for a volunteer to go with him to get the food to the men.[28]

John A. Harvey of Company I volunteered to go with McKinley and later described their ride to the front.

We started by the way of a by road through a heavy piece of woods. After driving along the road for some distance from the camp, we met an Army officer with his staff and he told (then Sergeant) McKinley that he must not try to go to the Regiment as it would be impossible to run the blockade, as the Rebel forces had command of an open strip in the woods. The road being so narrow that we could not turn around Sergeant McKinley thought we had better try to go on a little farther. Before we came to the open space in the woods, and close to the brow of the hill we met another Commanding Officer who ordered us to immediately turn back. We stopped and considered the matter and the Officer and his body guard went in the opposite direction. This left Sergeant McKinley to decide what was best to do. The Regiment was almost in sight of us and Sergeant McKinley was so anxious to carry out his point and give the half-starved boys something to eat. He made one more appeal to me to run the blockade; he himself risking his life in taking the lead, I following and the horses going at full speed past the blockade. We had the back end of the wagon shot away by a small cannon shot. In a very few minutes we were safe in the midst of the half-famished regiment.[29]

The soldiers in McKinley's regiment noticed an army wagon approaching from the rear "at breakneck speed, through a terrific fire of musketry and artillery that seemed to threaten annihilation to everything within its range." When the wagon drew up, they saw that it was McKinley, who leaped from the wagon and reported his arrival to Major Comly (commanding the 23d Regiment after Lieutenant Colonel Hayes was wounded). Colonel Scammon, hearing men cheering on the left of his line, sent Lt. James Botsford to find out the reason. Botsford found both officers and enlisted men cheering McKinley and the hot rations he had brought them.

Sergeant McKinley, a bronze tablet by James Edward Kelly, depicting
McKinley bringing rations to the soldiers at the Battle of Antietam. The
tablet was erected in Wilmington, Delaware, in 1908. From *Munsey's
Magazine. Courtesy of the Prints and Photographs Division, Library of
Congress.*

The men fell back to the wagon in groups of ten to receive their share. One
man who had been severely wounded in the battle was heard to murmur,
"God bless the lad!" After the war, McKinley liked to say that those words
"were the highest reward that he could possibly have received" for what he
had done.[30]

The 23d's casualties at Antietam were less than at South Mountain, although they were severe enough: eight men were killed, fifty-nine wounded,
and two missing. The regiment's losses at the two battles created vacancies
among the officers, and Major Comly, impressed with McKinley's actions,
recommended him for a promotion. He wrote to Hayes, who was recuper-
ating in Ohio, that McKinley "showed ability and energy of the first class,

in not only keeping us *fully supplied* with rations throughout the fight, but in having them fully prepared for eating, also. We had *plenty* when every body else was short. He delivered them to us *under fire,* in two instances, with perfect method and coolness. . . . I feel greatly indebted to McKinley. No promotion could be made which would give more general satisfaction." McKinley, too, was thinking about a promotion. Hayes's brother-in-law Joseph T. Webb, who was a surgeon in the 23d, also wrote to Hayes: "Our young friend McKinley[,] Commissary Sergeant, would be pleased with a promotion, and would not object to your recommendation for it. Without wishing to interfere in this matter it strikes me he is about the brightest chap spoken of for the place." Thirty-four years later, some of McKinley's comrades sought a greater recognition for him: the Congressional Medal of Honor. Shortly after McKinley's election to the presidency, they appealed to President Grover Cleveland to award the medal, and Nelson Miles, the major general commanding the army, recommended the award, but when McKinley learned about it, he asked that no action be taken, and the matter was dropped. Two years after McKinley's death, the state of Ohio erected a thirty-three and a half foot monument near the Burnside Bridge on the Antietam battlefield to commemorate McKinley's "valiant act" during the battle.[31]

The 23d remained on the battlefield the night after the battle. At the Burnside Bridge, the dead and dying "strewed the ground, and all about was the wreckage of battle." It was not long before "the blackened faces and bloated bodies" of the dead "were beyond recognition, and were disgusting to look upon for a moment." But someone had looked at them; everything of value had been taken from most of the bodies. Their pockets had been cut open and their shoes removed from their feet. Surgeons were soon at work on the wounded, and "hundreds of amputated limbs lay strewn everywhere." McKinley's work of feeding the living went on; the wagons and teams the Kanawha Division had brought from western Virginia proved useful in supplying provisions for the Ninth Corps, whose trains were insufficient for the task.[32]

The day after the battle, the men awaited the order to advance, but McClellan chose not to resume the battle, and that night Lee withdrew his army, crossed the Potomac, and returned to Virginia. That same night, the Kanawha Division was relieved, and the following day it moved to a location across Antietam Creek, near its mouth on the Potomac River, about seven miles from Harpers Ferry, where it remained for almost three weeks. While they were there, the men were diverted by watching Thaddeus Lowe make balloon ascensions. They also showed a renewed interest in religion; on Sundays and two or three times during the week, large numbers attended religious services held in the Kanawha Division.[33]

President Lincoln visited South Mountain and Antietam in early October. On October 3, accompanied by Generals McClellan and Burnside, he reviewed the Kanawha Division at its camp on the Potomac. As he approached each regiment, the men were permitted to cheer, and then they presented arms while Lincoln passed by. The president rode past some of the regiments with his head "turned rigidly to the front," not looking at the men or their officers. One soldier thought he seemed to be hurrying through "a distasteful undertaking." But when Lincoln came to the 23d Regiment, Burnside pointed to it and made some remark, and Lincoln turned his horse and rode over to the regiment's flag, which the color sergeant held out to him. It was riddled with bullet holes, and the blue field was almost destroyed by shells and bullets. Lincoln appeared to be moved by the account Burnside gave him of the regiment's losses, particularly those at South Mountain.[34]

The men were amused that, in riding, Lincoln's pants had worked up nearly to the top of his boots, "presenting a comical appearance." If McKinley noticed, he said nothing about it. What impressed him and remained in his memory was the expression on Lincoln's face. Speaking at a celebration of Lincoln's birthday in 1896, he said: "I remember, as though it were but yesterday, and thousands of my comrades will recall, how, when he reviewed the Army of the Potomac immediately after the battle of Antietam, his indescribably sad, thoughtful, far-seeing expression pierced every man's soul." When, during his presidency, McKinley visited the battlefield at Antietam, he confided to friends that Lincoln's review of the army was his most vivid memory of Antietam and that "the sadness of President Lincoln's face on that occasion made more impression upon him as a boy than all the carnage of that dreadful day."[35]

On July 4, 1861, when the 23d Regiment was still at Camp Chase, Lincoln had submitted a message on the war to Congress. He called attention to the volunteer army and said that "there are many single Regiments whose members, one and another, possess full practical knowledge of all the arts, sciences, professions, and whatever else, whether useful or elegant, is known in the world; and there is scarcely one, from which there could not be selected, a President, a Cabinet, a Congress, and perhaps a Court, abundantly competent to administer the government itself." At Antietam, Lincoln found just such a regiment in the 23d Ohio. It produced two governors of Ohio who went on to become presidents of the United

States, Hayes and McKinley; two lieutenant governors of Ohio, Robert P. Kennedy and William C. Lyon; four United States congressmen, Hayes, McKinley, Kennedy, and William S. Rosecrans; and a United States senator who later became an associate justice of the United States Supreme Court, Stanley Matthews.[36]

Much to the dislike of many of the men, who had taken pride in the *New York Herald*'s description of them as "the keen Damascus blade of the Army of the Potomac," the Kanawha Division was ordered to leave the Army of the Potomac and return to western Virginia. Although Cox had left five thousand men there under Col. Joseph A. J. Lightburn, they proved inadequate. Confederate forces under Maj. Gen. William W. Loring occupied Charleston in September, and the Union force retreated back to the Ohio River. With General Lee's army back in Virginia, the Kanawha Division could be spared to strengthen the Union forces in western Virginia.[37]

The division began a three-day march to Hancock, Maryland, on October 8. The men passed through the village of Sharpsburg, where few of the citizens came out to see them—the doors of the houses were closed and the blinds drawn—and over the Antietam battlefield, which was ravaged by the fighting and covered with discarded equipment. For miles on both sides of the road, they marched past freshly dug graves. The limestone that had been used to macadamize the Sharpsburg Turnpike was pulverized from the wagon trains of both armies, and the dust was suffocating. Marching at what the men thought an unnecessarily rapid pace in the hot sun while breathing the limestone dust made the march one of the worst they experienced during the war. The division reached Hancock on the third day, and the men waded across the Potomac into Virginia. There they boarded trains bound for the West, but before they left, they learned that Confederate cavalry under J. E. B. Stuart had crossed the river nearby, heading for Pennsylvania. The 23d Regiment with the rest of the First Brigade was ordered to pursue the Confederates, and though the men thought it foolish for infantry to pursue cavalry, they followed orders and marched about twenty miles into Franklin County, Pennsylvania. Finding nothing, they returned the next day to Hancock and again waded the Potomac into Virginia. But the "little chase into Pennsylvania," as McKinley called it, gave the soldiers a story they told for years, how on the march that day they had eaten breakfast in Pennsylvania, dinner in Maryland, and supper in Virginia.[38]

The soldiers boarded cattle and freight cars on the Baltimore and Ohio Railroad, which carried them to Clarksburg. There McKinley was able to furnish the men with a better quality of hard crackers than had been available in the East and, for only the fourth time since leaving Camp Chase, soft bread. While other troops quickly forced the Confederates out of the Kanawha Valley, the Kanawha Division went south from Clarksburg, through Weston, Bulltown, Sutton, and Summersville, marching down the same roads the 23d had traveled when it first arrived in western Virginia. Despite a general expectation of hard fighting, the Confederates retreated ahead of the Union troops, and the division followed them as far as Gauley Bridge. Near there, at Camp Maskell, at the falls of the Kanawha River, the division made its winter quarters.[39]

While the division was still at Summersville, McKinley was ordered back to Mahoning County, Ohio, his home county, to recruit for the 23d. Deaths, wounds, and sickness had taken their toll on the regiment. It had marched out of Camp Chase with more than a thousand men; now it had no more than four hundred fit for duty. McKinley was one of eleven sergeants from three regiments who were placed under the direction of Lt. Gordon Lofland and sent to Ohio as recruiters. His orders specified that when he had recruited nine men he would be commissioned as a second lieutenant.[40]

McKinley and the other sergeants traveled to Columbus, where they went to the newly completed statehouse and were received by Governor David Tod, the War Democrat from Mahoning County who had succeeded William Dennison. As they were leaving the governor's office, Tod surprised McKinley and Sgt. Milton DeShong by presenting them with commissions as second lieutenants for their services at Antietam.[41]

Governor Tod had learned about McKinley's performance at Antietam from Rutherford Hayes. Hayes reported Tod's reaction: "with the emphasis that distinguished that great war governor, he said: 'Let McKinley be promoted from sergeant to lieutenant,' and that I might not forget he requested me to put it upon the roster of the regiment, which I did, and McKinley was promoted." In 1888, after a distinguished career in Congress and efforts to nominate him for the presidency, McKinley told Hayes that "the proudest and happiest period of my life was when in 1862 I was sent from the regiment on recruiting service with other sergeants, and upon arriving at Columbus found that you had my commission as 2nd lieutenant, and that it had been issued upon your personal recommendation, for what as a boy, I had done at Antietam."[42]

The proud new second lieutenant, however, had to borrow money from DeShong to get home to Poland. DeShong lent him $3.45, which left DeShong short for his own trip home. From Columbus, McKinley traveled to Cleveland, where he met Lt. Russell Hastings, who was also recruiting for the 23d. As Hastings told about their meeting:

> It took me but a few minutes to find that he had only money enough to buy a soldier's railway ticket to his home at Poland, Ohio. I said[,] "McKinley, how would you like to go home to your Mother in your second Lieutenant's uniform, with your sword by your side". How his eyes sparkled when I said, "You ought to and shall". "Stay with me two or three days, and I will fit you out". What a proud boy he was (then 19) when he first donned his uniform.[43]

He arrived home on November 18, "bubbling over with enthusiasm," his sister Sarah said, happy about his commission, talking about his experiences in the war, describing his exploits at Antietam, and seeming quite proud of what he had done.[44]

Poland had changed in the seventeen months McKinley had been away. The romance had gone out of the war. Eleven of the men who left home with the Poland Guards had been wounded, one had died of illness, two were killed at South Mountain, and three more were killed at Antietam. Six weeks before McKinley arrived home, the townspeople had gathered for the funeral of Charles Long, a member of the Poland Guards who had been killed at Antietam. A week before that, they had gathered for the funeral of Gaylord Hawkins, the Methodist minister who visited the Poland Guards at Camp Chase. Hawkins had enlisted as a chaplain in the 2d Ohio Cavalry and had died of typhoid fever at Fort Scott, Kansas. The townspeople were also accustomed to gathering as the Poland Soldiers' Aid Society to raise money and prepare food and clothing for the sick and wounded; shortly after McKinley arrived home, James Botsford's father went from Poland to visit the soldiers at Camp Maskell, bringing supplies from home. In September, the town had been aroused at night by news of a Confederate threat to Cincinnati, and seventy or eighty men from Poland joined the "Squirrel Hunters" from around the state who responded to the governor's appeal for volunteers to defend the city.[45]

McKinley set up a recruiting office in the drugstore in Poland owned by his brother-in-law, Daniel May, advertising the office in the Youngstown newspaper and offering a forty-two-dollar bounty for volunteers. As a recruiter, McKinley was to ascertain the age of any potential recruit, "his former habits as to sobriety, and his general character," and to obtain a surgeon's examination. Then he was to read the Twentieth Article of War to the volunteers, which specified the death penalty for desertion, and if they

Recruits Wanted

FOR THE

TWENTY-THIRD OHIO.

LIEUT. WM. McKINLEY, 23d Ohio Volunteers, is authorized to recruit for the 23d Reg't O. V.

$42 Bounty will be Paid

upon being mustered into the service.

Office in Daniel May's Drug Store, Poland, O.
November 27, 1862.-3t

A notice McKinley placed in the *Mahoning Register*, published at Youngstown, Ohio, when he was recruiting for the 23d Ohio Volunteer Infantry in November 1862. *Courtesy of the Ohio Historical Society, Columbus.*

still wanted to enlist, he was to have a magistrate administer the same oath he had taken at Camp Chase. And he was to report to Columbus daily about his activities. Although no record of McKinley's success in recruiting has survived, Poland prided itself in always meeting its military quotas with volunteers; the township was never subject to a draft. McKinley returned to the army a full four weeks before his orders required him to, probably because he had reached his quota of recruits but perhaps too because of the enthusiasm for the army he had exhibited to his sister Sarah.[46]

When McKinley arrived at Camp Maskell, Rutherford Hayes, well again and back in camp with a promotion to colonel, noted in his diary that "our new second lieutenant, McKinley, returned today—an exceedingly bright, intelligent, and gentlemanly young officer. He promises to be one of our best." The next day, Hayes wrote about McKinley to his wife, Lucy Webb Hayes.

> One of our new second lieutenants—McKinley—a handsome bright, gallant boy, got back last night. He went to Ohio to recruit with the other orderly sergeants of the regiment. He tells good stories of their travels. The Thirtieth and Twelfth sergeants stopped at second-class hotels, but the Twenty-third boys "splurged." They stopped at the American and swung by the big figure. Very proper. They are the generals of the next war.[47]

THREE *Quartermaster*

[McKinley] had unusual character for the mere business of war. . . .
Young as he was, we soon found that in business, in executive ability,
young McKinley was of rare capacity, of unusual and unsurpassed
capacity, especially for a boy of his age.

—Rutherford B. Hayes

As an officer, McKinley was set apart from his former comrades. His officer's sword and sky-blue shoulder straps were signs of his office and were to be respected by the men in the ranks. But McKinley managed to keep on good terms with the enlisted men. John Ellen said that he always retained "close touch" with his "first associates in army life," the common soldiers of the 23d. (After he was commissioned, he impressed his old company by sharing a cake he had received from home just as he would have done before he was an officer.) And he had the respect of all the soldiers. One of the men in Company G said that he was "esteemed and respected by all his comrades and was recognized as a young man in whom could be placed implicit confidence." Another soldier also spoke approvingly about him:

> He was a model officer, and a good fellow to boot. To be sure, there
> was a certain reserve about him, so that one couldn't get too famil-
> iar, but he was never harsh, and he never swore at us as some officers
> did. He never seemed to care for rough stories, and I don't think he ever
> told such a story in his life, even though he would occasionally make
> a good-natured joke. He was a great fellow to read and to watch how

matters were going in camp, and he kept his uniform and equipments as clean as the cleanest.[1]

The new second lieutenant was assigned to Company D, the former Cleveland Rifle Grenadiers, and two days after he arrived in camp he was busy directing a working party that was clearing the camp's parade ground. The camp required a good deal of work. The men ditched the camp grounds and sanded the streets. They were busy for a month building sixty log cabins with large fireplaces for the winter, cutting trees on the mountainside and sliding the logs down to the building sites. In the evenings, when their work was done, the men gathered about fires for conversation, which usually turned to the battles in Maryland—"how this one fought, or that one fell." Their dead comrades were often on their minds, and the men of the 23d Regiment resolved to build a monument after the war to bear the name of every man who had fallen and every one who would fall before the war was over. The city of Cleveland donated a lot in Woodland Cemetery for the monument, and the soldiers raised two thousand dollars for it; McKinley contributed fifteen dollars. One soldier in particular was on Colonel Hayes's mind; Hayes renamed the camp Camp Reynolds in memory of the regiment's sergeant major, Eugene Reynolds, taken prisoner at South Mountain and shot and bayoneted in trying to escape.[2]

The soldiers celebrated New Year's Eve by "making all the noise possible, firing muskets, blowing up old shells, and 'raising Ned' generally." The beginning of 1863 brought changes in the commands in western Virginia. The old Kanawha Division was divided, and the First Kanawha Division, commanded by George Crook, was sent west to assist General Burnside. The Second Kanawha Division, under General Scammon, remained in western Virginia. Hayes was given command of the First Brigade in Scammon's division, consisting of the 23d and 89th Ohio Infantry Regiments and two companies of cavalry. It was a small brigade, numbering 1,859 on paper but with only 1,350 present for duty. On January 7, 1863, when he assumed command of the brigade, Hayes appointed McKinley as the brigade's acting assistant quartermaster.[3]

The favoritism Hayes showed to McKinley was not appreciated by everyone. John Ellen, who had recently been appointed quartermaster of the 23d Regiment, suspected that Hayes and his brother-in-law Dr. Joe Webb did not approve of his appointment; "I presume 'Mc' was their choice." But then, Ellen had become cynical about much in army life. After only a few weeks in the Quartermaster's Department, he found it "all

Second Lt. William McKinley Jr. After McKinley received his
commission, Col. Rutherford B. Hayes selected him for his military staff.
Courtesy of the Rutherford B. Hayes Presidential Center.

wrangle and confusion." Throughout the army, he thought, everyone was "trying to *get*, without any apparent desire to *do*. . . . Self! Self! Self is the rule, and true patriotism the exception." Later, Ellen noted that McKinley accompanied Hayes at a review of the 23d and described the review as "a puny burlesque of military display; a kind of farce."[4]

McKinley was aware of the duties of a quartermaster from serving as clerk to the brigade quartermaster. But now the responsibility for supplying the needs of the men in the brigade was his, and he would be held accountable not only to Colonel Hayes but also to the chief quartermaster at Charleston. Hayes also assigned McKinley the duties of commissary of subsistence—familiar to him from his experience as commissary sergeant—but his main assignment was as quartermaster of the brigade.[5]

All the materials the soldiers needed, except ordnance, were supplied through the quartermaster: clothing, equipment, tents, stoves, fuel, flags, musical instruments, building materials, tools, wagons, horses, and mules—and the animals' shoes, saddles, harnesses, combs, medicine, and feed. In one month, McKinley provided 30,720 pounds of corn, 52,266 pounds of oats, and 95,226 pounds of hay for 469 horses and mules. His work involved countless details. In one case, he wrote about cavalry coats: "In drawing clothing of you on the 24th inst. 6 Six Cavalry Great Coats were issued & upon examination turn out to be Inf[antry] Overcoats with two row Buttons. I sent my clerk to your forage House this morning & your storekeeper refuses to exchange & give me what my requisition calls for." In another case, he wrote to John Ellen about a mistake on one of Ellen's reports: "Respectfully returned for correction in the *total* number of animals being *53* instead of *54*, makeing a difference in the hay." In still another case, he wrote about missing tools: "I furnished your command with 17 Axes, 7 Pick Axes & 5 shovels. . . . I left instructions with QM Sgt. Webb to ship them to me from Gauley. . . . They have never reached me, nor have I been able to hear anything of their whereabouts."[6]

The supplies McKinley received and issued had to be accounted for on endless forms: "Quarterly Return of Quartermaster's Stores"; "List of Articles Lost or Destroyed in the Public Service"; "Statement of Forage Issued to and Consumed by the Public Animals under My Direction"; "Monthly Return of Clothing, Camp and Garrison Equipage"; and on and on. Moreover, the reports had to be submitted on time: "Hereafter no excuse will be received for not rendering the Dept. Reports at times prescribed in the Dept. Circular No. 1." He was required to send copies of the reports to Washington for the quartermaster general (in triplicate) and the third auditor in the Treasury Department. In August 1869, four years after the end of the war, the Third Auditor's Office suspended McKinley's "Returns of Quartermaster's Stores" for the period January 1863 to July 1864 and returned them to him for explanations. McKinley appears to have ignored the request and filed the returns away rather than attempting to provide the auditor with explanations for minute matters five and six years old. (The quartermaster of the 34th Massachusetts Infantry had a similar experience; the officials at Washington returned his accounts because he had issued three more lead pencils than he was authorized to issue.)[7]

Enlisted men were detailed to assist the new quartermaster. At one time, Hayes had put under McKinley's direction a clerk, a carpenter, a foragemaster, a wagonmaster, a harnessmaster, two blacksmiths, and five teamsters. The skills of the men reflected the importance of the transportation of supplies, which was also the quartermaster's responsibility. Supplies were sent from a depot at Gallipolis, Ohio, up the Kanawha River by steamboats, which came close to Camp Reynolds if the river was high, farther away if it was low. Then they had to be transported to the camp by bateaux or by wagons—heavy, lumbering army wagons, covered with white canvas and usually pulled by teams of six mules, with the drivers, mounted on the left-hand mules nearest the wagons, urging them on with their whips. A quartermaster was often surrounded by the sounds of wagons rumbling, harnesses creaking, whips cracking, mules braying, and teamsters swearing. Though no longer a commissary sergeant, McKinley still spent much of his time among the mules.[8]

His clerks prepared some of his paperwork for him, but McKinley had to review their work and sign the forms. The paperwork required all the supplies of a commercial office; at different times, for his use in the Quartermaster's Department, he was issued official forms and envelopes, letter papers, foolscap papers, sealing wax, ink, blotting paper, lead pencils, pens, pen holders, and office tape (the original red tape, used to tie bundles of official papers). He made good use of them; his letters and reports were consistently orderly and businesslike—despite the third auditor's faultfinding.[9]

Inevitably, supplies for the brigade came up missing and had to be accounted for. Army regulations permitted Hayes to appoint a board of survey to investigate the losses and, if the board found that McKinley was not responsible for them, to provide a statement freeing him of the responsibility. McKinley himself had served on such a board before he became a quartermaster. Boards met frequently to review losses; a typical one dealt with articles McKinley said were "worn out lost and destroyed" and determined that McKinley was not responsible for their loss. Certifying that supplies were "worn out lost and destroyed" was one of the ways dishonest quartermasters used to enrich themselves. One exposé of those practices, published in 1862, was titled *Nine Months in the Quartermaster's Department on the Chance of Making a Million!* But McKinley was not one to abuse his office; once, after he found it necessary to destroy some of the brigade's property to keep it from falling into enemy hands, McKinley told a friend, "This is where the quartermasters make their money, but I don't want a dollar of Uncle Sam's that doesn't belong to me."[10]

McKinley soon learned the routine of supplying the camp, and he was usually able to do it in six days and to rest on Sunday, for, as he told his sister Sarah, "I suspend all unnecessary business on that day." He also served on a general court-martial assembled to try one of the privates, and he managed to find time for reading, choosing history and the biographies of military men; he was beginning to think of making the army his profession. Hayes added to his store of military books by giving him a copy of Silas Casey's *Tactics* with a personal inscription. And McKinley received another promotion. Maj. James McIlrath wrote to Governor Tod to make recommendations for promotions in the 23d Regiment, including one for a promotion to first lieutenant for William McKinley Jr., which he received on March 30. "He deserves it," one old soldier said. "Watch him, and some day you'll see him a general."[11]

Camp Reynolds was a quiet place in the early months of 1863. The nearest Confederate forces were at Lewisburg, too far away to be a threat, and the soldiers were able to relax. A visit from the paymaster raised their spirits, and they broke the monotony by organizing lyceums and literary exercises, sailing small sailboats on the river, and fishing at the falls, where three- to ten-pound pike could be caught. The main topic of conversation was the Peace Democrats, or Copperheads, in the North, and the men frequently wrote to their hometown newspapers to vent their anger against those who opposed the war. "Were it not for the fact that such cowards and traitors would disgrace the service," one of them said, he hoped they would be drafted so they could experience the hardships the soldiers had endured "for their safety and comfort." Another correspondent was more blunt: "These men ought to be provided with hempen collars."[12]

The interlude in the war encouraged Colonel Hayes to invite his wife, Lucy, to visit the camp, and she arrived at Camp Reynolds on January 24 with their two oldest sons, Birchard and Webb. Despite the lull in the fighting, it took some courage for them to travel to western Virginia. An earlier traveler described the steamboat that carried him up the Kanawha River.

The doors and windows, the smokestacks, and some of the cabin walls had bullet holes in them, and the pilothouse, engines, and boilers were armored with thick planks of wood. After their arrival, Lucy showed her fearlessness by riding as much as four or five miles outside the lines. "Lucy says she thinks the Rebels can't get her," her husband wrote. "I am not so sure."[13]

Lucy and the boys joined Hayes in his double log cabin, whose open shake roof let the snow through "in clouds." With the soldiers, they enjoyed the fishing and boating on the river, rode horseback, read, played cards, and made the camp into what Hayes called "a happy abiding place." They stayed at Camp Reynolds for two months, and during that time they were part of the colonel's mess, which included, among other officers, Lieutenant McKinley.[14]

As Lucy Hayes and her sons prepared to return to Ohio, her husband was also preparing to move his headquarters. After four months at Camp Reynolds, the brigade headquarters and the part of the brigade stationed with it were to be moved "out of the wilderness" to Charleston. Two companies were sent ahead, and then on March 15 the rest of the men marched four miles to Loup Creek, where they boarded steamboats bound for Charleston. They stayed in churches in the city for two nights and then crossed the Kanawha River and went into camp near the mouth of the Elk River, with small wedge tents for the men and wall tents for the officers. Camp White, as it was called, was to be their home for more than a year.[15]

A few days later, Lucy Hayes and her boys continued on their way to Ohio. They left none too soon. Nine days after they left, two boats loaded with passengers and troops were attacked on their way north from Charleston. One person was killed and several wounded. More than three hundred bullet holes were counted in one of the boats and two hundred in the other.[16]

Portions of the brigade were scattered about the state, from Gauley Bridge to the Kentucky line, making the issuing of supplies more difficult for McKinley, but his location in Charleston made the drawing of supplies much easier; steamboats passed the camp two or three times a day, and the supply depot at Gallipolis was only five or six hours away. McKinley had a skiff assigned to him, which allowed him easy access to Gallipolis as well as to the troops stationed upriver from Charleston. A Confederate raid on Point Pleasant, at the mouth of the Kanawha, destroyed some stores and interrupted traffic on the river, and raids at other outlying points, including the Jones and Imboden raids, raised enough concern that a fort was built near the camp and an ironclad gunboat placed on the river, but for the most part, McKinley and the other soldiers led a peaceful life at Camp White during the spring and early summer of 1863.[17]

One soldier described Charleston, across the river from the camp, as "a very pretty place of about 3,000 inhabitants, who, to almost a man, are of Secession sentiments." The large number of soldiers stationed there encouraged investors, and Charleston businesses flourished, including "billiard saloons" and gambling halls. Despite rudeness from some of the inhabitants, the soldiers managed to go to parties and dances in the city as often as once or twice a week. (A year before, the men of the 12th Ohio Infantry attended so many parties in Charleston that "it was barely possible to keep men enough in quarters to protect the camp from being pillaged by thieves.") The men also played ball and went boating on the river. McKinley, who was ambidextrous, entertained his comrades with demonstrations of his ability to shave with his straight razor using his left hand as well as his right—after they had laid bets that he could not. On at least one occasion, McKinley was invited to go riding with Colonel Hayes and Dr. Webb, and both Hayes and McKinley were guests at Sarah Robinson's boardinghouse on Virginia Street in Charleston, preferring her cooking to that in camp. The wives of some of the officers visited the camp, and Lucy Hayes returned, with her mother and all four of her sons, but they had been there only a few days when the Hayeses' youngest son, eighteen-month-old Joseph, sickened and died, and the family soon returned to Ohio.[18]

Salutes from the brigade's batteries marked Independence Day, a day that held special meaning that year because the new state of West Virginia had been added to the Union just two weeks before. Three days later, one hundred guns were fired in celebration of the capture of Vicksburg. And soon after that, Scammon's division made a rapid movement south to Raleigh, where a heavy concentration of Confederates had been reported. The Confederates had constructed fortifications near Raleigh, but on the approach of the Union troops, they fled, and Hayes's brigade, after destroying the fortifications, began its return to Charleston. Colonel Hayes thought it "a very lively and pleasant raid."[19]

At Fayetteville, on the return from Raleigh, Hayes learned from a telegrapher that Confederate general John Hunt Morgan and his cavalry had entered Ohio and were approaching Gallipolis with its great store of supplies. Hayes convinced General Scammon to let him take two infantry regiments—the 23d Ohio and the 13th West Virginia—to go to the defense of Gallipolis, arranged for two steamboats to transport his men, and informed the soldiers, who, despite having just marched seventeen miles on a hot day, received the news "with cheers and great delight, and with cries that they were off for God's country." Not finding Morgan at Gallipolis, the troops went up the Ohio River to Pomeroy, Ohio, where they landed and formed in battle line, "amid the cheers and many smiles of the inhabitants." When the Confederates approached and realized that they were facing more than militiamen, they started for Buffington Island, where they hoped to cross the river into West Virginia. Hayes put his men back on the steamboats and met the Confederates at Buffington Island. On the foggy morning of July 19, Hayes's troops landed on the West Virginia side of the river and assisted Union militia, federal cavalrymen, and U.S. Navy gunboats in preventing the crossing and capturing more than 2,300 of the raiders. Hayes's brigade captured 208 of the prisoners, including 145 who surrendered to two soldiers of the 23d Regiment, Alfred Arthur and David Kimberly, who were in a small group of 6 Union soldiers separated from their commands. Morgan and 336 men who continued their raid northward into Ohio were finally captured near West Point, Ohio. After guarding fords and searching for more of Morgan's men as far up the river as Hockingport, Ohio, the brigade concluded what McKinley called its "whirl through Ohio" and returned to Camp White.[20]

As the men were making themselves comfortable again in their old camp (too comfortable, perhaps; an order was issued to "'clean out' all bawdy houses"), McKinley was ordered to Ohio to procure arms and equipment for the 13th West Virginia Infantry. When he had completed his assignment, he stopped at the Hayes residence, leaving a note for Lucy Hayes, and then, despite orders to "return as soon as possible," he made a visit to his home in Poland.[21]

Poland was still astir from the Morgan raid. McKinley's brother-in-law, Daniel May, had been roused from his bed on July 26—just a few days before McKinley's arrival—by men who had heard that Morgan and his cavalry were approaching and who wanted to buy lead from May's store for ammunition. Nearly every able-bodied man, including May, left for neighboring Columbiana County but soon learned that Morgan and his men had surrendered. The site of the surrender, near West Point in Columbiana County, the northernmost point reached by Confederate troops during the war, was no more than twenty-five miles from Poland. Niles, McKinley's former home, and the surrounding communities had been similarly aroused and armed. At Salem, the churches were dismissed, and the women went home to mold bullets and bake bread for the men who were going out to "lick Morgan." At Youngstown, the money and records of the banks were hurried off by a special train to Cleveland for protection.[22]

McKinley was soon back at Camp White and settled into its routine: light duties with plenty of time for visiting Charleston, swimming, boating, riding, reading, music by the regiment's band—and with soft bread instead of crackers for rations. Still, reminders of the war sometimes interrupted the routine. Two members of the 23d were murdered near Gauley Bridge on their return from a scout.[23]

The officers' wives returned to camp, and some of the unmarried officers came back from furloughs bringing brides with them. In September, Lucy Hayes returned to Camp White and stayed for a month. Women were on many of the soldiers' minds. Some of them, "destitute of sweethearts," wrote to the *Holmes County Republican* asking for female correspondents. "Three of Uncle Sam's youths, who have fought and suffered for their country, wish to correspond with any number of Union-loving sisters, with a view to fun and mutual improvement." Another soldier, not to be outdone, said he wanted to "correspond with a dozen young ladies with a view to fun, love and the consequences." And prostitutes still clung to the camp. One soldier wrote to his family about the "deba[u]chery and disease" he had observed:

> There are some of the hardest looking specimens of female kind in the Kanawha Valley that I ever saw or expect to see and they are here of all grades and colors and draw their supplies from officers as well as privates and scatter their disease among all without regard to rank. It seems in this country that since the war has broke out there is a Strumpet to almost every soldier or officer. Every few days some of the worst are arrested and sent down the river somewhere.[24]

McKinley and one of his fellow officers were also showing an interest in the opposite sex. He had become friends with twenty-eight-year-old Russell Hastings, formerly a lieutenant in the Ohio Union Savers but now a captain and an aide-de-camp to General Scammon. The two had become "bunkies," having tented together, the five-foot, six-inch McKinley and the six-foot, four-inch Hastings—whom McKinley had once called a "clothes pin of an officer"—frequently sharing a blanket. Hastings later described his and McKinley's social life while they were at Camp White:

> During this period of inaction McKinley and I became much interested in the young ladies of Charleston and surrounding country. At Malden five miles above, our horses (caparisoned steeds) were frequently seen

at the door of a wealthy salt maker's house. It was dangerous to be so far away from camp without guard, as the people of Malden were all Confederate sympathizers; some having relatives in the Southern Army. We were always gladly received in our many calls, and were really never suspicious of any collusion with their Confederate army friends. We were very careful to instruct our orderlies as they held our horses, to never go away from the front gate, to never dismount, to be alert, and to alarm us in haste if anything suspicious should occur. The young ladies of this household frequently visited a married sister in Charleston and as the summer wore on we became quite chummy (Platonic).[25]

Hastings said that he and McKinley had "the entrance to the houses of the aristocracy" of Charleston and were out somewhere every evening. But eventually, McKinley reached the limits of General Scammon's tolerance for social life in the army. At Scammon's direction, his adjutant—and McKinley's friend—James Botsford wrote to Colonel Hayes telling him that his staff officers were not to visit Charleston at night for pleasure and adding: "You will call Lieut. McKinley's attention to this. I have been directed to notify him, and afterwards should he disobey the order to arrest him."[26]

Other forms of recreation also had their risks. McKinley and John Ellen were in a group that went boating one day. They had crossed the river and were returning when their boat capsized. McKinley and one of his companions swam to shore; the others were rescued by boat. Ellen's comment on the accident was a casual "Very chilly bath." But accidents on the river were a serious matter. Three months earlier, at Camp White, two men had drowned, one while swimming, the other while boating. In all, eight men in the 23d Regiment drowned during their military service.[27]

The men were increasingly agitated by the political news from Ohio. The Democratic Party had nominated Clement Vallandigham for governor. Vallandigham was a Peace Democrat who had been arrested for his criticisms of the war, convicted of treason, and banished to the Confederacy. John Cracraft, at home in Mahoning County on furlough, said that "his old friends, the Democracy of Ohio, are in mighty mean business, supporting Vallandigham." A soldier from Cleveland said the men generally were disgusted with the Democrats for nominating "that chief of traitors Vallandigham." One man in Company C wrote to his hometown newspaper that the soldiers thought someone should "string him up to the first tree that they would come to." The soldiers, he said, hated him "like a black snake."[28]

The election for governor was held on October 13, with the soldiers voting by absentee ballot. When the results reached Camp White, McKinley woke Hayes with the good news that Vallandigham had been decisively defeated by the Union candidate, John Brough. John Ellen, the regimental quartermaster, celebrated the victory by issuing whiskey to the men. The 23d had voted unanimously for Brough, as had Hayes's entire brigade. (It is possible that some fraud was involved; a veteran of the 107th Ohio Infantry admitted after the war that the opponents of Vallandigham in that regiment found ways to keep his supporters from voting. But it appears that few in Hayes's brigade would have voted for Vallandigham in any case.) Despite vast differences in their politics, McKinley had a special interest in the Vallandigham candidacy, for his parents, his grandfather, and his great-grandfather were all well acquainted with the Vallandigham family. His grandfather James McKinley was an elder of the Presbyterian church in New Lisbon (now Lisbon), Ohio, when Vallandigham's father, the Reverend Clement Vallandigham, was the church's pastor. McKinley's great-grandfather David McKinley taught school in New Lisbon, and both of McKinley's parents and the Vallandigham children, including young Clement, were among his students.[29]

A Union cavalryman stationed in West Virginia considered the fall of 1863 "the most pleasant time we experienced during the war." It was an opportune time for the government to ask the men to reenlist, offering them a bounty of $402, the promise of a thirty-day furlough, and the privilege of calling themselves "veteran volunteers" and wearing chevrons that showed their new status. McKinley was one of those who reenlisted, as he said later, "with the determination to remain at the front until treason was destroyed and the unity of the Nation was established." When three-fourths of the 23d had reenlisted—the first Ohio regiment to do so—it became the 23d Regiment Ohio Veteran Volunteer Infantry.[30]

Lucy Hayes returned to camp in November with her mother and two of her sons, Webb and Rud, and stayed for two and a half months, giving McKinley a further opportunity to get acquainted with the Hayes family. He had already developed a great respect for Rutherford Hayes. At a political rally in 1876, McKinley spoke about the impressions he had formed of Hayes while they were both in uniform: "I saw him in all his varied positions and trials, in Camp, on the march, in the thickest of the battle, in full strength, and when crushed by rebel bullets, in all these we found him the brave, big souled, firm, wise, intrepid leader. No shams—no gauze—no dress parade—great in his simplicity, beloved by all, honored by all."[31]

McKinley may also have had Hayes to thank for one of his lifelong habits, cigar smoking. McKinley's father and brothers all smoked, but Andrew Duncan said that McKinley himself learned to smoke in the army. Duncan recalled the example their commander set. After he had gone to Hayes's headquarters in November 1863 to receive a commission, Hayes and his staff and several other officers smoked cigars, and the room was soon filled with smoke, "so murky that those present could hardly be distinguished." Just then Lucy Hayes appeared, looking for her boys, who were "hid away somewhere in the room." After she had found them, she said to her husband, "Rutherford[,] you should set these children a better example, I am surprised." Maj. James McIlrath of Cleveland also learned to smoke in the 23d Regiment. After Hayes and McKinley became public figures, McIlrath's six nonsmoking brothers liked to tease him by saying he would not have acquired the habit if he had not gotten into the "bad company" of people like Hayes and McKinley.[32]

Seven-year-old Webb Hayes was fascinated with military life. His mother had brought her sewing machine with her and made him a blue uniform with shoulder straps, and Captain Botsford gave him an old, broken sword. He was a familiar sight riding about camp or driving some soldier's team. After General Crook returned from serving under Burnside in the West, Webb attached himself to him, remembering him as "the kindest-hearted man" he had ever known. When Crook told him he could never be a soldier with his long, carefully kept curls, he had the curls cut off—much to his parents' displeasure.[33]

McKinley always rode a little brown horse, and Webb used to call out to him, "Hullo Billy McKinley on a bobtail nag." After the war, when McKinley was making a political speech in an Ohio town, an army veteran followed the crowd to where McKinley was speaking. Recognizing his old comrade on the platform, the veteran startled the crowd by calling out in the middle of the speech, "Billy McKinley on a bobtail hoss, by gee!" McKinley graciously acknowledged his comrade, told the story of the bobtail horse, and wove the incident into some "eloquent, impassioned remarks" about patriotism.[34]

Lucy Hayes, with her sunny disposition, charm, and tact, was a favorite of every soldier who knew her. Robert P. Kennedy, the officer who escorted her from the boat when she first came to camp, cautioned her about the mud underfoot. "Oh," she said, "you must know I came prepared for everything, and I am ready for it." Kennedy said that her gentle presence made the soldiers' hardships seem easier and their duties lighter.

One of the soldiers wrote to his wife that he had been to headquarters to get some chicken and chicken soup Lucy Hayes had made for the sick. "She is always looking after the welfare of the boys. They are the best couple that I ever saw and are well matched and well liked by almost everyone." Lucy Hayes came to be thought of as the "Mother" of the regiment.[35]

Lucy's good-natured response to a request from James Parker became a legend in the regiment. Parker was a young private from rural Mesopotamia in Trumbull County, Ohio. Before Lucy's arrival was generally known in camp, Parker told his comrades he was looking for someone to mend his blouse and put pockets in it. One of them mischievously told him there was a woman in the colonel's tent who did sewing for the regiment and encouraged him to take his blouse to her. The naive Parker took his blouse to Colonel Hayes and asked for the woman who did mending. Hayes realized that the young private was the victim of a joke, but he unhesitatingly called Lucy, who cheerfully did the work. When Parker returned to his company with his blouse mended and pockets added, his comrades were not sure if the joke was on him or on them.[36]

Lucy Hayes became fond of Lieutenant McKinley. His appearance may have first attracted her attention. Charles Manchester, a private from Wellington, Ohio, admired McKinley's "upstanding carriage and appearance," describing him as "very neat in apparel, the ideal type of private soldier" and considering him "quite good looking." He thought Lucy Hayes also noticed McKinley because of his good looks. With light brown hair, hazel-tinted, deep gray eyes, a musical voice, an easy, swinging gait, and health renewed by army life, McKinley was indeed a handsome young man. On one of her trips back to Ohio, Lucy wrote to Rutherford to tell him she had heard reports of a "mania" for marrying in the regiment and added, "do *not let Lt McKinley* venture to *Ohio—he would* not return alone." Manchester said Lucy also told her husband that McKinley "seems like such a fine young man. You ought to help him climb."[37]

Lucy went riding on McKinley's bobtail horse, and she and McKinley were among a group that often sat around a fire on the lawn in front of Hayes's headquarters. The wife of Asst. Surg. Joseph Barrett, who described McKinley as a "happy jolly boy" and a favorite of all the officers, said that on those occasions he loved to stir the fire. She said Lucy Hayes called him Casabianca because he was so faithful with the fire (referring to the popular poem of that name that begins, "The boy stood on the burning deck"). Mrs. Barrett also said that Lucy was always mothering McKinley and that on one occasion McKinley reminded Rutherford and Lucy that when the three of them were together on a steamboat, fellow passengers thought McKinley was their son. McKinley and the Hayeses were close enough that, while they were staying at what McKinley called "that scolding widow's house" at Camp White, McKinley succeeded in getting Rutherford and Lucy to promise to attend his wedding when he got married.[38]

The quiet of Camp White was broken in December, when General Scammon set out with four thousand men for Lewisburg in support of a cavalry raid on the Virginia and Tennessee Railroad at Salem, Virginia. Only part of Colonel Hayes's brigade participated, but McKinley was among them. An army on the march meant additional work for the quartermaster. Wagons had to be obtained and loaded with tents, baggage, hospital stores, tools, supplies for the blacksmiths, cooking gear, and rations. One army wagon could carry food for one day for nine hundred men; another wagon had to be added for each day of a march. And in places like the mountainous regions of West Virginia that lacked forage for the animals, that had to be transported too. After the wagons were loaded, the quartermaster also had the task of keeping the wagon train moving, riding back and forth along the train, seeing that it kept closed up, and dealing with wagons that were broken or bogged down in the mud.[39]

Paperwork accompanied the quartermaster in the field. Supplies received, issued, and remaining on hand had to be reported; supplies lost or destroyed had to be accounted for; and receipts had to be given for food and supplies foraged from the countryside. Even stationery issued in the field had to be reported on monthly forms—in duplicate.[40]

The hundred-mile march to Lewisburg and the return trip were made in ten days. On the way there, guerrillas attacked the advance guard and were "a serious annoyance" to the wagon train but were driven off by Union cavalry. The wagon train stopped at Meadow Bluff—fifteen miles west of Lewisburg—while McKinley went on with the troops to Lewisburg, where they skirmished with the Confederates. McKinley ordered the train forward, only to send it back again when it had almost reached its destination. Concerned by rumors of Confederate reinforcements in front and by guerrillas in the rear, Scammon had decided to take most of his troops out of Lewisburg. One of Scammon's three brigades remained, while the other two, including Hayes's brigade, returned to Loup Creek, where steamboats took them back to Camp White. On the march to Loup Creek, the men—followed by a large number of slaves seeking freedom—marched through cold rain and snow, singing to keep warm, and amusing themselves by calling out, "Show me the man who wants us to reenlist!" and "Show me the damned fool who will reenlist." Colonel Hayes telegraphed ahead to have fires built and coffee and supper ready, and after the men were warm and fed, he again appealed to them to reenlist, promising to get them to Cleveland by Christmas Eve for a ball if they did, and despite their jesting, many reenlisted on the spot.[41]

On his return to Camp White, McKinley was given an additional assignment on Hayes's staff, that of adjutant, writing letters and orders for Colonel Hayes and signing them as acting assistant adjutant general. The extra duty was no hardship; many of the men were on furlough, and apart from completing barracks for winter quarters, there was little activity in camp. Winter had come in full force. The river froze over, and for a week the camp was "cut off from the civilized world." McKinley celebrated his twenty-first birthday on January 29, 1864, by having his picture taken and then prepared to go home on furlough, presumably the thirty-day furlough due him on his reenlistment.[42]

So many soldiers were on furlough in Poland at the time McKinley reached home that a dance was held for them at the Sparrow House and the Methodist minister preached a sermon primarily for them. The civilians were busy doing their part for the war, drilling in militia companies and contributing funds to be paid as bounties to volunteers. Most of the townspeople were pleased with the results of the recent election. Poland had voted overwhelmingly for John Brough for governor, and nearly every house in town had been illuminated in celebration of his victory. While he was home, McKinley visited with his family but missed seeing his father, who had been away on business for the past six months. On February 28, McKinley left home for Camp White. His eighteen-year-old brother, Abner, may have traveled back with him, for a few weeks later he was visiting at Camp White. Having seen something of military life, Abner later enlisted in the 155th Ohio Volunteer Infantry, a hundred-day regiment composed of two battalions of the Ohio National Guard. Others who were close to McKinley were also being drawn into the war. Aaron Morton, the minister who baptized him, had volunteered as a delegate of the United States Christian Commission and later that year became the chaplain of the 105th Ohio Infantry. McKinley's cousin Joseph Osborne, Will Osborne's brother, enlisted in the 171st Ohio Infantry. Thirty-seven days after he was mustered into the service, Osborne was killed in a battle with Gen. John Morgan's cavalry at Keller's Bridge near Cynthiana, Kentucky.[43]

McKinley found a new commander in the division when he returned to West Virginia. During his furlough in Ohio, guerrillas had attacked a steamboat on the Kanawha River and captured General Scammon and two members of his staff. Scammon was eventually exchanged but never returned to West Virginia; George Crook was assigned to take his place. In late March, Crook was called to the headquarters of Lt. Gen. Ulysses S. Grant to participate in the planning of the spring campaign. While the forces of Grant, William T. Sherman, Benjamin F. Butler, and Nathaniel P. Banks advanced on the Confederates in other parts of the country, Gen. Franz Sigel, in command of the Department of West Virginia, would move his troops up the Shenandoah Valley toward Staunton, and Crook would take his division south to the Virginia and Tennessee Railroad, the infantry and cavalry going by separate routes. After destroying the railroad, Crook was to move east and join Sigel's forces for a movement toward Lynchburg.[44]

Steamboats soon began to arrive at Camp White with large quantities of wagons, mules, rations, and ammunition. McKinley wrote orders to remove the blockade on the Lewisburg Pike—"thirty to fifty axes will be enough"—and to prepare the various regiments to move, "without exciting the least suspicion of any military movement." He supplied the troops with rations for part of the march, but after that they would have to live off the country; the distances were so great and forage for the animals so scarce along the way that the teams could not haul rations and forage for the entire trip. As the movement began, Hayes changed McKinley's duties; the responsibilities of commissary of subsistence and adjutant were given to other officers, and he was named Hayes's acting aide-de-camp as well as the brigade's acting assistant quartermaster.[45]

On April 29, Crook's division of 6,155—a third of them in Hayes's brigade—began its march south. Russell Hastings, who had been serving with McKinley on Hayes's staff since General Scammon's capture, remembered that "cheer after cheer went up and when Col. Hayes with his Staff took his position at the head of the column and the band struck up 'Dixie' all our hearts were stirred to their depths." Birchard and Webb Hayes marched the first five miles with the troops, while their mother and grandmother followed on a steamboat. At Loup Creek, Lucy Hayes sat on the roadside and watched the troops marching off; only when the last soldier had passed did she reboard the boat to return with her family to Ohio, even though the boat's captain was impatiently blowing the whistle for her.[46]

Much of the march was over familiar territory, through Camp Reynolds, Fayetteville, and Raleigh, and over Flat Top Mountain to Princeton. McKinley called it "a rough and trying march over mountains and through deep ravines and dense woods, with snows and rains that would have checked the advance of any but the most determined. Daily we were brought in contact with the enemy. We penetrated a country where guerillas were abundant and where it was not an unusual thing for our men to be shot from the underbrush—murdered in cold blood."[47]

While climbing a mountain, one tired soldier slipped and rolled some two hundred feet into a hollow below. McKinley, who had been "hustling" the troops along and helping stragglers, called to another soldier, "Come on, let's help him up!" and the soldier followed him down the hillside. McKinley's companion said "it was a tough climb down into the hole, and a worse climb back. But we got him on his feet, and then two or three others joined hands with us, and in that way we got him up to the path." They revived him with coffee and liquor, and eventually he was all right again.[48]

On May 9, the Union troops finally encountered the Confederates under Gen. Albert Jenkins entrenched across the road at Cloyd's Mountain, five miles from Dublin, Virginia. When Crook's troops were in position, he ordered a charge across a meadow a quarter of a mile wide, through a waist-deep stream, and up the steep, thickly wooded mountain to where the Confederates were positioned. Hayes and his staff joined the charge on foot, the difficulty of the terrain having forced them to abandon their horses. McKinley described the charge at one of his regiment's reunions:

> Over the beautiful meadow which intervened, the troops move grandly at a double-quick—the ball and canister of the enemy having little perceptible effect upon their well-formed line; down to the ugly stream which interposed its obstruction, in full sight and range of the Confederates. Without a halt, on they dash into it and across it. "Then with a yell, amidst shrapnel and shell," the ascent is commenced—quick and furious the charge is continued amid heavy fire of musketry; the enemy's works are taken, their artillery captured, and another great victory is added to the regiment's scroll of fame.

On another occasion, McKinley said that the "hand-to-hand combat in the fort was as desperate as any witnessed during the war."[49]

The veterans of the 23d long remembered Pvt. John Kosht, the first man to reach the enemy guns, who "sprang from the ranks, with a boyish shout, and hung his hat over the muzzle of one of the guns." Twice the Confederates fell back and tried to resist, but they were soon forced to retreat. The battle was costly to both sides. Confederate dead were found "in heaps" behind their works; Union troops buried more than 200 of their enemies. Some of the Confederate dead were prisoners bayoneted by Union soldiers before their officers could stop the killing. Crook's command lost 108 killed, 508 wounded, and 72 missing.[50]

With Hayes's brigade in the lead, Crook's troops pressed on to Dublin Depot on the Virginia and Tennessee Railroad. There they burned the railroad station, the telegraph office, and a large accumulation of military stores and the next day moved on to the covered railroad bridge over the New River, destroying culverts and tearing up the track as they went. After a brief artillery duel across the river, Crook's men set fire to the four-hundred-foot bridge, which was the goal of the raid. While it burned, the 23d Regiment's band played and the men cheered; as one of them wrote, "the great backbone of the Confederacy [was] broken." Then the Union troops began a retreat through Blacksburg and Union to Meadow Bluff, where they could be resupplied.[51]

The retreat was grueling for everyone, including the Confederate prisoners who accompanied the army. The hardships began with the crossing of the New River, a "tediously-slow process," the whole command having to wait in turn to cross in one small ferryboat, "with the rain pouring down and dashing in the men's faces all night." McKinley's wagon train crossed at a ford nearby, where one of the wagons tipped over, drowning one man and six mules. The route led over Salt Pond Mountain, with Mountain Lake at its top. McKinley described the trail as "a rocky, mountain pass, where every boulder in the road was like a little mountain; it was enough to appal the stoutest hearts." It had rained every day since the men left the railroad, and on the six-mile ascent of Salt Pond Mountain horses gave out and many of the wagons bogged down in the mud. Some of the supplies had to be abandoned or destroyed to lighten the wagons; so much ammunition was left at one place that the local residents called it Minié Ball Hill. Some one hundred empty wagons—half the train—were backed over the edge of the road and allowed to tumble down the mountainside, the mules being double-teamed to the wagons that were left. Despite the losses, Crook said after the campaign that he regarded bringing the trains through with so little loss "one of the most remarkable features of the expedition" and one that reflected "great credit" on the Quartermaster Department.[52]

Many of the men had worn out their shoes and were barefoot. The rations were used up after the first nine days of the raid, and the men lived on what they could find along the road. And they were harassed by guerrillas. One of General Crook's aides was shot and wounded, and Crook himself received a slight wound. When one of the guerrillas was captured, Crook ordered him shot, and the men of his old regiment, the 36th Ohio, carried out the execution and left the body lying in the road with a note pinned on it, saying, "This is the fate of all bushwhackers." After twenty-one days of "constant marching, frequent fighting, and much hardship, and some starvation," they reached Meadow Bluff. Two days later a wagon train met them with supplies, and 150 wounded men and 266 prisoners were sent back to Gauley Bridge. As exhausted as the men were, they were pleased with what they had accomplished and pleased with their new commander. "Brigadier General George Crook is a soldier," one of the officers wrote, "always in advance of his column, ready to fight or assist the pioneers in removing obstructions from the road; in a word always at his post." Colonel Hayes said simply: "General Crook is the best general I have ever known."[53]

On their retreat to Meadow Bluff, the troops had been joined by several hundred fugitive slaves. They were of all ages and traveled "uncomplainingly along after and with the army," some on foot and others "on horseback, on muleback, in some instances a whole family on the back of a single mule, in carts drawn by cows, in the old family coach drawn perhaps by a team composed of a mule and a cow." When the teams of those who had vehicles gave out, they too were forced to walk through the mud and rain, carrying their supplies and their children. One of the veterans of the Dublin Raid remembered the attention given to them by Colonel Hayes's quartermaster.

Major McKinley was with us,—he was only a lieutenant then,—and he had to take his dose of the disagreeable the same as all of us. Everybody in the ranks was covered with mud, and the officers weren't any better off, although the major always was a sticker to keep his uniform bright. He helped around the supply wagons,—he was used to that kind of work, having been a commissary sergeant himself,—and once I saw him help a poor contraband who had his wife and three children with him, and several heavy bundles of household goods, probably everything the poor fellow had in the world. McKinley helped carry one of the children along the road for at least a mile, and helped the woman over more than one ditch. And he did those things just as if he thought it was no more than his duty to do them.[54]

At Meadow Bluff, Crook learned that General Sigel's forces had been defeated at New Market and that Gen. David Hunter had replaced him as commander of the Department of West Virginia. Grant ordered Hunter to attack Lynchburg to destroy the railroad and the canal there, saying it would be of great value to take Lynchburg even for a single day. In preparation for the movement toward Lynchburg, Hunter ordered Crook's division to join him at Staunton, Virginia, and on May 31, after twelve days at Meadow Bluff, Crook's troops began the march to Staunton. They made the march in nine days, skirmishing with guerrillas, stopping to admire the beauty of the resort at White Sulphur Springs, and finding plenty of food and forage along the way. The soldiers tore up the railroad and destroyed furnaces, forges, and saltpeter works as they went. When they arrived at Staunton, they found Hunter's troops, who had arrived there after defeating a Confederate force at the Battle of Piedmont and had burned factories, shops, and supplies in Staunton after they arrived.[55]

Not all of McKinley's regiment had reenlisted, and at Staunton 160 men and 9 officers who had completed their three years of service left for home, taking with them a group of prisoners and the regiment's tattered battle flags, no longer fit for service. They stopped at Columbus, where Lt. John Cracraft, one of the original members of the Poland Guards, presented the flags to the state.[56]

As Crook's division was preparing to leave Staunton, William Averell, the cavalry commander, ordered the execution of fifty-five-year-old David S. Creigh, a citizen of Greenbrier County, West Virginia, who had been convicted of murdering a Union soldier in November, and Creigh was hanged on a tree at the head of the column and left hanging with a card pinned to his breast that said, "Murderer of a Union Soldier." A few days later, Matthew White, who was suspected of spying, was shot by Averell's orders and his body left lying in the road as a warning to others, as was the body of a guerrilla killed along the way. A black man attached to Averell's command who attempted to rape a white woman was also shot.[57]

Hunter's army of eighteen thousand, with Crook's men as one division, left Staunton on June 10 and reached Lexington the next day. After a three-hour "artillery and sharpshooter fight," Lexington was taken, with Hayes's brigade leading the way into the city. The army stayed in Lexington for two and a half days, leaving bitter memories behind when it left. General Hunter, a fierce opponent of slavery, had issued orders freeing and arming slaves when he commanded the Department of the South, and the Confederacy had branded him an outlaw and announced that he would be executed if captured. Undaunted, Hunter believed that the enemy should pay a price for the rebellion and ordered the burning of the arsenal, warehouses, mills, canal boats, and wagons in Lexington and all but one of the buildings at the Virginia Military Institute: the library, the barracks, the professors' quarters, the mess hall, and the hospital. He also ordered the burning of former governor John Letcher's home, giving his wife and children only ten minutes' notice. Hunter had been angered when his soldiers discovered a proclamation by Letcher calling on citizens to resist the "foul Yankee invader" with guerrilla warfare. Despite the provocation, Hayes said that Crook's officers and men "were all disgusted" with the burning of Letcher's home, and few of them supported the burning of the institute. A veteran of the 91st Ohio Infantry put the feelings of the men into poetry: "And few there were to give assent / To Hunter's modes of punishment." Estimates of the value of the property destroyed by Hunter's army in Lexington ran as high as $3 million. One of the losses was the Virginia Military Institute's bronze statue of George Washington, carted away by Hunter's soldiers.[58]

Among the buildings burned at the Virginia Military Institute was the home of Maj. William Gilham, one of the professors. General Hunter himself told Gilham's wife to remove her furniture because he intended to burn her house the next morning. David Strother, Hunter's chief of staff, said that Mrs. Gilham was troubled about the order, "but she was a soldier's wife and a soldier's daughter so she set us out some good applejack, apologizing she had nothing better, and then went to move out her furniture to the lawn." McKinley was one of a group of Union officers who helped her carry some of her possessions—tables, sofas, and other furniture—out to the parade ground. The next day, when her house was burned, she was seen seated in the midst of her possessions, "firm and ladylike." Sympathetic Union officers provided wagons to move her goods, a supply of rations, and a guard at her new lodgings.[59]

When Hunter's army left Lexington, it advanced to Buchanan, where it destroyed a branch of the Tredegar Iron Works and other furnaces and foundries and then crossed the Blue Ridge at the Peaks of Otter, losing wagons and animals that tumbled off the narrow roadway during the crossing. The mountainside was covered with rhododendrons, and the soldiers put bouquets in the muzzles of their rifles, making the troops seem like "a moving bank of flowers." At Liberty (now Bedford), they again set about destroying the railroad and burned houses from which shots were fired. As the army approached Lynchburg, Crook's soldiers engaged the city's defenders near an old Quaker meetinghouse, some three miles from the city. The defenders retired into the fortifications, but the Union army, instead of pursuing them, went into camp on the night of June 17.[60]

Hunter and Crook made their headquarters at Sandusky, the home of Maj. George C. Hutter, a former U.S. Army officer known to Hunter from their service together as army paymasters but who had resigned from the army when the war began. Hayes and McKinley were among the officers who stayed overnight at Sandusky. Hutter and his family were allowed to stay in the house, and the major's daughter made a vivid impression on the Union officers. Despite her loyalty to the South, for which her three brothers were fighting, her sweet voice, "clear olive-pink" cheeks, and pleasant manner were much admired; one of the officers called her "the divine." During the night, the men could hear railroad trains, drums beating, and the sounds of troops moving, which convinced them that Confederate reinforcements were arriving in the city. The next day, the battle resumed, but before the day's end, Hunter, fearing he was outnumbered and realizing he was short of rations and ammunition and far from his base of supplies, ordered a retreat, back across the mountains into West Virginia. When Hunter left Sandusky, he abandoned some ninety wounded soldiers in Major Hutter's barn. Some of his soldiers left with "various ornaments and valuables" they had stolen from the major's daughter.[61]

Many of the soldiers thought that a more resolute commander than Hunter—Crook, for example—could have taken Lynchburg. After the war, when McKinley spoke to his comrades about the Lynchburg campaign, he did not even mention Hunter's name.

Acknowledging no impediments and yielding to no resistance, nothing could then have stood between our advance column and Lynchburg but command to halt from one higher in command than a Crook, a Hayes or a Duval. Lynchburg, that coveted prize, was within its grasp; but lo! in the morning it was too late; the shades of night had safely guided re-enforcements from Richmond to that beleaguered garrison, the opportunity of the previous night was gone, and we were at the mercy of the enemy. . . . It took the genius of a Crook, the steady, vigorous hand of a Hayes, and the thorough discipline of the troops to save us from complete capture or a dreadful slaughter.[62]

Pursued by Confederate cavalry, Hunter's army began its retreat, followed by hundreds of the "ever faithful colored people," who shared their provisions with the soldiers and showed them where other provisions had been hidden. The army went through Liberty and Salem, over the "wild, waterless, and abrupt" mountains, back through White Sulphur Springs and Meadow Bluff to Gauley Bridge, and reached Camp Piatt, near Charleston, eleven days later. At the beginning of the retreat, the army was still concerned with destroying railroad tracks and burning mills, furnaces, and factories. By the third day, the men had little but their "gaunt and half-famished cattle" left to eat, and when the cattle were gone, hunger and fatigue became their greatest concerns. They ransacked houses and gardens along the road, looking for food. Men were seen "staggering along, half asleep, occasionally falling down on their faces," keeping themselves going only out of fear of being captured. Hundreds of horses and mules that could not keep up were left along the road to be shot by the rear guard, and eighty wagons were burned. Even when the men had moved beyond the Confederate forces, they were still in danger; signs of guerrilla activity surrounded them: dead horses, burned wagons, bridges, and farmhouses. Finally, a supply train met them at Big Sewell Mountain; the men "crowded around like hungry hogs" and fought over the rations; many of them ate all night. The empty supply wagons were filled with sick and exhausted soldiers, and ambulances were loaded with food and sent back to the men who had fallen by the wayside.[63]

The retreat left the soldiers with haunting memories. One remembered the deaths of the animals. "I stumbled nearly every rod against a horse or mule either standing or lying down to die. I could hear them as they fell or were thrown from the road, as they rolled and tumbled over and over down the side of the mountain among the bushes. Such crackling and groaning as they made that night I can never forget." For another, it was hearing a shot and a woman's scream. A toddler had wandered into camp and knocked over a stack of muskets, one of which discharged, hitting the child. The soldier never forgot the sight of the mother wringing her hands and the tear-streaked face of the soldier holding the child. Others remembered picking through manure for undigested grain and peeling the inner bark from trees to satisfy their hunger.[64]

McKinley remembered the fatigue and the hunger. "Two days and two nights, without sleep or rest, part of the time wholly without food; fighting and marching and suffering, it seems to me, as I recall it, almost unreal and incredible that men could or would suffer such discomforts or hardships."[65]

Rutherford Hayes, whose brigade was in the rear of the retreating army, remembered an attempt to check the Confederate pursuit. He ordered a barricade built across the road behind the army, with regiments behind the barricade and others on the mountains on both sides for protection. When they were ready to withdraw the regiments and move on, Hayes sent McKinley up the mountain on one side and Russell Hastings up the other side to bring the men down. It was dark, and both aides were carefully instructed to bring the men down behind the barricade lest they be mistaken for the enemy. As Hayes was waiting for McKinley and Hastings to return, he heard the order to fire and was sure that his men had come down on the wrong side of the barricade and were about to be shot by their comrades. He rushed out to the troops guarding the barricade. "My soul was on fire," he said. "I was too choked to cry out: 'Our men! Our men! Don't fire!'" But he was too late; a volley was heard and then groans and cries and curses. Fearing the worst, Hayes jumped over the barricade and grabbed one man after another, shouting, "What regiment?" One wounded man answered faintly, "——th Virginia; Early's army." To his great relief, Hayes realized that they were not his men. He learned later that McKinley and Hastings had brought the men down properly, and they had gone on after the army.[66]

Hunter's exhausted soldiers, "weakened," "footsore," and "discouraged," were finally allowed to rest at Charleston. Crook's men were particularly in need of rest. They had marched almost continuously for nearly two months, crossing the three ranges of the Alleghenies four times and the Blue Ridge twice. But they were not to rest long. When Hunter's army retreated into West Virginia, General Early quickly moved his army down the unguarded Shenandoah Valley and crossed the Potomac into Maryland. After defeating a Union force at the Battle of Monocacy, Early's army moved on to the outskirts of Washington, D.C. Even when Early retired from Washington, he continued to be a threat, and Maj. Gen. Horatio G. Wright was put in command of the forces opposing him. The troops in West Virginia, including Hayes's brigade, were placed under the command of George Crook, who named them the Army of the Kanawha, and were called east to join Wright's command.[67]

Only a few days after Crook's men arrived at Charleston and while many of them were still in tattered clothes, barefoot, and ill with diarrhea, they left for the East. As they had two years earlier when Robert E. Lee's army invaded Maryland, the infantry traveled by steamboats to Parkersburg, receiving cheers and food from Ohio citizens as they went up the Ohio River. The artillery, cavalry, and baggage trains went overland to Parkersburg. From there the whole command traveled on the Baltimore and Ohio Railroad to Martinsburg. The men and the line officers were crammed into "filthy old" cattle and freight cars, but General Crook found a day car and shared it with his division and brigade commanders and their staffs, which made McKinley's trip more comfortable than that of most of the soldiers. Soon after the army's arrival in the East, it joined the fight with Early's army at Snicker's Ferry. Hayes's brigade, however, stopped at Martinsburg, arriving there in the middle of the night, and Hayes and his staff slept on the veranda of a German saloon. From Martinsburg, they went on to Harpers Ferry, where they looked over the burned arsenal and the fire engine house where John Brown was captured. Moving on to Kabletown, West Virginia, the brigade engaged the enemy and took the town. From Kabletown, it too advanced toward Snicker's Ferry but was surrounded and, fighting its way free, fell back to Charles Town, West Virginia, camping there in the field where John Brown had been hanged. Finally, the brigade joined Crook and the rest of his army at Kernstown, four miles south of Winchester, Virginia. Early had gone back up the Shenandoah Valley, and General Grant, thinking that Early was no longer a threat, withdrew Wright's forces, leaving only Crook's Army of the Kanawha in front of Early's army. When Early learned that Wright and his troops were gone, he immediately ordered his army to advance and attack the Army of the Kanawha at Kernstown.[68]

The Battle of Kernstown was fought on Sunday, July 24, 1864. When General Crook received reports that a large Confederate force was approaching, he put his troops in line, with Colonel Hayes's brigade of four regiments on the left. At first, the brigade advanced on the Confederates but soon realized that was futile. The Confederates were advancing in two long lines "in almost the form of a horseshoe," overlapping the Union line more than half a mile and "almost enclosing us as it were like a huge boa," in one man's words, or "as a nutcracker might a nut," in another's. Then Hayes's brigade was attacked on its left by Confederates "yelling like demons" and "pouring volley after volley" as well as artillery fire into it and was forced to retreat toward Winchester. Staff officers were galloping in all directions, giving orders for the retreat. One of Hayes's four regiments, the 13th West Virginia Infantry commanded by Col. William R. Brown, had been posted in an orchard to the rear as a reserve. Hayes realized that in the confusion of the battle, Brown's regiment had been left in the orchard, and to prevent its being overrun and captured, Hayes directed McKinley to go and bring it back.[69]

Russell Hastings, who served as Hayes's adjutant during the battle, later described the scene. He said that McKinley set off at a "fierce gallop obliquely" toward the advancing Confederates. As he did so, "a sad look came over Hayes's face," convinced as he was that he had sent his young aide on a mission that could well mean his death.

> None of us expected to see him again, as we watched him push his horse through the open fields, over fences, through ditches, while a well-directed fire from the enemy was poured upon him, with shells exploding around, about and over him. Once he was completely enveloped in

the smoke of an exploding shell, and we thought he had gone down; but no, he was saved for better work for his country in his future years. Out of this smoke emerged his wiry little brown horse, with McKinley still firmly seated, and as erect as a hussar. Now he had passed under cover from the enemy's fire, and a sense of relief came to us all.[70]

McKinley reached Brown and gave him the order to fall back, adding, "I supposed you would have gone to the rear without orders." Brown said he had decided that he should retire without orders, but now that McKinley was there, he was ready to follow McKinley out. "But," he said, "I 'pintedly' believe I ought to give those fellows a volley or two before I go," to which McKinley replied, "Then up and at them as quickly as possible." The regiment fired a volley at the advancing Confederates and then slowly retreated to some woods in the rear, and McKinley led it through the woods toward Winchester. When McKinley made his report to Hayes, Hastings heard Hayes say to him, "I never expected to see you in life again."[71]

The brigade fell back to Winchester, suffering heavy losses, and marched through the city. Most of the inhabitants were Southern sympathizers and showed their pleasure at the Union defeat, but one old Quaker woman, known to the troops as a supporter of the Union, was seen standing at her gate, with tears running down her cheeks. The Union soldiers, concerned for her safety among her neighbors, hesitated to show their sympathy for her, but Hastings said that McKinley "in his great kindness of heart, reined his horse to the curbstone and in a low voice said, 'Don't worry, my dear madam, we are not hurt as much as it seems, and we shall be back here again in a few days,'" which brought a smile to her face.[72]

With Hayes's brigade as rear guard, Crook's army continued its retreat north from Winchester toward Martinsburg, harassed by cavalry, halting occasionally to fire on the pursuing infantry, and making one last stand that finally drove the enemy away. The soldiers found abandoned wagons along the road and burned them. Hayes's brigade also found an abandoned battery of artillery, four cannons with their caissons, and McKinley asked permission to take the guns along rather than leaving them for the enemy. The men were exhausted and apparently unable to do the work involved, but McKinley insisted that it could be done and thought that his regiment would help him do it. When Hayes agreed to let him try, McKinley went to his old comrades in Company E and asked for volunteers. They readily agreed to help and, assisted by others in the regiment, hauled the guns to that night's camp, where they handed them over to the artillery captain. The captain, Hastings said, "cried like a baby."[73]

William McKinley Jr. as a staff officer. *Courtesy of the McKinley Memorial Library and Museum, Niles, Ohio.*

Over the next two days, Crook's army continued its retreat, crossing the Potomac River into Maryland, while the Confederates resumed the destruction of the Baltimore and Ohio Railroad that they had begun earlier in July. Crook's men found themselves in familiar places when they once again crossed the Burnside Bridge, marched across the Antietam battlefield, and went into camp near Sharpsburg. Here they had an opportunity to count the army's losses; Crook's army had been greatly outnumbered at Kernstown, and its losses were severe: 100 were killed, 606 wounded, and 479 captured or missing. Hayes's brigade suffered one-third of the casualties.[74]

The day after the battle, McKinley was promoted to captain. One member of his regiment said, "Nobody begrudged him his promotion, and plenty of us thought he ought to be a major or a colonel. Perhaps he was looking for something higher, but if he was, he never said so." The promotion was often said to have been given for his services at Kernstown, but Lieutenant Colonel Comly had written to the adjutant general of Ohio a week before the battle, recommending a captaincy for McKinley, and promotions in the Ohio regiments were granted in Columbus, not in the field. Nevertheless, McKinley had proved his worth as a staff officer at Kernstown, and Hayes was able to report to his wife, Lucy, after the battle that "McKinley and Hastings were very gallant."[75]

FOUR   *Adjutant*

McKinley was always keen, quick, and alert, and so was naturally
fitted for staff service, a fact his superiors soon realized and took
advantage of, so that during the greater part of the war he served on
the staff of the general officers, one of the most dangerous positions
in the army, one which required the utmost readiness of resource and
bravery of the highest order.

—*Russell Hastings*

When McKinley was promoted to captain, George Crook was promoted to brevet major general. Soon after their promotions, Crook asked
to have McKinley transferred from Hayes's staff to his own as an acting assistant adjutant general. Hayes was reluctant to let him go. He had grown
fond of McKinley. He once said he had found him "a clean-cut, bright
fellow, honest to the core, and always willing to do anything asked of him.
Sometimes he fairly seemed to anticipate my wishes, and he always carried them out, no matter what the cost." But Hayes realized, "of course it
was my duty to tell McKinley he must leave me." He said he was "sorry to
lose McKinley but I couldn't as a friend advise him to do otherwise. He is
taken *out* of [the] quartermaster's department and *that* is good, and *into*
[the] adjutant-general's office, and that is good."[1]

James Botsford may have played a part in McKinley's transfer. Botsford was an assistant adjutant general on Crook's staff at the time, and ac-
cording to Hayes, McKinley was to be an assistant to Botsford. But Crook
was either aware of McKinley's abilities himself or soon became aware of
them. Impressed with McKinley's thoroughness, Crook was accustomed
to say, "McKinley never slops over. When he makes a report that there

76

were twenty men in a skirmish, there were twenty men in the skirmish, for he had counted them and knew. He does not exaggerate and does not take anything for granted, as do many of the officers in the army."[2]

Leaving Hayes's staff did not end McKinley's association with Hayes or with the 23d Ohio Infantry. Hayes's brigade continued to be part of Crook's army. That army was not large—about seven thousand men when McKinley joined Crook's staff—and McKinley continued to have close relations with Hayes and his old comrades.[3]

McKinley had served as Hayes's adjutant for a time, so his duties on Crook's staff were not new to him. With the help of his clerk, he wrote reports, letters, and orders for Crook, issuing the orders in Crook's name and signing them "William McKinley, Jr., Acting Assistant Adjutant General." Much of the work was routine—detailing guards and pickets, detaching men to serve as teamsters or blacksmiths or clerks, issuing passes and furloughs, requesting reports—but McKinley believed in doing even routine work with care. During the Spanish-American War, he drew on his experience as an adjutant to advise his nephew Lt. James F. McKinley how to be a good soldier. "Be attentive to all your duties. Do everything the best you know how and if you are in doubt ask some superior officer the best way to do it. Be careful about your writing. See that your words are spelled correctly. Better have a little pocket dictionary with you. It mars an official paper or letter to have a word misspelled."[4]

Although an adjutant's work in camp tended to be routine, McKinley began his service with Crook while the army was in the field, and there the staff was a vital part of the communication system. Staff officers carried orders, directed troop movements, and sought out information, following their commanding officers' orders. On the battlefield, staff officers could be seen galloping here and there, with large official envelopes tucked in their belts—orders from their commanders. Ambrose Bierce described the life of a staff officer in battle as "precarious," subject at any time to being dispatched "with an order to some commander of a prone regiment in the front line—a person for the moment inconspicuous and not always easy to find without a deal of search among men somewhat preoccupied, and in a din in which question and answer alike must be imparted in the sign language. It is customary in such cases to duck the head and scuttle away on a keen run, an object of lively interest to some thousands of admiring marksmen." Good riding was a necessity, and McKinley became an excellent horseman during the course of the war, as well as an efficient adjutant.[5]

A staff officer's life could be exciting, and it put him in a good position to observe men of high rank, but any glory it had was merely the reflected glory of the officer's commander. One adjutant said that "one has opportunities on the staff of seeing a great deal that is interesting, still staff officers are simply satellites of the General." Russell Hastings described a staff officer as "a kind of high toned lackey who simply follows his General about and takes and carries orders here and there over the battlefield." McKinley was fortunate in his general. Crook was a favorite of officers and men alike. Thirty-four years old, he was a graduate of West Point and a professional soldier, having served in the Pacific Northwest before the war and in both the eastern and western theaters during the war. But he was also wise enough to treat his volunteer soldiers as equals and quickly won their trust and devotion. After seeing him in action at the Battle of Cloyd's Mountain, one of his soldiers said that "all have faith in our General George Crook[.] He makes his camp in the field without display[,] puts on no style and sees to all movements in person, is the first and foremost on the battle field cheering on his men and takeing his chances with them." Hayes thought enough of Crook to name one of his sons after him.[6]

Crook's army moved from Sharpsburg to Harpers Ferry but remained there only a few days before returning to Maryland. General Early had sent cavalry under John McCausland into Pennsylvania, where they burned the city of Chambersburg in retaliation for Hunter's burnings in Virginia, and Crook's army was sent into Maryland to provide protection against an invasion of that state. Seeing nothing of the Confederates, the army marched through Frederick, Maryland, and camped at Monocacy Junction, three miles south of Frederick. A Union officer who saw the army there said that Crook's men were "in a fagged-out and demoralized condition, ragged, famished, discouraged, sulky, and half of them in ambulances. They have been marched to tatters, they say, besides being overwhelmed and beaten." The men were surprised to find that part of the Nineteenth Corps was also at Monocacy Junction. General Grant had determined to deal firmly with Early's army and was assembling troops there in sufficient force to oppose it.[7]

On August 5, General Grant himself appeared at Monocacy Junction to consult with General Hunter and with the man he had chosen to replace Hunter in command of the troops assembled there, Philip Sheridan, the thirty-three-year-old commander of the cavalry of the Army of the Potomac and a soldier McKinley later compared with Stonewall Jackson, saying "he was to our army what Jackson was to the other side." Sheridan was placed in command of a new Middle Military Division that included the Department of West Virginia, with George Crook replacing David Hunter in command of the department. Crook's Army of the Kanawha was given

Maj. Gen. George Crook. *Courtesy of the Massachusetts Commandery, Military Order of the Loyal Legion and the U.S. Army Military History Institute, Carlisle Barracks, Pennsylvania.*

a new name; it was to be the Army of West Virginia. That army and the Sixth and Nineteenth Corps made up the infantry of Sheridan's Army of the Shenandoah.[8]

At sunset on the same day Grant arrived at Monocacy Junction, a soldier in the 23d Ohio was executed there by order of General Crook. It was the only execution in the regiment during the war. Isaac B. Whitlow, also known as John Hall, enlisted in Company D of the 23d after deserting from the Confederate army. Five days later, he deserted from the 23d, only to be captured, wearing a Confederate uniform, at the Battle of Cloyd's Mountain. He escaped from prison and then reenlisted in the Union army, to get the bounty paid to volunteers. He thought he would be joining the 12th Ohio Infantry, but the 12th had been consolidated with the 23d, and on arriving at Monocacy Junction, he found himself assigned not only to his old regiment but to his old company, where he was immediately recognized and charged with desertion. Crook authorized a drumhead court-martial, and James Botsford issued the order for it on August 4. The court met the next day and found Whitlow guilty. Crook ordered him shot at sundown.[9]

Lieutenant Colonel Comly was to have had charge of the execution, but the thought of it made him so sick that he was unable to leave his tent, and the task fell to Maj. Edward Carey. Crook's three divisions were drawn up on three sides of a hollow square, and the prisoner, with his arm over the neck of the chaplain who accompanied him, was brought to the front by an armed guard, while the band of the 34th Ohio Infantry played a dirge. An ambulance brought Whitlow's coffin, and he knelt on it about ten paces from a firing squad made up of ten men from the 23d. Eight of the ten balls they fired hit him in the chest. General Crook and his staff were assembled near the place of the execution, "intently watching the proceeding."[10]

Sheridan immediately moved his army to Sandy Hook, near Harpers Ferry, and then up the Shenandoah Valley, driving the Confederates to Cedar Creek, near Strasburg. Then, having learned that the Confederates were being reinforced, the army, followed by the Confederates, moved back down the valley to a position at Halltown, again near Harpers Ferry. McKinley called the movements "a waltz up and down the valley, fighting and skirmishing, first at this point, and then at another, intrenching ourselves for a little while here and then over yonder." At Halltown, Hayes's brigade made reconnaissances on three successive days and on one of them captured a small regiment of South Carolina troops on outpost duty, doing it so quickly that one of the astonished prisoners called out to his captors, "Who the hell are you'uns?" McKinley described the engagement as "a sharp and decisive conflict between Hayes' brigade and Kershaw's division, resulting in a marked victory, routing the enemy and capturing many prisoners. I witnessed nothing through the war more plucky and determined than the affair just mentioned."[11]

Sheridan's army began to move up the valley again on August 28. When the men reached Charles Town, West Virginia, they sang "John Brown's Body," for they were all aware that Charles Town was the site of Brown's hanging. Late in the afternoon of September 3, Crook's army engaged Maj. Gen. Joseph Kershaw's division of Early's army at Berryville, Virginia. Rutherford Hayes called it one of the fiercest fights he had ever been in.[12]

The men had just been cheered by news that General Sherman's army had taken Atlanta when Union pickets encountered Confederates on the Winchester Pike and skirmished with them. Crook's command was called out, and heavy firing began, musketry, artillery, and hand-to-hand fighting as well. It was an unusual battle in that it was fought in the dark—until after ten o'clock at night. McKinley called it "a grand spectacle! the flashes from the musketry and artillery illuminating the field with the brilliancy of a thousand gas jets." The Union forces drove the Confederates back to an entrenched position. After the fighting ended, the surgeons and burial parties of both sides began to move over the field with lanterns, mingling with each other as they worked.[13]

During the fighting, McKinley's horse was shot under him, but he was not injured. This was apparently not the only time that happened, for Hayes later told his son Birchard that McKinley had "two or three horses" shot under him. He also told Birchard that "every one admires [McKinley] as one of the bravest and finest young officers in the army."[14]

McKinley liked to tell about another incident of the fighting at Berryville. He said that before the armies retired he was ordered to direct a regiment some distance away to a new position. It was dark, and he knew nothing of the country around him. He did know, however, that the army was almost surrounded by Confederates, and riding in the darkness, he said his heart "jumped into his throat" when he heard the words, "Halt! Who goes thar?" in a pronounced Southern accent. He turned his horse and hurried away. Soon he was stopped again, but this time the words were "Halt! Who goes there?" with a Yankee twang, and he said that as soon as he heard the word "there" pronounced in that way he knew he was among friends. He gave the countersign and soon had the regiment moving.[15]

After the engagement on September 3, the Army of the Shenandoah remained at Berryville in entrenchments, while Early's army remained between the Union army and Winchester. Sheridan was cautious about engaging Early's troops. The presidential election was approaching, and a defeat in battle would be costly politically as well as militarily, so Sheridan waited for an opportune time to attack the Confederates. While he waited,

McKinley was busy at Crook's side, writing the letters and orders necessary for an army in the field, directives about guards, pickets, and escorts for wagon trains, and requests for the reports he needed to make up his own reports.[16]

When Sheridan learned from a young Quaker schoolteacher, Rebecca Wright, that Early had sent some of his troops to Richmond, he decided it was time to strike. At the same time, General Grant again visited Sheridan at Charles Town. Grant had prepared a battle plan for Sheridan, but when he heard Sheridan's plans, he said nothing about his own plans but only told Sheridan to "Go in!"[17]

The resulting engagement—the Battle of Opequon, or the Third Battle of Winchester—was fought on September 19. Sheridan planned to attack the Confederate line, which was about two miles east of Winchester. Crook's Army of West Virginia was to be held in reserve while the Sixth and the Nineteenth Corps made the attack, and then it was to move south to cut off any Confederate retreat. After the battle had begun, Crook and Hayes, with their staffs, were lying in a field of clover at the Opequon Ford on the Berryville Pike, waiting for orders, when McKinley suddenly sprang to his feet, saying, "I think I see one of Sheridan's staff officers riding full tilt for us." The Sixth and the Nineteenth Corps had been driven back, and the staff officer brought changed orders: Crook's army was to come to their support. The men joked that they had known something was about to happen; Hayes said he had seen the moon over his left shoulder, and McKinley said that one of his stockings was on inside out.[18]

The First Division of Crook's army, commanded by Col. Joseph Thoburn, moved toward the front, past ambulances with wounded men and tents where surgeons were already amputating limbs. At one place the Berryville Pike passed through a long, wooded ravine—the Berryville canyon—that was blocked with horses, ambulances, broken caissons, artillery, and stragglers, and the First Division was delayed in getting through it. Sheridan and Crook sent McKinley back to bring Col. Isaac Duval's Second Division to the front. McKinley, noting the difficulty the First Division was having in passing through the ravine, urged it to hurry and then informed Duval about the obstructions in the road. McKinley advised him to move up a creek running parallel to the road so that his troops could get to the front quickly. Duval replied that he would take the other route only if commanded by General Crook. McKinley had no such order from Crook, but realizing that the division was urgently needed, he sat up straight in his saddle and said, "Then, by order of General Crook, I command you." Duval did what McKinley told him to do, and the division's prompt arrival allowed it to play an important part in the battle. McKinley often said that he had never suffered more than he did during the hour it took for the division to reach the front, when he could be sure he had not been mistaken in giving the order. When McKinley reported what he had done to General Crook, he was told that it was all right but only because the movement had been successful.[19]

When Colonel Duval's division reached its place on the right of the line, it was sent even farther to the right to find and break the Confederate left. Crook and McKinley accompanied the division, and when a long line of cavalry was seen a mile or more to the north, McKinley was sent to see if it was Confederate or Union troops. Russell Hastings described his ride:

> Away went McKinley, accompanied by his orderly, down the hill, through a cornfield, over an open field, getting closer and closer to this body of cavalry. Soon he was seen to halt, hesitate a moment and then turn and ride rapidly away, toward his command. Now there was no need to question who these troopers were, as a heavy carbine fire was opened upon McKinley, and his orderly was seen to reel and fall from his saddle.

Just as McKinley returned, unhurt, the left of the enemy's infantry line came into view, and Crook's troops found themselves caught between the Confederate cavalry and infantry. But then Union cavalry appeared and began to drive off the Confederate cavalry, and Crook sent McKinley to Colonel Thoburn of the First Division to tell him that Crook and the Second Division were going to attack the Confederate infantry and that he and his division should support them. Then McKinley went to Sheridan to inform him about the attack and to ask that it be supported by an advance of the entire Union line.[20]

As Duval's division advanced toward the Confederate line, under heavy fire, it found the way obstructed by "a deep creek with high banks, boggy, and perhaps twenty-five yards wide," with thick soft mud on the bottom and overgrown with moss on the surface, a slough some called it; McKinley called it a "deep and insurpassable morass." Without hesitating, Hayes rode his horse into the morass, calling out, "Come on, boys!" The men followed him through the mud and slime and pushed the Confederates back. McKinley was again with the division, and he too forced his way through the morass. As Crook's troops continued the assault, Union cavalry that had been pursuing the Confederate cavalry came up, and Sheridan ordered a charge against the retreating Confederates. With bands playing and guidons fluttering, the cavalry descended on the enemy. "No man ever saw a more thrilling sight than that cavalry charge," one infantryman said. "Every man's saber was waving above his head," another soldier said, as the cavalry charged the enemy with "a savage yell." Several of the younger staff officers—McKinley among them—were caught up in the excitement of the charge and left their commanders to join it. When McKinley returned and was being gently chided by Hayes for his breach of discipline in joining the charge without orders, he said simply, "How could anybody help it?"[21]

Crook brought up his First Division, and with the help of the cavalry his army pushed the Confederates back, the Sixth and Nineteenth Corps joining in the assault all along the line. Crook's army drove the Confederates through Winchester and went into camp south of the city. Sheridan's chief of staff reported that the army had sent the Confederates "whirling through Winchester," and President Lincoln telegraphed his congratulations: "Have just heard of your great victory. God bless you all, officers and men." Both sides suffered heavy losses; there were some five thousand Union and four thousand Confederate casualties. It took five days to bury the dead, and Winchester was one vast hospital for the wounded. Among the casualties were Colonel Duval, who was shot in the thigh and was succeeded in command of the Second Division by Rutherford Hayes, and Russell Hastings, so seriously wounded above the right knee that McKinley did not think he would survive.[22]

The Confederates fled up the Shenandoah Valley to a strong defensive position at Fisher's Hill, south of Strasburg. It was "the Gibraltar of the Valley," a high bluff that blocked the valley at its narrowest point. The Army of the Shenandoah followed and on September 22 defeated them again, and again Crook's Army of West Virginia played a leading role in the victory. Crook suggested using his army in a flanking movement, and Sheridan agreed. Crook led his two divisions, concealed in the woods, along Little North Mountain to the west of the Confederate line, over what McKinley said "appeared to be an impassable route, over the mountain side, where it seemed the foot of man had never trod." Then, while the Sixth and Nineteenth Corps attacked from the front, Crook's men charged down the mountainside, "with fixed bayonets, yelling like devils," one soldier said, and the Confederates "ran in flocks like sheep" up the valley. McKinley spoke later of the Confederates' "utter rout and demoralization. Thinking only of personal safety, they left camp, equipage, artillery, and stores, giving us undisputed possession of what was believed to be an impregnable position." He also said that the flanking movement, "strategic in its conception, impetuous in its execution," stamped Crook as "one of the foremost Generals in the war." Sheridan reported that Crook and his army had "turned the tide of battle in our favor both at Winchester and Fisher's Hill." Crook, in his report, noted his indebtedness to his staff, including McKinley, for their assistance "by carrying orders and for cheering the men forward during the thickest of the fight."[23]

Sheridan's cavalry pursued the Confederates as far as Staunton and Waynesboro, but the infantry went into camp at Harrisonburg. On the way there, Crook's Army of West Virginia stopped at New Market. As it was preparing to leave for Harrisonburg, an artist for *Frank Leslie's Illustrated Newspaper,* James Taylor, was introduced to Crook and his staff and described them in his diary. Crook, or "Gray Fox" as he was called from his days of Indian fighting, was "conspicuous in his white felt hat, astride his favorite war horse Bully, surrounded by his staff." McKinley and the other members of the staff were, he said, "gentlemen all, without pretensions to airs." "Now," Taylor wrote, "the bugle sounds and the regiments move into line amidst inspiring music of brigade bands," to resume their march to Harrisonburg.[24]

As the army moved south, some ugly events clouded the Shenandoah Valley. Some of John S. Mosby's Partisan Rangers, who had harassed Sheridan's forces since they arrived in the valley, killed a wounded Union cavalry officer—after he had been captured, according to some of the Union cavalrymen. General Grant had authorized the hanging of partisans, without trial, and the Union cavalry hanged and shot six captured men at Front Royal in retaliation and later hanged another captive. Mosby later responded by ordering the execution of seven of Gen. George Armstrong Custer's men chosen by lot from a group of captives, although four of the seven escaped death.[25]

Confederate partisans were a constant threat even to staff officers. At Harrisonburg, Lt. John R. Meigs, Sheridan's chief engineer and the son of Montgomery Meigs, the quartermaster general of the United States Army, stopped at Crook's headquarters before starting on a survey for Sheridan, and James Taylor sketched him there with Crook, McKinley, and other officers. While still within the Union lines and less than three miles from camp, Meigs was shot and killed by Confederates wearing blue overcoats, and Sheridan retaliated by ordering the burning of all the houses within five miles of the place of his killing, although in the end only a few houses were burned. Two days later, an ambulance with Meigs's body stopped at Sheridan's headquarters and then at Crook's headquarters, where Crook and his staff paid their respects before the ambulance began its journey to the North. A few days later, partisans also killed Emil Ohlenschlager, Sheridan's medical inspector, and Cornelius W. Tolles, his chief quartermaster. Another member of Sheridan's staff said that "almost everywhere in Virginia the staff officers felt that they carried their lives in their hands together with their dispatches, and if a twig cracked by the roadside it seemed ominous of bullets and sudden death."[26]

With the defeat of Early's army, Sheridan turned his attention to the other object of his campaign. Grant wanted to eliminate the Shenandoah Valley as a source of food and supplies for the Confederacy, and he had ordered Sheridan to destroy railroads and crops in the valley, saying, "If the war is to last another year, we want the Shenandoah Valley to remain a barren waste." When Sheridan's army first entered the valley, in August, it burned some buildings and crops, and after the Battle of Fisher's Hill, the Union cavalry destroyed crops, herds, and buildings south of Harrisonburg, but now the destruction began in earnest.[27]

On October 6, the Army of the Shenandoah began to move back down the valley from Harrisonburg, with the cavalry in the rear, spread across the entire valley, under orders to burn all forage and drive off all livestock. Some of the infantry was also ordered to participate, the 23d Ohio among them, but they did not all participate wholeheartedly. Lieutenant Colonel Comly said that although it was proper to destroy the enemy's supplies, he hated the assignment. "It does not seem real soldierly work. We ought to enlist a force of damned scoundrels for such work." But the destruction went on for three days, the troops burning barns, haystacks, granaries, mills, and store houses. James Taylor called it a "harrowing spectacle. . . . The Valley was filled with somber pillars of grimy smoke towering upwards and darkening the sky with a pall, amid wailings and lamentations of the husbandman." Taylor noted that there was little of the usual levity among Crook's staff, both because of the retreat back down the valley and the "sad panorama of destruction" that surrounded them. Sheridan reported from Woodstock that more than seventy mills and two thousand barns filled with crops had been burned and thousands of animals driven off or killed.[28]

Early's cavalry followed the Union army but was decisively beaten off at Tom's Brook. Sheridan's army went as far as Cedar Creek, near Strasburg, where it camped in a position that seemed secure, although Crook's headquarters was shelled on one occasion, and when Crook's troops were called out, one of his brigade commanders, Col. George Wells, was killed. Early's forces quickly withdrew, and Sheridan, thinking they were no longer a threat, went to Washington for consultations with Secretary of War Edwin Stanton and General in Chief Henry Halleck. McKinley said later that the victory at Fisher's Hill "was thought to be the last of Early, but it was not. His silence and seeming inertness following Fisher's Hill were only the cover of a well planned and skillfully executed assault upon our lines upon the morning of October 19, 1864, at Cedar Creek."[29]

Without warning, just before daylight on October 19, the Confederates charged through a thick fog, striking the First Division of Crook's army, which was on the extreme left of the Army of the Shenandoah, and then rolling the entire Union army back before them. The Union commanders and their staffs were in the midst of the fighting. Maj. Gen. Horatio G. Wright was in command in Sheridan's absence, and he and Crook and their staffs were at Sheridan's headquarters, Belle Grove, which the Confederates attempted to take in the hope of capturing Sheridan. Wright and Crook and their staffs rushed out and tried to rally their troops, but Wright was wounded, and Capt. Philip Bier was killed. Bier was an adjutant on Crook's staff who worked with McKinley, "a Wheeling boy, a model adjutant, ever prompt with his reports; had fiery red hair, was strictly temperate and religious, and held in the highest esteem by all with whom he came in contact." Col. Joseph Thoburn, commanding Crook's First Division, was also killed while trying to rally his troops.[30]

The demoralized Union army fell back through Middletown and formed a defensive line behind stone fences on a ridge north of the town. The Confederates, however, did not attack. They were exhausted, and some had stopped to plunder the Union camps. And Early had become indecisive, giving the Union forces time to regroup. As the Union army waited, loud cheering was heard from the rear. General Sheridan had returned to his army.[31]

Sheridan had come back from Washington and spent the night in Winchester. In the morning, he heard reports of heavy firing at the front, and when he had ridden out of Winchester, he could hear the sound of cannonading. Riding on, he encountered supply trains halted by reports of a battle and then soldiers retreating from the battlefield. Spurring his black horse, Rienzi, Sheridan hurried toward Cedar Creek, waving his hat and calling on his men to return to the front. They responded with cheers and began to follow him back to Cedar Creek. After Sheridan arrived at the battlefield, he rode down the Union line to let everyone know he was back. James Comly said that Sheridan was "magnetism incarnate" and that his presence stirred the men "like the crackle from an electric battery." Invigorated by Sheridan's return, the Union army repelled an attack by the

Confederates and then advanced and defeated them, ending once and for all the Confederate threat in the Shenandoah Valley and adding greatly to Lincoln's prospects in the election that was held only three weeks after the battle.[32]

Sheridan's ride became one of the best-known events of the war. Thomas Buchanan Read celebrated it in a poem called "Sheridan's Ride" that gained great popularity. The poem begins with Sheridan in Winchester, "twenty miles away," and has Rienzi bringing him closer and closer to the battlefield until the poem's climax:

> The first that the general saw were the groups
> Of stragglers, and then the retreating troops;
> What was done? what to do? A glance told him both.
> Then striking his spurs, with a terrible oath,
> He dashed down the line 'mid a storm of huzzas,
> And the wave of retreat checked its course there,
>   because
> The sight of the master compelled it to pause.
> With foam and with dust the black charger was gray;
> By the flash of his eye and the red nostril's play,
> He seemed to the whole great army to say,
> "I have brought you Sheridan all the way
>   From Winchester down to save the day!"[33]

McKinley played a part in Sheridan's celebrated return. At Newtown (now Stephens City), Sheridan found the streets too crowded to go through. He said in his *Memoirs* that in going around the town he met "Major McKinley, of Crook's staff," who "spread the news of my return through the motley throng there." A half hour later, James Taylor found McKinley and some guards at Newtown, announcing Sheridan's return and doing their best to turn the soldiers back toward the front. When McKinley was governor of Ohio, he wrote his own account of the meeting with Sheridan and the ride Sheridan later took down the Union lines.

> I had been across the pike to put in position Colonel Dupont's battery, by order of General Crook, and as I returned I met Sheridan dashing up, and he asked me where Crook was. I took Sheridan to Crook, and they and the staff went back of the red barn. It was there determined by Sheridan to make the charge. Then it was suggested that Sheridan should ride down the lines of the disheartened troops. His overcoat was

McKinley announcing General Sheridan's return to stragglers at
Newtown and directing them to return to the battlefield at Cedar Creek,
October 19, 1864. Drawing by James E. Taylor. *Courtesy of the Western
Reserve Historical Society, Cleveland, Ohio.*

pulled off him, and somebody took his epaulettes out of a box. The
epaulettes were placed upon his shoulders—and my recollection is that
this was done by Colonel Forsythe and another officer. Then Sheridan
rode down the lines. He was dressed in a new uniform.

Another account says it was McKinley who suggested that Sheridan take
off the common soldier's blue overcoat he was wearing, so the men could
more easily recognize him, and McKinley who helped him take the coat
off. McKinley often said that Sheridan—whom he called "that gallant little
Irishman"—never looked more like a soldier than he did then. On one occasion, McKinley described Sheridan's expression that day. "He did not
appear excited. I might say he was calm, but there was a tightening of the
muscles of the face and a look in the eye that denoted determination.
There was a set purpose in his face, and it meant fight." He said that Sheridan's arrival at Cedar Creek was "like the reinforcement of a thousand

men. When he rode down the line to show that he was there every man saw fight and victory in his presence."[34]

George A. Forsyth, who was a member of Sheridan's staff, remembered seeing McKinley and Rutherford Hayes standing with the troops as Sheridan rode down the infantry line. He said McKinley and Hayes joined in the cheering, and as a color-bearer near McKinley raised a tattered battle flag, the two men saluted and then swung their caps. (Forsyth also remembered being with McKinley on a cold, damp, and "thoroughly disagreeable" day during the campaign, when McKinley offered him half of what he had to eat—two pieces of hardtack and a piece of meat—which they ate sitting on the trunk of a fallen tree. Forsyth said that he was "devilish hungry" and that he never afterward ate with McKinley when the food was more appetizing.)[35]

After the battle, the army went into camp near Belle Grove. There was still work to be done: prisoners to be sent north, some of the dead reburied, and the wounded attended to. James Taylor noted a mass of "maimed soldiers" in the churchyard in Middletown, "with wounds bound up, stretched in rows, all bloodless and pale." Gen. George Armstrong Custer was sent to Washington with captured Confederate flags and returned with his wife, Libbie, to visit the army's headquarters. The sight of Libbie, in her "long black riding habit with a tight-fitting jacket of velvet" and her "wealth of brown hair, all free to the breeze, about her shoulders" was a welcome distraction from the glut of bloodshed and death the soldiers had seen.[36]

McKinley was busy with his work as Crook's adjutant. Philip Bier was dead, James Botsford had been transferred to the department headquarters at Cumberland, Maryland, and McKinley was the sole adjutant left with Crook in the field. The work of accounting for men and equipment and of resupplying the army after a battle fell heavily on the adjutant. McKinley also received reports of the battle from the commanders of the various units in the Army of West Virginia and used them to make up his own reports. And he issued orders for Crook, most of them routine, but at least on one occasion written with a touch of youthful enthusiasm. He sent a telegram to Col. John H. Oley at Charleston, West Virginia, saying: "Your telegram received. The general commanding directs that you hold out, fight, clean out, and destroy all in your front, as Breckinridge is in Kentucky, and there can be nothing but bushwhackers in that country. You must not permit yourself to be frightened by them. You have force enough; none can be spared from here."[37]

Guerrillas continued to harass the Union army, and the soldiers showed them no mercy. When George Briggs, of the 6th Michigan Cavalry, was shot by guerrillas, Union soldiers arrested two men who were thought to have been the killers. The first lieutenant of Briggs's company burned the men's houses and, when he heard cartridges explode in the fires, was convinced that the houses had concealed arms, which he took as proof that one of the men was the killer. He said that he tried to get ropes to hang the men but finding none asked for volunteers to shoot them. His troopers "rode forward as one man." He gave the men time to say their prayers, and then they were both shot.[38]

The Army of the Shenandoah was still at Cedar Creek on election day, November 8, and McKinley voted for the first time in a presidential election. The Ohio elections had been held in October, and McKinley may have voted then as well. In that election the Ohio soldiers in the Army of West Virginia voted overwhelmingly for the Union candidates. One of the candidates elected to Congress was Rutherford Hayes, even though he refused to leave the field to campaign for the office. In the presidential election, McKinley voted in the company of Rutherford Hayes, George Crook, and Philip Sheridan. It was also Sheridan's first vote; even though Sheridan had never voted before, he wanted to cast his vote for Lincoln (as did a large majority of the soldiers in his army). McKinley, Hayes, Crook, and Sheridan voted at the polling place of the 34th Ohio Infantry, an army ambulance parked in a woods amid autumn foliage that was beautiful even on a drizzly, gloomy day. The ambulance held the election officials as well as an old cartridge box that served as a receptacle for the ballots. Hayes showed the new voters how to cast a ballot, while the onlookers cheered and the regimental band played "Hail to the Chief Who in Triumph Advances." Years later, Senator Nathan B. Scott said he was present when McKinley voted and had a conversation with him. He said McKinley "spoke of his study of the law, and speculated in regard to his future. It was a special wonder with him whether he could reach a position which would bring him influence enough to elect him a probate judge in his native county."[39]

On the same day as the presidential election, McKinley issued orders for the Army of West Virginia to join the rest of Sheridan's army in moving back to Kernstown, where the troops would be closer to their supplies. The march was made in one day, and the army went into quarters at a camp it called Camp Russell. The arrival at Camp Russell and the building of log huts marked the beginning of a quiet winter for most of the men. Supplies were plentiful; among those that arrived was a large wagon train full

McKinley voting with Generals Philip Sheridan and George Crook during the presidential election of 1864. Sheridan is handing his ballot to the official in the ambulance. Crook, with the light-colored, broad brimmed hat, is standing beneath the flag, with McKinley, partially hidden, directly behind him. Drawing by James E. Taylor. *Courtesy of the Western Reserve Historical Society.*

of poultry, fruits, and mince pies for the army's Thanksgiving dinner, sent by grateful citizens of the North. Along with their usual drills and guard duty, the soldiers enjoyed horse races, music, religious services, current periodicals, regular mail, the presence of female visitors, "and festive times generally." Camp Russell was near Winchester, and McKinley rode with Rutherford Hayes into the city, where they stopped at a law office and, because of the proposed amendment to abolish slavery, read the constitutional provisions about amendments. They also visited their friend Russell Hastings, who was recovering from the wound he received at the Battle of Opequon.[40]

Heavy snows in December made sleighing possible, and McKinley took a sleigh ride with Hayes—recently promoted to brigadier general—into Winchester, where they visited Hastings again and were pleased to find him in "capital spirits" over his continued improvement. With little military action of its own, the Army of the Shenandoah followed the news from Gen. William T. Sherman's army in Georgia and Gen. George H. Thomas's army in Tennessee. James Taylor was surprised to hear cannon fire on December 16, but when he went to Crook's headquarters, he learned from McKinley that the cannons were being fired in celebration of Thomas's victory at Nashville. The camp, he said, was in a "high state of elation from General Crook down," and plans had been made for a victory celebration with a serenade and bonfires that night.[41]

In December, the Sixth Corps left to join Grant's army at Petersburg, and soon plans were under way for the Army of West Virginia to move as well. McKinley issued orders for the First Division to travel to Washington, where it was assigned to Gen. Benjamin F. Butler's Army of the James. Parts of the Second Division were ordered to Martinsburg and Beverly, West Virginia, and part to Cumberland, Maryland. James Taylor visited Crook's headquarters again on December 19, where he found "a busy scene." McKinley and three other members of Crook's staff, "especially upon whom evolved the work of looking after the corps needs, were up to their eyes, as the command was to move out by night." His visit was short because "none had time to waste in long conversations." Despite his busyness, McKinley found time to visit Russell Hastings one more time before he left Camp Russell. Crook and his staff left for the department headquarters at Cumberland, Maryland, on December 28.[42]

Cumberland had been chosen as the headquarters of the Department of West Virginia earlier in the war because of its location on the National Road, the Chesapeake and Ohio Canal, and especially the Baltimore and Ohio Railroad. When Crook and his staff moved there, Hayes's brigade of the Second Division accompanied them to guard the railroad against attacks by guerrillas. While Hayes's brigade settled into huts on the hillside near Cumberland—a camp that Hayes called Camp Hastings—Crook and his staff moved into the city's hotels. Some of the staff had already been stationed at Cumberland, including Maj. Robert P. Kennedy, an adjutant who ranked McKinley, and Capt. W. I. Mathews, another adjutant on the staff. James Botsford was still on the staff but was serving as assistant inspector general. The eagle was adopted as the department symbol, and McKinley and the other men connected with headquarters were entitled to wear a gilt or golden eagle as their badge. The department headquarters was identified by a large red and blue flag adorned with a gilt spread eagle and a gilt fringe.[43]

In mid-January, Confederate cavalry surprised and captured the Union post at Beverly, West Virginia, and the 23d Ohio was sent by rail to Grafton, West Virginia, to protect the railroad. They stayed there, in bitterly cold weather, some without tents, for five days before returning to Cumberland. McKinley accompanied the regiment. One night he told the pickets to "keep a sharp eye" on a certain barn. Although he did not give a reason, they followed his orders. On the third night, they saw three men going back of the barn toward a railroad trestle, carrying something that looked like a milk can. The pickets called on them to halt and, when they did not, fired on them, hitting one, although all three escaped. The soldiers discovered that the can the men were carrying was filled with turpentine and had been overturned on a nearby handcar. A bag of cotton was also on the handcar, and the soldiers were sure that the men were planning to set the cotton on fire and send the burning handcar hurtling down the track. A veteran who recounted the incident said he "often wondered how Captain McKinley got the information that led him to give orders that we watch the barn, but I was never able to find out. But I think he was doing some scouting work on the quiet, with the hope of receiving a promotion."[44]

Apart from guard duty, drills, and occasional scouts along the railroad, the soldiers had few duties at Cumberland, and they were able to enjoy sleighing, educational classes, religious services, "young ladies, a pretty town, parties, balls, etc." Hayes and McKinley were among a group of officers who went on a ten-mile sleigh ride to a hospital on the Cumberland Road. Hayes recorded that they had "a great time snowballing." General Crook himself sponsored balls at the Revere House in Cumberland in January and again in February, with McKinley a member of the Committee of Invitation for one of them. James Comly described the January ball to Hayes, who was at home on a furlough, as "a grand party." "The belle of the evening was the Chf. Quartermaster Farnsworth, who parts his hair in the middle. Gardner was the best dancer—and from what Kennedy tells me of the latter end of the thing, McKinley must have been the drunkest. I guess they had a little difficulty about it." That brief mention is the only reference to McKinley drinking during the war, although the subject was raised later and magnified by his political opponents.[45]

A young woman also had McKinley's attention at Cumberland. Russell Hastings was well enough to return to his home at Willoughby, Ohio, and Cyrus Roberts of Crook's staff wrote to him there about their friend McKinley. "Persons who did no[t] know him as well as I were seriously alarmed for his peace of mind, for true to his old reputation, he fell in love (to all appearances) with a young & beautiful 'damsel' as soon as he reached Cumberland & had not the young lady taken her departure for her home, even I who know McK so well, would not have answered for the consequences, & as it is, it is a debatable point whether he has escaped scot free or not."[46]

The balls and young women at Cumberland may have distracted the officers from their duties, for on the early morning of February 21 a raiding party of McNeill's Rangers stole into Cumberland and captured General Crook and Gen. Benjamin F. Kelley, the commander of the post. Overrunning the pickets and obtaining the countersign by threatening to hang one of them, the raiders entered Cumberland despite the eight thousand troops stationed there to prevent such incursions. They took Crook from the Revere House and Kelley and his adjutant, Capt. Thayer Melvin, from the St. Nicholas Hotel, entered the telegraph office, cut the wires and disabled the equipment, stole some horses, and quickly headed for Richmond with their captives.[47]

McKinley was staying at the St. Nicholas Hotel and could easily have been captured. One Confederate veteran said he had participated in a raid in Berkeley County, West Virginia, in which McKinley escaped capture only because he was away at a dance that night. McKinley's social life may have saved him at Cumberland as well. His sister Anna wrote to him about the capture of the generals suggesting that "more *vigilance* on the part of [the] *military* might have prevented it." Then she could not resist teasing her brother by asking, "Didn't it lower *your feathers* considerably? Quite a come down from *balls*, parties and *general* gayety, I think."[48]

With Crook's capture, Brig. Gen. John D. Stevenson, who was commanding the Military District of Harpers Ferry, became the senior officer in the Department of West Virginia, and Sheridan assigned him to command the department until someone was named to replace Crook. Stevenson, a forty-three-year-old lawyer and former president of the Missouri state senate who had served in the West before being assigned to Harpers Ferry, immediately went to Cumberland. He retained Crook's staff, and McKinley was soon issuing orders in Stevenson's name.[49]

A few days later, Sheridan left Winchester to go up the Shenandoah Valley and eventually to join Grant's army, and Maj. Gen. Winfield Scott Hancock was placed in command of the Department of West Virginia and the troops of the Middle Military Division who had not accompanied Sheridan. Hancock then named Brig. Gen. Samuel Sprigg Carroll to replace Stevenson at Cumberland and to command the Department of West Virginia in Hancock's absence.[50]

One week after Stevenson arrived at Cumberland, Carroll came to take his place. He too retained Crook's staff, and McKinley began to work for him. But eight days later, Hancock revoked Carroll's assignment. Hancock had mistakenly thought that Carroll was a brevet major general, and when he learned about his mistake, he realized that he should not have assigned him to the command at Cumberland. Not wanting to send Stevenson back to Cumberland, Hancock decided to go there himself. When he got to Cumberland, he too retained Crook's staff. McKinley found himself serving on the staffs of four different generals—Crook, Stevenson, Carroll, and Hancock—all in a period of fifteen days.[51]

Hancock stayed in Cumberland only a few days and then returned to Winchester, taking McKinley with him. Although McKinley was at the headquarters of the Middle Military Division at Winchester, he was assisting Hancock in the work of the Department of West Virginia. While they were at Winchester, General Crook, freed from military prison, returned to Cumberland and took command of the Department of West Virginia. Hancock insisted that Crook had no right to do so, and after two days at Cumberland, Crook was dispatched to join Grant's army at Petersburg.[52]

In late March, Hancock and McKinley returned to Cumberland, where McKinley continued to serve on Hancock's staff. Hancock, a West Point graduate and a veteran of the Mexican War, had commanded the Second Corps in the Army of the Potomac, becoming known as "Hancock the Superb." A severe wound at Gettysburg had limited his service, and he was organizing a new corps to be composed entirely of veterans when he was called on to replace Sheridan. Hancock was respected for his courage and ability, but he was not an easy man to work for. One staff officer, who noted that Hancock had once been a quartermaster and had a lingering "taste for military papers," called him "a terror to adjutants, having a singular penchant for going over everything himself about two or three times a week. He usually goes into his adjutant's office about 11 P.M. and asks for the books, papers and correspondence, when an immediate tempest invariably occurs, and the adjutant general is badgered in great style." The badgering was apt to be laced with some choice language; one of Hancock's chaplains was appalled by the example the general set with his use of the "grossest profanity" and the "most horrid oaths."[53]

McKinley had served with Hancock for only about one month when he received a new assignment. Grant requested a reorganization of the Army of the Shenandoah so that all the troops that were not required to protect the Baltimore and Ohio Railroad could be placed in units ready for service in the field. In the reorganization, a new division was created, the Fourth Provisional Division, which was to be commanded by Samuel Carroll.

Maj. Gen. Winfield Scott Hancock. *Courtesy of the Massachusetts Commandery and the USAMHI.*

The division was made up of a brigade from the Army of West Virginia at Cumberland, commanded by Brig. Gen. Isaac Duval, and one brigade of Hancock's veteran volunteers. When Carroll accepted the command, he asked that McKinley be assigned as his adjutant, and on April 6, McKinley and his orderly left for Winchester, where the division was to be stationed. McKinley would still be associated with the 23d Ohio, for it was part of

Duval's brigade, but his close association with Rutherford Hayes ended with his move to Winchester; Hayes was given a new command and was sent to New Creek, West Virginia.[54]

Samuel Sprigg Carroll replaced Hayes as McKinley's sponsor and mentor. Carroll was the son of William Thomas Carroll, for many years the clerk of the U.S. Supreme Court and a grandnephew of Charles Carroll of Carrollton. Thirty-two years old and a graduate of West Point, he had served as colonel of the 8th Ohio Infantry and, later, as a brigade commander under Hancock in the Second Corps. One of the men who served under Carroll said that his only fault, "if fault it may be called, was that he was too daring, regardless of his own life and welfare." That daring behavior had led to five different wounds, the last time in the left arm at Spotsylvania, "knocking his elbow all to pieces." Hancock said that Carroll was "crippled for life, and in infirm health, but proud of his reputation, is ready and anxious to devote his remaining strength to the service." McKinley called Carroll "a distinguished soldier . . . whose almost countless wounds attest his courage and devotion."[55]

When McKinley had joined Crook's staff, he was one of several adjutants, and even when changes in assignments left him the only adjutant with Crook in the field, others served Crook at department headquarters. But when McKinley went to Carroll's Fourth Provisional Division, it was as the sole adjutant. The order announcing Carroll's staff named McKinley first, which reflected the fact that an adjutant served as a commanding officer's chief of staff, directing the service of all the other departments of the staff and of the whole command. Jacob Cox said that the adjutant was "the centre of the formal organization, keeping its records, carrying on its correspondence, and formulating the orders of his chief." If an adjutant had his commander's confidence, he could issue orders in routine matters on his own, sure that his commander would not interfere and that the orders would be obeyed. An adjutant also read his commander's orders and the many others received from higher commands to the soldiers on dress parade. McKinley did so in the voice widely admired later in his career for its carrying power. James Boyle, his private secretary when he was governor of Ohio, said it was "a wonderful voice, which, when in full swing, was as clear and penetrating as a bugle and as rich and sonorous as a big bronze bell."[56]

McKinley's new position presented new challenges. Another officer who served as an adjutant complained about the "steady stream" of orderlies who came to him, "their arms piled high with letters, requisitions, charges, returns, reports, requests—all demanding attention, all demanding decisions," and the officers who crowded around his desk with their own demands, "each believing his case to be unique and more urgent than anyone else's." Another adjutant said he was "expected to know everything" and "give opinions on every conceivable question," which required him to study army regulations "both early and late."[57]

When McKinley was preparing for his new assignment, Robert Kennedy ordered supplies for him: order books, letter books, endorsement books, blank books, and a letterpress. McKinley ordered still more supplies: ink, inkstands, pens, pen racks, writing paper, envelopes, and erasers. The War Department issued twenty additional pounds of candles each month for his use as adjutant. It appeared that McKinley's mission was to fight the war—day and night—with paperwork. But the war was nearly over. Three days after McKinley joined the Fourth Provisional Division at Winchester, Gen. Robert E. Lee surrendered, an event that was celebrated at Winchester with great cheering and the firing of two hundred guns. One of the first orders McKinley issued was in celebration of Lee's surrender. "In honor of the crowning victory of our arms, and the prospect of a speedy peace, the City of Winchester will be thoroughly illuminated this evening. All citizens are called upon to bear their part in the illumination. Those not having the means can obtain them by calling upon the Provost Marshal of the City of Winchester." Most of the citizens had Southern sympathies and few were inclined to help celebrate the Union victory, but someone recognized that McKinley's order was a bit of history, and a copy of it was kept and displayed for years in Winchester's public library.[58]

McKinley furnished the division with information about the death of John Wilkes Booth and the surrender of Gen. Joseph Johnston's army. He also issued orders about the division's relationship with the city of Winchester. Even though the fighting was over, soldiers visiting Winchester were required to wear their side arms and were not permitted to remain in the city after tattoo. Civilians were forbidden to carry arms on the city streets or to be on the streets after 9:00 P.M. without the permission of the provost marshal.[59]

McKinley issued order after order to his division, but with the fighting over, army regulations and routine were resented more than ever. Dr. Joe Webb, writing to Hayes, complained about "all kinds of silly orders, Reviews innumerable, First Carroll reviews every body. Then Hancock. Hancock leaves and Torbert, just breaks his neck, rides that White Horse and his Staff (21 in number) almost to death. . . . Cotton (white) Gloves, all the rage." The army had little to do at Winchester, and it was soon dispersed. Duval's brigade was sent to Staunton, which for the first time separated McKinley from the 23d Ohio. General Hancock moved his head-quarters to Washington, D.C., and Carroll was given a new command, the First Division of the First Army Corps, or as it was commonly known, Hancock's Corps. Carroll named McKinley as his adjutant and aide-de-camp in his new division.[60]

The First Army Corps was stationed at Camp Stoneman, in the District of Columbia, just south of the Anacostia River. The Second Brigade of Carroll's Fourth Provisional Division—made up of three regiments of Hancock's veteran volunteers—was to be part of Carroll's new command, and McKinley issued orders for it to be ready to march from Winchester to Camp Stoneman on May 4. In the midst of the preparations for the march, McKinley was hurriedly initiated into the Masonic Lodge.[61]

McKinley became acquainted with Masonry after the Battle of Opequon when he accompanied one of the surgeons on a visit to the Confederates taken prisoner at the battle. He later told a fellow Mason about the experience:

Almost as soon as we passed the guard, I noticed that the doctor shook hands cordially with a number of Confederate prisoners. He also took from his pocket a roll of bills and distributed all he had among them. Boy-like, I looked on in wonderment; I didn't know what it meant. On the way back to our camp I asked him, "Did you know these men or ever see them before?" "No," replied the doctor, "I never saw them before." "But how did you know them, and why did you give them money?", I asked. "They are Masons, and we Masons have ways of finding that out." "But," I persisted, "you gave them a lot of money, all you had about you. Do you ever expect to get it back?" "Well," said the doctor, "if they are ever able to pay it back, they will. But it makes no difference to me; they are brother Masons in trouble, and I am only doing my duty." I said to myself, "If that is Masonry I will take some of it myself."[62]

McKinley was initiated into Masonry at Hiram Lodge No. 21, Free and Accepted Masons, in Winchester. The activities of the Winchester lodge had been interrupted during the war, but after the Battle of Cedar Creek, its officers asked General Sheridan for permission to reopen the lodge. One of Sheridan's surgeons, who was himself a Mason, urged Sheridan to grant the request, arguing that it would give the soldiers an opportunity to mingle with the local people and remove some of the bitter feeling between them, and Sheridan agreed. The soldiers showed considerable interest in Masonry, and more than two hundred were initiated into the Winchester lodge. John B. T. Reed, the master of the lodge, an "intensely Southern man," conferred McKinley's degrees on him on the three days before he left Winchester for Camp Stoneman, May 1, 2, and 3. On May 3, McKinley was given a release of his membership, and when he returned to Ohio, he resumed his association with Masonry and continued it the rest of his life.[63]

Carroll and his staff and the three regiments of veteran volunteers began their five-day march to Camp Stoneman on May 4, an uneventful march except for the surrender of some four hundred Confederate soldiers along the way. The other six regiments of veteran volunteers were already at Camp Stoneman, and all nine regiments were soon organized as the First Division, First Army Corps.[64]

The veteran volunteers in the First Army Corps had been recruited from honorably discharged soldiers with at least two years of military service. They were to serve as U.S. Volunteers rather than serving in state organizations as previous volunteers had. To encourage enlistments, the popular General Hancock was selected to organize the corps, which became known as Hancock's Corps. Volunteers were promised a special bounty of three hundred dollars and the right to keep their breech-loading or repeating rifles when they were discharged. Although Hancock and his staff had their headquarters in Washington, all the volunteers that had been raised—about eight thousand men—were stationed at Camp Stoneman, and all were included in General Carroll's First Division, the only division in the First Army Corps. To establish the new corps' identity, badges were issued to all the men, who were ordered to wear them on the tops of their caps under penalty of being "tied up 24 hours by the thumbs."[65]

The organization of the division was completed in time for the Grand Review of the Union armies in Washington in late May, but Carroll's request to have the division included in the review was not granted. Instead, General Hancock reviewed the division at nearby Giesboro Point in the company of Governor Andrew Curtin of Pennsylvania and Maj. Gen. Christopher C. Augur, who commanded the Department of Washington. Even though McKinley did not participate in the Grand Review, he was able to go into Washington to observe it. He was struck by a motto displayed at the Capitol that said, "The only debt this government can never pay is the debt it owes the brave men who saved the nation," a statement he often quoted in postwar speeches.[66]

Two weeks later, Hancock again reviewed the division, this time accompanied by Q.M. Gen. Montgomery Meigs and a large group of general officers and their wives. Almost inconspicuous among the visitors was "a

Maj. Gen. Samuel Sprigg Carroll and the staff of the First Division, First Army Corps, 1865. Standing *(from left)*: Lieutenant Nolan, Maj. William McKinley Jr., Capt. H. C. Cherrington, Captain Bronson, Maj. Ivan Tailof. Seated *(from left)*: unidentified, Lt. John Wesley Eckles, Maj. Gen. Samuel Sprigg Carroll, Lieutenant von Stamp, Surgeon Thomas F. Betton. *Courtesy of the Massachusetts Commandery and the USAMHI.*

modest-looking civilian, on foot, in the line of spectators," President Andrew Johnson. During the review, Hancock and Carroll and their staffs passed along the entire line, "inspecting the men closely," and then took their positions while the troops passed before them. After the review, President Johnson, the generals and their staffs, and the invited guests "repaired to General Carroll's headquarters, and spent an hour or two very pleasantly in social intercourse, in which the ladies bore the most conspicuous and entertaining part. A delicate and appropriate collation was served, and the scene was charming and interesting."[67]

Unfortunately, the veteran volunteers were given little to do besides participating in reviews, and the inactivity began to affect morale. "We Are still laying heare in Camp," one soldier in the 4th Regiment wrote, "hav nothing to Doo But Bee inspected or Reviewed & that is Allmoste evry Day. . . . But the worst trouble with us now is we Donte Get enough to eate." He said that many of the men were deserting "& Going home just on Acount of the way thare Are used it is A Disgrase to humanaty." To stem the desertions, Carroll ordered four roll calls daily and directed all guards and pickets to have their weapons loaded. At the same time, the officers were kept busy with drills in the use of the sword by the division's "instructor of sword exercise." McKinley was occupied with the paperwork that crossed his desk, but even he was underemployed, and on June 19 he was given twenty days' leave. He used it to return to Poland— his fourth trip home during the war.[68]

When McKinley returned to Camp Stoneman, he received notice of his appointment as a brevet major—an honor that gave him the name of the higher rank without changing his actual rank or pay. Crook had recommended McKinley for a brevet in January, and his recommendation was endorsed by Sheridan. The brevet, which was to date from March 13, 1865, was given for "gallant and meritorious service during the campaign in West Virginia and the Shenandoah Valley." McKinley did not receive the actual commission until November 1866, but as soon as he signed his oath of office on July 11, 1865, he called himself and was addressed as Major McKinley. It was a title he cherished. After he had been elected president, Charles Manchester, another veteran of the 23d Ohio, confessed confusion about what to call him. "I am at a loss to know how to address you," he said. "I knew you as a soldier, as a congressman, as governor, and now as President-elect. How shall I address you?" "Call me Major," McKinley replied. "I earned that. I am not so sure of the rest."[69]

Even though the veteran volunteers were little needed at Camp Stoneman, there was use for them elsewhere. Some were sent to the battlefields of Spotsylvania and the Wilderness to bury the dead. The Second Brigade went to Washington on guard duty when the four conspirators in Lincoln's assassination were executed. The men guarded all the approaches to the Old Penitentiary where the executions were held and were stationed in the building, in the yard, and on the surrounding walls. They also conducted the burials: "We eased the bodies down and put them in a straight rough box with the same clothes on and put them in their graves." During July, all nine regiments were sent to other parts of the country, the remaining officers and men of the First Division were ordered to be mustered out of the service, and on July 19 both Carroll and McKinley were relieved of their duties.[70]

On the same day that McKinley was relieved of his duties, he made an official application for an appointment as a captain in the First Army Corps. The War Department was seeking officers as well as enlisted men for the veteran volunteer corps, and General Carroll had encouraged him to apply for a commission that would allow him to stay in the army when his regiment was mustered out of the service. Carroll endorsed his application, saying that "Maj. McKinley has been promoted from a Private to his present rank for gallant & efficient conduct in the field, and I can vouch for his capability in every respect." Hancock also endorsed the application: "I think the applicant will make an excellent officer. I recommend that he be appointed Captain at once, the examination to be deferred. I am in need of more officers for the troops already raised."[71]

Despite Hancock's recommendation to defer the usual examination in McKinley's case, military routine prevailed. McKinley was ordered to appear before a board of examination in Washington on July 29. The board, headed by Brig. Gen. Thomas H. Neill, was made up of officers who had served in the First Army Corps' First Division: the commanders of the three brigades, colonels of two of the regiments, and the division's surgeon in chief. The members of the board expressed their satisfaction with McKinley's examination and recommended him for a captaincy. Then the War Department informed him that he would be appointed a captain in the First Army Corps when the War Department was notified that he had been mustered out of the service. (In fact, he had already been mustered out, with the 23d Ohio Infantry on July 26.) But then, unexpectedly, McKinley declined the commission that had been offered to him.[72]

It was his parents' objection that kept McKinley from a career in the army. When McKinley was governor of Ohio, a reporter, Frank G. Carpenter, asked him how he had liked military life. "Very much indeed," he replied. "I wanted to remain in the army. My friends among the officers

Mathew Brady photograph of
William McKinley Jr. taken in
Washington, D.C., in 1865.
*Courtesy of the Western
Reserve Historical Society.*

urged me to do so, and I would probably be in the military service to-day if
my father and mother had not seriously objected. Somehow or other, they
did not think much of my being in the army in the time of peace. The result
was that I came home and studied law." Carpenter interviewed McKinley
again when he was president and reported then that McKinley had come
home to Poland "full of the idea of joining the regular army and making
war his profession for life." But when he proposed the idea to his father,
the response was, "Well, William, you may do as you please, but I have
never thought that soldiers amounted to much in times of peace." And
McKinley, either impressed by his father's opinion or simply deferring to
his judgment, dropped his plans for a life in the army.[73]

McKinley returned to his home in Poland in August, too late to attend the dedication of the 23d Ohio's monument to its dead in Woodland Cemetery in Cleveland on July 29. McKinley marveled that his old
regiment—and the entire volunteer army—simply disbanded, the hard-
ened warriors going peacefully to their homes. He said:

We had a million soldiers in the field when the war terminated, and the highest testimony to their character is found in the fact that when the muster hour came, and that vast army, which for years had been accustomed to wars and carnage, returned to their homes, they dropped into the quiet walks of citizenship, and no trace of them was ever discernible except in their integrity of character, their intense patriotism, and their participation in the growth and development and maintenance of the Government which they had contributed so much to save.[74]

McKinley, too, quietly turned from what he called "the most sacred cause in history" to civilian life. But he was indelibly marked by his wartime experiences. The war that had interrupted his education instructed him in other, deeper ways. Murat Halstead, one of McKinley's early biographers, said that "the [military] camp was to him a university. . . . When the combat closed, Major McKinley was an officer and a gentleman, who had builded in his diversified education wiser than he knew, and taken a degree beyond any the colleges could confer." He was wiser when he left the army, not only about military matters and business practices but about the human condition in both its noblest and its most debased expressions. The seasoned veteran, home from the war, was twenty-two years old.[75]

FIVE *Veteran*

There is perhaps no part of [McKinley's] career, or no other
associations of his life in which he takes greater pride, and justly so,
than in his army service, . . . and none which have had greater
influence in shaping his subsequent career.

—*Robert B. Wilson*

McKinley's later life and career were profoundly affected by his military service. Proud of his status as a Union veteran, he displayed his officer's sword over his desk, frequented gatherings of veterans, spoke and acted on veterans' behalf, and kept his army comrades as his best friends. Believing that one of the most important results of the war was the ending of slavery and the new rights of the freedmen, he championed those rights through most of his career. Later, he began to reach out to the Southern whites who had fought against him, an endeavor that gradually crowded out his concern for the rights of black Americans. Drawing on his experience as a staff officer during the war, McKinley slipped easily into the role of a military commander, both as governor of Ohio during civil unrest in that state and as president during the Spanish-American War. The following account of McKinley's postwar years is not intended as a full description—that is available elsewhere—but only to show how deeply he was affected by the four years he spent in uniform.

The citizens of Poland arranged a soldiers' reunion and picnic shortly after McKinley came home and invited veterans of the 23d, 60th, and 105th Ohio Infantry Regiments, their families, the families of deceased soldiers, the clergy, the public, and veterans of the War of 1812. About five hundred people responded by gathering in Henry Kirtland's Grove, where they were welcomed by H. G. Leslie, a local attorney; and Judge Charles E. Glidden, who had inspired McKinley by his speech at the Sparrow House in Poland at the outbreak of the war. Two members of the old Poland Guards were invited to respond to the welcome, Lt. Albert B. Logan and Maj. William McKinley Jr. It was McKinley's first public speech.

Having decided on a legal career, McKinley began to read law with Judge Glidden, his mind full, he said, of "the solemnities of the marriage contract" and the "old customs of the Saxons & Danes." But his military comrades were often on his mind. He wrote to Russell Hastings that he found Poland "very tame, but I have banished myself. I often feel that I would like to have Hastings & Webb step in & talk over old matters or new ones. . . . Whenever you can make it convenient come & see me." Yet even tame Poland held reminders of the war; no more than three months after McKinley's return, Thomas Buchanan Read's poem "Sheridan's Ride" was recited at the Poland academy.[2]

After a little more than a year with Judge Glidden, McKinley left to study for a term at the Albany Law School in Albany, New York. The class McKinley entered, known as the "War Class," was exceptionally large and was said to include veterans of every rank in the army, from major general down to private. McKinley was in Albany when he received his commission as a brevet major, signed by President Andrew Johnson and Secretary of War Edwin M. Stanton. About this time he should also have received the bronze medal the state of Ohio presented to those who reenlisted for a second term, "without any hope or expectation of large bounties, and actuated only by the purest love of country."[3]

McKinley left the Albany Law School early in 1867, and late in March he moved to Canton, in Stark County, Ohio, where his cousin and her husband, Sarah and William K. Miller, were living and where his sister Anna was teaching school. McKinley soon entered into a law partnership in Canton with Judge George W. Belden and became active in Republican politics. Rutherford Hayes was the Republican candidate for governor in the fall of 1867, and McKinley spoke in support of him, making the first political speech of his career from the top of a dry goods box at New Berlin (now North Canton) and then repeating the speech all around Stark County. He recited Hayes's war record, describing his wound at South Mountain, telling how he had "waded[,] swam, and floundered across the dense marsh" at Opequon, and noting that "he served his country until the *last* rebel stronghold had been surrendered although months before elected to Congress by the 2d District of Ohio." McKinley dismissed Hayes's

Democratic opponent, Allen G. Thurman, as a Peace Democrat during the war and a prominent member of the convention that nominated the despised Clement Vallandigham for governor. "Every energy of his mind was directed against the war measures of the Union party. Every effort which he could employ, was used against the administration and its policy." For McKinley, the election offered only one choice: "This nation for the present at least must be confided to none but its preservers, its enemies must be kept out of the counsel chambers."[4]

In his maiden speech, McKinley also addressed what he considered an even more compelling issue than Hayes's candidacy. In that same election, Ohioans were asked to vote on an amendment to the state constitution that would grant the vote to black as well as white male citizens. William Lynch, a leading Stark County Democrat, said that McKinley "declared that there was one candidate on the ticket for whose success he was especially anxious." Lynch said people assumed that McKinley meant his friend Hayes, but McKinley said, "No, my especial candidate is Negro Suffrage." On that issue, Lynch said, McKinley "was counted a radical."[5]

McKinley made various arguments for giving blacks the vote, emphasizing their participation in the war. Even though McKinley had not served alongside black troops, he was well aware of their service and considered them comrades. They "enlisted in our armies [and] were made soldiers," he said, "they served with distinction in the field, they marched [and] countermarched and fought side by side with our white soldiers." And he stressed other services of blacks during the war, some of which he had witnessed himself. "They not only were soldiers, but see the services they rendered as guides to our armies, as spies to the Enemy's camp, and greatest of all their kindness[,] sympathy and assistance to our soldiers attempting an escape from the prison hells of the south. I tell you was there nothing else to recommend them their services alone should be sufficient." The young veteran was indeed radical on the subject of black suffrage—too radical for most Ohioans. Although Hayes was elected governor, the constitutional amendment his former quartermaster supported so forcefully was soundly defeated. Even McKinley's own Stark County was among the majority of counties that voted against it. Nevertheless, McKinley's voice would be heard again and again in support of voting rights for blacks.[6]

In 1868, McKinley became the chairman of the Republican Central Committee of Stark County, and during that fall's presidential campaign between the Democratic candidate, Horatio Seymour, and the Republican Ulysses S. Grant, he organized Grant clubs and was a frequent speaker on behalf of the general. Here, too, he was radical, bringing the war into the campaign by accusing the Democratic Party of supporting the Confederacy during the rebellion. The Southern Democrats, he said, fought against the Union, and "the democrats of the North with many happy exceptions aided their southern allies in the field with their sympathy as well as their material aid[.] Too cowardly to enlist in the Southern Army and fight from the front, they entrenched themselves in the rear of the Union Army, and while it was battling with rebellious [hosts?] who were in the front, these covert, cowardly, stay at home rebels were firing upon our rear, shooting us in the back, proclaiming the war a failure." The voters, McKinley said, had a clear choice in the election: one party "sought to destroy the government of our Fathers, and erect on its ruins an Autocracy of Caste & Color: the other met, fought, and defeated their fiendish schemes and saved our homes, our friends, our constitution, [and] our country. . . . Let us fight now upon the same line upon which our brave boys fell, and as they died to save our nation let us vote to keep it saved."[7]

He also spoke strongly for a military presence in the South to maintain the results of the war. "Ever since Mr. Johnson undertook in his own way and pursuant to his own policy to reward treason and promote rebels, the south has been one constant scene of local violence and notorious butcheries." Military force, he said, was the only way to meet offenses like the race riots at New Orleans and Memphis and the violence of the Ku Klux Klan.[8]

McKinley himself was a candidate for office in 1869, running for the office of Stark County prosecutor against William Lynch. He won the election and then, two years later, was defeated by Lynch when he ran for reelection. McKinley's supporters, aware that a good record in the war was attractive to veterans, drew attention to his military service in both campaigns. The *Canton Repository* noted that while McKinley was fighting "side by side with Governor R. B. Hayes, earning distinction and the gratitude of his countrymen on many a bloody battle-field," Lynch "was making Vallandigham speeches in the villages of Stark County. He was the enemy in the rear, using all his puny efforts to neutralize what McKinley achieved at the front." McKinley himself brought the war into the campaign. The Democrats, he said, "may change their garments, they may appear in a new dress . . . but it[']s as transparent as the clear crystal stream. We see under it all the grey coat, the stars and bars, the butternut, the incendiary's torch, the assassin's knife[,] all . . . ineffaceable marks which time don't cover up."[9]

McKinley's military record was an issue again in 1876 when he was a Republican candidate for Congress. The *Canton Repository* continued to emphasize his wartime service, stressing his association with Hayes and telling the story of his feeding the troops at the Battle of Antietam. But the Democratic newspapers mocked him by calling him the "little Majah" and the "Little Tin Major" and referring to him as "a military man, who is better accustomed to swearing than praying." And they accused him of campaigning by "waving the bloody shirt." One newspaper reported on a McKinley campaign speech by saying he had "jumped squarely for that old 'bloody-shirt,' and how he did wring and tear it! It was so completely used up, in his endeavors to twist a little more war spirit out of it, that it will hardly be presentable for him or any other political speaker to wrap them-selves within its terrible folds." The Democrats continued the mockery in 1878 by referring to McKinley as a "late army kitchen mechanic" and say-ing that his "entire stock of gallantry consists of on one occasion having dealt out 'hot coffee and fixings' to the boys that carried knapsacks" and did the fighting.[10]

The most serious accusation against McKinley during the 1876 cam-paign charged him with lying "drunk half the time" while he was in the army. If the accusation was not a complete fabrication, it could have come from someone who knew of his drunkenness at Cumberland—which, although apparently true, hardly constituted a pattern of behavior—but it could also have come from someone who confused him with another McKinley in the 23d Regiment, Sgt. John McKinley. That McKinley, ac-cording to Rutherford Hayes, was indeed a drinker, "a nuisance, a dan-gerous one too, when drunk . . . a savage when in liquor!" John McKinley was once reduced to the ranks and twice sentenced to hard labor for being drunk on duty. McKinley simply ignored the charges, and they did not affect the outcome of the election.[11]

In that same election, Rutherford Hayes was a candidate for the presidency, and his military record was also under attack. His opponents claimed that when Isaac Whitlow was executed at Monocacy Junction, Hayes had taken $400 that was Whitlow's bounty money and kept it for his own use. Hayes defended himself by saying he had used the money to obtain another recruit for the 23d Regiment. When a reporter interviewed Hayes about the matter, Hayes included some of the regiment's former officers in the interview. McKinley and Russell Hastings were Hayes's guests at the time and were among those who helped him defend himself against the charges. The *Stark County Democrat* attempted to draw McKin-ley into the alleged theft of the money by claiming that his and Hastings's names were "in one way or another, connected with" what it called "Hayes' Haul."[12]

The veterans of the 23d Regiment had begun to hold annual reunions on the anniversary of the Battle of South Mountain, and McKinley attended the reunion held in Cleveland during the 1876 campaign. He used the occasion to praise Rutherford Hayes as "one of the best officers the old Twenty-third ever had" and to encourage his comrades to vote for Hayes in the November election. McKinley returned to Cleveland to speak just before the election, where he characterized the Democratic Party as "tainted with treason, hypocrisy and repudiation, while the Republican party had always shone resplendent in loyalty, was covered with glory, and had spent its best blood in behalf of the Union." He said that the recent Democratic convention had been controlled by Southerners who "hooted" when the name of his old commander Winfield Scott Hancock was mentioned. "They wanted men whose war record was unexceptionable to the people of the South, and so they chose Tilden." Members of the 23d were present as he made a last appeal for votes for their comrade Rutherford Hayes.[13]

Both Hayes and McKinley were elected, and they traveled together to Washington early in 1877. McKinley was accompanied by his wife, Ida Saxton McKinley, whom he had married six years earlier and who showed the public her admiration for his service in the war by always calling him "Major." (Before their marriage, Ida had shown an interest in another attorney, John W. Wright, who had also served as a major during the war— but in the Confederate army!) Two daughters were born to the McKinleys, but neither of them lived to go to Washington with them. The couple moved into the Ebbitt House, which was "well known as the home of army and navy people." Later that year, Russell Hastings—McKinley's best friend from his army days—also came to Washington and moved into the Ebbitt House to be near the McKinleys. Hastings and the McKinleys were frequent visitors at the White House, and President Hayes and his family became their closest Washington friends.[14]

McKinley's specialty in Congress was the tariff, and although his speeches and discussions on that subject contained little that reflected his military service, they did display a remarkable grasp of detail—of facts and figures about tin plate, hoop iron, wool, binding twine, glassware, anvils, anchors, and much more—that showed the mind of an old quartermaster at work in a new field. One of his congressional assignments, however, related more directly to his military service. The Speaker of the House of Representatives appointed him to serve for one term on the U.S. Military Academy's Board of Visitors. With the rest of the board, he attended the annual examinations at West Point in June 1880. While there, he

served on the board's Education and Library Committee, which strongly
urged that the academy's standard for admission be "materially raised"
or that, at least, candidates be compelled to meet the current low standard.
McKinley himself, however, preferred that, instead of raising the standard of admission, competitive examinations be held in each congressional
district. "The standard," he said, "should not be so high as to shut out
the poorer young men of the country whose educational advantages are
limited."[15]

McKinley's visit to West Point came only two months after Johnson
Chesnut Whittaker, the only black cadet then enrolled, was found bleeding and unconscious in his room. Whittaker said he had been attacked by
three masked assailants. The black cadet, however, was not a welcome
presence at West Point; like the other blacks who had attended the academy, he had been completely ostracized by the staff and the cadets, and the
story was soon circulated that Whittaker had mutilated himself. A court
of inquiry agreed on Whittaker's guilt, but the Board of Visitors, arriving
in the midst of the controversy, sought to establish the truth themselves.
A subcommittee of the board, including McKinley, interviewed Whittaker
and others and later reported to Congress. Without expressing an opinion
on the assault itself, McKinley did express his agreement with the minority
report submitted by another board member, Senator George F. Edmunds,
who went further than the rest of the board by objecting to the treatment
of black cadets at the academy. "No one," Edmunds admitted, "is under
any obligation to cultivate intimacy, or offer polite hospitality to any other;
but it is equally true that every one who has an honest heart and a well-
balanced mind will show to all others, and especially to those who are his
equals in right and in station, the common and kindly sympathy of everyday life." Edmunds thought the officers and instructors at the academy
could remedy the situation by "showing to the white boys that the color of
one's skin, or the race or family from which he comes, is no test whatever
by which gentlemen, in the best sense of the term, regulate their conduct
towards others."[16]

All through his years in Congress, McKinley continued to speak out
for the rights of blacks, and his arguments usually derived from the war.
The war had ended slavery, which he considered "the giant evil and cause
of the war," and he was determined that slavery would remain "buried in
the sepulchre of the rebellion forever." The war had also led to new constitutional rights for the freedmen, which McKinley insisted had to be preserved. When the Democrats gained control of the House of Representatives in the mid-1870s, he spoke out against "their unholy work of striking

the last vestige of our war measures from the statute-books." In 1880, he spoke forcefully against the disfranchisement of blacks in the South, saying that "the whole power of the Federal Government must be exhausted in securing to every citizen, black or white, rich or poor, everywhere within the limits of the Union, every right, civil and political, guaranteed by the Constitution and the laws. Nothing short of this will satisfy public conscience, public morals, and public justice." In a speech titled "Equal Suffrage" in 1885, he decried the "outrages" against voters in the South and said that in view of them the war

> would seem to have determined nothing, to have settled nothing. Donelson, Antietam, Vicksburg, and Gettysburg accomplished nothing but the needless slaughter of brave men; the surrender at Appomattox was an idle ceremony; and the Democratic declaration at Chicago, in 1864, that "the war is a failure," is painfully true. Are we ready to admit it? I trust in God that we are not! The settlements of the war must stand as the irreversible judgment of history, the inflexible decree of this Nation of free men. . . . The war is over, the flag of the lost and wicked cause went down at Appomattox more than twenty years ago; but that does not prevent us from insisting that all that was gained in war shall not be lost in peace. . . . That which was secured by so much blood, suffering, and sacrifice must be cheerfully accorded by every patriotic citizen. . . . The freedom and political equality of all men must be fully and honorably recognized wherever our flag floats.[17]

What McKinley said in the North, he was also willing to say in the South. At Petersburg, Virginia, in 1885, he spoke about the Democratic criticisms of Republicans who were "waving the bloody shirt." He said that if the Democrats meant that the Republicans were insisting "that every man in this country is the equal of every other man politically," then he confessed that Republicans had waved the bloody shirt and would continue to wave it

> until every citizen of this Republic shall enjoy every right guaranteed to him by the Constitution of the United States. I have said that in Ohio. I say it in Virginia, in sight of the battlefields upon which we fought. We say it in the North, and we say it in the South, that not only shall the black man, but the white man, the native-born and the naturalized, enjoy equally every right guaranteed by the Constitution of the United States.[18]

About the time of his Petersburg speech, McKinley visited Rutherford Hayes. Hayes was critical of the "bloody-shirt course of the canvas," believing that it was bad politics and that the people were weary of it. But McKinley carried on, and when others accused him of "reviving the recollections of the war," he said he was only insisting that "the settlement made between Grant and Lee, at Appomattox, and which afterward found voice and recognition in the Constitution of the United States, shall stand irrevocable, and be respected and obeyed in every part of the Republic." He advocated the enforcement of the constitutional provision for reducing the representation of states that limited the right to vote and, in 1890, spoke strongly for a bill that would have provided supervision of federal elections to guarantee the rights of black voters.[19]

In his speeches, McKinley fell easily into military images. In his "Equal Suffrage" speech, he dismissed Republicans who were less radical than he was as "only useful to the enemy; they only retard the movement of our advancing columns; they are the stragglers moving with the baggage train—enrolled among us, but never ready for duty and always ready to surrender without resistance." Speaking on public education, he challenged his audience by saying: "You can not make progress with a substitute. Every man must do his own fighting." When he spoke in Petersburg, Virginia, with two other Northerners, he referred to the trio as "hardly a corporal's guard." In using those images, he was reflecting his own military experience, but he could be sure that most of the men who heard him, North and South, would readily understand. Many of his speeches also included a favorite wartime story about a color-bearer who advanced beyond the troops and was told by the general commanding, "Bring those colors back to the line." McKinley said that the color-bearer answered "with the voice of command that went back to the general quicker than a minié ball: 'Bring the line up to the colors.'" It was a story that was always well received by men who had served in the ranks.[20]

McKinley continued to attend the reunions of the 23d Regiment whenever he could. He played a prominent part in two of the more memorable reunions. In 1877, when veterans of the regiment were guests of President and Mrs. Hayes in Fremont, Ohio, McKinley was the main speaker for the occasion, giving a history of the regiment from the time it was mustered into service at Camp Chase until Lee's surrender at Appomattox. His comrades of the 23d were joined in the audience by Secretary of War George Washington McCrary, Chief Justice of the United States Morrison R. Waite, and Union generals Philip Sheridan, William S. Rosecrans, James A. Garfield, Jacob D. Cox, E. Parker Scammon, Isaac Duval, and

Samuel S. Carroll. In 1880, McKinley hosted the reunion in Canton, which coincided with a Soldiers and Sailors Reunion for veterans of nine regiments and three independent artillery batteries. McKinley's guests included George Crook, William T. Sherman, President Hayes, and James A. Garfield, who was then campaigning for the presidency against McKinley's former commander Winfield Scott Hancock. The veterans who attended passed a resolution thanking McKinley for his hospitality and Ida McKinley for the decorations, the reception, and the "splendid repast spread before us in the evening, proving that she was as good a commissary as the Major—whom we were well satisfied with in the dark days, amid the strife and turmoil of war."[21]

Other veterans groups frequently invited McKinley to speak. On Memorial Day 1877, he spoke at Woodland Cemetery in Cleveland, the site of the monument erected by the 23d Regiment. In October 1887, he returned to Poland to speak at the dedication of the monument erected in Riverside Cemetery in memory of the thirty-nine men from Poland who had died in the war, nine of them from McKinley's regiment. In an 1891 speech at a soldiers' and sailors' reunion at Bowling Green, Ohio, McKinley defended pensions for the veterans against their critics. The veterans, he said, had waited for their pensions so that the war debt could be paid first; now they deserved the country's consideration. "Is there anybody," he asked, "who thinks the debt due the creditors was more sacred than the debt due the soldiers?" And he challenged his opponents to debate the issue. "If there is anybody in Wood county who objects to that let him hold up his hand. Let him step upon this platform. I would like to exhibit him and ask him where he was during the war." He returned to the subject of pensions in a speech at a reunion of the 51st Ohio Infantry at New Philadelphia, Ohio. "Some things," he said, "are so priceless that only blood and death can procure them. Liberty and union are these priceless things. The debt this government owes to the brave boys who saved the Union can never be paid."[22]

On Memorial Day 1889, McKinley spoke at the Metropolitan Opera House in New York City on "The American Volunteer Soldier," using the occasion to praise "the elevated patriotism of the rank and file of the army and their unselfish consecration to the country." Knowing nothing of war, he said, but only that the Union was threatened, the men had volunteered in such numbers that "the whole North was turned into a camp for muster and military instruction." Their object in the war was only to save the Union, but, McKinley said, that object was overruled by "Him who is the Sovereign of soul and life" so that the war also brought the end of slavery and new rights for the freedmen. McKinley went on to praise the black soldiers. "Our black allies must neither be deserted nor forsaken. And every right secured them by the Constitution must be as surely given to them as though God had put upon their faces the color of the Anglo-Saxon race. They fought for the flag in the war, and that flag, with all it represents and stands for, must secure them every constitutional right in peace."[23]

McKinley's respect for blacks was more than a political posture. By all accounts he dealt respectfully with them in peacetime just as he had with those he met following the army during the war. A spokesman for a group of Stark County blacks that visited McKinley's home when he was campaigning for the presidency told him, "You have always treated us, just as you do everybody else, with great consideration and kindness, and on every occasion have been our friend, champion and protector." The single recorded exception to that consideration was a time when McKinley's brother-in-law Marshall Barber succeeded in getting him to don blackface and participate in a minstrel show on a private camping expedition. But even then, someone who was there thought that "nothing at Cedar Creek or Antietam so appalled McKinley" or caused him so much discomfort and embarrassment as that one performance.[24]

More characteristic was his meeting with John Mercer Langston, the Ohio attorney who was the first black elected to public office in the country. The two met at Alliance, Ohio, shortly after the war. After hearing Langston speak, McKinley asked to be introduced. He took Langston "warmly by the hand" and said, "Mr. Langston, if I could speak like you my chief ambition would be realized." Remembering McKinley's sincerity, Langston followed his career, noting his speeches championing voting rights for blacks and benefiting from McKinley's support when he himself sought a seat in Congress. In 1891, when McKinley was a candidate for governor, Langston said: "I was never in my life more interested for any man than I am for McKinley. I am going to do all in my power to help him along." Langston said that black voters in Ohio generally supported McKinley and that "no man could possibly have been nominated who stands higher in the estimation of the colored people than McKinley."[25]

John P. Green, a Cleveland attorney who had served in both houses of the Ohio legislature, was another black who strongly supported McKinley's candidacy for governor. During the campaign, Green—who was the author of the bill making Labor Day a legal holiday in Ohio—was invited to speak at a Labor Day celebration in Cincinnati, but when he arrived in the city, he was denied entrance to the dining room at the Gibson House and defiantly moved to another hotel. McKinley was also to speak at the celebration. Local Republicans quickly canceled McKinley's reservations at the Gibson House and arranged rooms for him where Green was staying. The next day, McKinley and Green rode together in a parade "and were loudly cheered." A reporter wrote that "McKinley's conduct has set the colored population wild. His name is heard on all sides, and casual groups of colored men on the streets cheer it at every opportunity."[26]

Even though twenty-six years had passed since the end of the war, McKinley's service in the army was prominently noted during the gubernatorial campaign. The *Canton Repository* published a summary of his service, along with his picture as a private in the army and a testimonial from one of his comrades about his bravery and his attention to duty during the war. The campaign opened at Niles, where two arches had been erected over the street, "mounted with guns and figures representing the Major's service in the army."[27]

In the midst of the campaign, McKinley spoke at Lakeside, Ohio, where former president Hayes, who had come to think of McKinley as his "young hero," introduced him. Hayes told how he had first met McKinley when he came to the 23d Regiment as a "boy," carrying his musket and knapsack. He spoke about the young soldier's ability and his dedication to duty. "When battles were fought or service was to be performed in warlike things he always took his place.... When I came to be commander of the regiment he soon came to be upon my staff, and he remained upon my staff for one or two years, so that I did literally and in fact, know him like a book and loved him like a brother." And he told about McKinley's exploit at Antietam and about the commission he had received for it from Governor Tod. Those were matters that still carried weight with voters in Ohio.[28]

McKinley defeated his Democratic opponent, James E. Campbell— himself a Union veteran—and was inaugurated as governor on January 11, 1892. More than three thousand Ohio soldiers participated in the inaugural parade. When the Cleveland Grays marched to a church service, McKinley joined them and was cheered when he had to "'catch step' just as many a veteran soldier who goes into a parade on memorial day." McKinley liked to be among soldiers, and a military presence marked both of his terms as governor. He attended encampments of the Ohio National Guard and was frequently escorted by military organizations and serenaded by military bands as he traveled around the state. Some two thousand Ohio troops accompanied him to the World's Fair in Chicago and one thousand on a visit to the Civil War battlefield at Chickamauga. As governor he had a uniformed military staff of sixteen, who often traveled with him; prominent among them was James L. Botsford, once a member of the Poland

Guards, whom McKinley had appointed brigadier general, commissary general of subsistence, and quartermaster general of Ohio.[29]

One of McKinley's first acts as governor was to have a portrait of David Tod moved from a corridor in the statehouse to a conspicuous place in his office. That room had also been Tod's office, where Tod had given McKinley his commission as a second lieutenant in 1862. A life-size portrait of Rutherford Hayes was among the other portraits McKinley chose for his office.[30]

As governor, McKinley continued to speak out for voting rights for blacks. In a speech in Cleveland's Gatling Gun Armory, where the polished muzzles of Gatling guns were visible around the hall, McKinley credited the Republican Party with freeing four million slaves and giving them the ballot. That ballot, he said, should never have been denied them as it had been in the South. He told another favorite story about the Civil War, one he had read in John A. Logan's history of the war. A black color-bearer in Louisiana who had been entrusted with the flag told his colonel that he would bring the flag back with honor "or I will report to God the reason why." He fell in the Battle of Port Hudson, McKinley said, "with the colors pressed to his bosom and his face to the front. Tell me that men made of that metal shall be deprived of their constitutional right! The fight will go on until every citizen will enjoy every right guaranteed by the constitution of the United States."[31]

Rutherford Hayes died during McKinley's first term as governor. They were both members of the Military Order of the Loyal Legion of the United States, an organization of former Union officers, and McKinley was one of the authors of the Legion's tribute to Hayes. "Every battlefield," it said, "which saw his presence witnessed his devotion. . . . Those who had served with or under him always found him the same generous, manly, and kind-hearted companion." Speaking at an encampment of the Grand Army of the Republic, the other veterans organization McKinley and Hayes belonged to, McKinley said that he "never saw a braver or a better soldier than Rutherford B. Hayes."[32]

McKinley was reelected governor in 1893. Members of the governor's military staff, "brilliant in the gold braid of full dress uniform," participated in the inaugural ceremonies. Because of the depressed economy, McKinley had said he did not expect the Ohio National Guard to take part in the inauguration, but the guardsmen still came. The governor called attention to the Guard in his inaugural address, noting that it numbered 6,117 officers and men. They were well represented in the inaugural parade, which a poet described as including "splendid columns," "ever blowing bugles," "noisy drums," and the glittering "bayonet and blade." The parade also included a sergeant who was carrying McKinley's Civil War musket, "an old fashioned flint lock adapted to percussion caps." McKinley had brought the musket home from the war and given it to his cousin's husband, William K. Miller, a resident of Canton. Miller kept the musket over his mantelpiece, proudly showed it to visitors to the city, and made it available for display at the inauguration.[33]

The Ohio National Guard was called to active duty fifteen times during McKinley's second term as governor. Major fires in Springfield and Toledo, lynch mobs, and labor disturbances, especially among coal miners, created demands for order that local authorities were unable to meet, and McKinley called the Guard into service repeatedly. At one time 3,647 guardsmen were on duty, patrolling what was said to be the largest area under military occupation since the Civil War.[34]

The Guard was called out three times to protect prisoners against lynch mobs. On one of those occasions, at Washington Court House in October 1894, the sheriff called out the local company when a crowd threatened William Dolby, a black man accused of raping a white woman and under arrest for the crime. Two additional companies under the command of Col. Alonzo B. Coit were sent from Columbus the next morning. A mob of two thousand defied Coit, calling out, "Hang the colonel if he won't give us the d——n nigger." During a confrontation with the mob, the guardsmen fired on it, killing five and wounding more than a dozen others. The arrival of still more troops finally restored order. McKinley was out of the state at the time of the shootings, but he strongly supported Coit and the actions of the Guard in protecting the prisoner. "Lynching," he said, "cannot be tolerated in Ohio. The law of the State must be supreme over all, and the agents of the law, acting within the law, must be sustained."[35]

McKinley also called the Guard out to deal with frequent labor disturbances among Ohio's coal miners, not as strikebreakers but simply to preserve public order. McKinley preferred arbitration in labor disputes and was cautious about dispatching troops, but when the disputes turned violent—when coal tipples and bridges were burned and miners who continued to work were attacked—he sent the Guard out in force, dispatching it quickly by rail, hoping to overawe the strikers and avoid bloodshed. One train alone carried twelve to fifteen hundred men, two Gatling guns, batteries, brass guns, ammunition, and equipment. Pontoon bridges, pickets, a field telegraph office, and signal lights soon dotted the countryside. McKinley said he had noted during the war that fighting was avoided when

a brigade found itself confronted by the strength of a division. "These outrages must stop," he said, "if it takes every soldier in Ohio." Feeling at ease
in military matters, McKinley took personal control of the operations and
was in constant telegraphic communication with commanders in the field.
At one time, he kept close watch over the troops for sixteen days, often remaining in his office long after midnight, sometimes telegraphing instructions as late as 3:00 A.M. The result of his diligence was that peace was
quickly restored, without bloodshed, throughout the state.[36]

The veterans of the Civil War continued to receive McKinley's attention. He appointed a commission to assist the National Battlefield Commission in marking the battlefield at Antietam, visited a reunion of the Army
of West Virginia and encampments of the Grand Army of the Republic,
spoke at a Memorial Day service at Grant's Tomb in New York City, and
attended the dedication of a monument at the Chickamauga battlefield. It
was good politics for McKinley to court the veterans, but it was also in their
company that he felt at home—"the men with whom I kept step from '61
to '65," as he called them, the men he could joke with about the way they
exaggerated their exploits in the war—and he used every opportunity
available to be among them. Reporters noted how McKinley would stop
anywhere to shake hands with a veteran, picking him out by his empty
sleeve or the bronze badge of the Grand Army of the Republic he wore,
and greeting him warmly as a comrade. Even his growing political association with Marcus Hanna was strengthened by military ties. Hanna too
was a veteran, having served as acting first lieutenant in a hundred-day
regiment, the 150th Ohio Infantry, assigned to the forts guarding Washington, D.C.[37]

McKinley's military record and his support among veterans were significant factors in his campaign for the presidency in 1896. His record as
a soldier was widely publicized. Some of his campaign buttons pictured
him as a Union private with the words "Our Comrade"; others bore the
slogan "The Boys in Blue Are for Wm. McKinley"; still others, suspended
from a miniature American flag, were inscribed "Maj. Wm. McKinley."
Campaign songs celebrated his military service. One of them included
the verse:

We "the boys" who breasted treason
  Through our country's darkest night,
With patriot pride and reason
  Claim our comrade is all right—
          Major McKinley.

IN 1861
WILLIAM MC KINLEY
WAS UPHOLDING HIS
COUNTRY'S HONOR,—
AND HE'S DOING
IT YET!

IN 1861
THIS IS WHAT
WILLIAM J. BRYAN
WAS DOING,—
AND HE'S DOING
IT YET!

THE DEADLY PARALLEL.

McKinley's military service was prominently noted in all his political campaigns. This cartoon was published in *Harper's Weekly* in 1896. *Courtesy of the Cleveland Public Library Photograph Collection.*

Harper's Weekly pictured McKinley in uniform beside William Jennings Bryan in a cradle; Bryan had been only fourteen months old when McKinley enlisted. A group of former Union generals, including Daniel E. Sickles, Horace Porter, Franz Sigel, Frederick Grant, O. O. Howard, and John C. Robinson (who had mustered McKinley into the army), campaigned for McKinley. They cast the Democratic platform as a conspiracy to "bring repudiation, dishonor and financial ruin" on the country and appealed to veterans to "rally to the support of our gallant Comrade, Major McKinley, the first private soldier who has ever been nominated for the high office of President of the United States." Some of them toured the country, traveling nearly seven thousand miles, speaking for "the Major." Sickles, who made a point of being carried onto platforms to show that he had lost a leg in the war, spoke bluntly to the veterans in one of his Ohio audiences: "If there is an old soldier in Ohio who will vote for Bryan he ought to be ashamed of himself."[38]

Inevitably, accusations were made about McKinley's service. He was forced to deny a statement that he had failed to deliver money that soldiers had entrusted to him during the war for their friends at home, and the commander of McKinley's Grand Army of the Republic post in Canton had to refute a statement that the members of the post were opposed to McKinley's candidacy. He said they were, in fact, proud to be associated with "the only presidential nominee who carried a musket."[39]

Many of the delegations that streamed into Canton during the Front Porch Campaign were made up of veterans. One typical group, on seeing McKinley, "went wild with enthusiasm, cheering as only soldiers know how to cheer." McKinley greeted the group warmly, assuring them of his great pleasure in meeting "at my home my comrades of the Civil War." But he gave an even warmer reception to the veterans of his own regiment, the 23d Ohio, when they came to Canton to congratulate their old comrade and to assure him that they stood "shoulder to shoulder" with him in the campaign just as they had during the war. These were the friends of his youth, the men to whom he was still "Mac." "Nothing," he told them, "gives me greater pride than to have been a private soldier with you in the great civil war."[40]

Surprisingly, one of the delegations that came to Canton was made up of nearly a thousand Confederate veterans from Virginia's Shenandoah Valley. They wore badges inscribed with "No North, No South, No East, No West—the Union Forever." The Virginians were received with cheers from Canton's citizens and veterans, and bands played both "Dixie" and "Marching Through Georgia." When McKinley spoke to them, he said he regarded their visit as an assurance that "complete reconciliation has come and that the South and North, as in the early lifetime of the Republic, are again together, in heart as well as in name." The reunion of old enemies was genuine, but it did not come easily. The Virginians came from the very valley McKinley and his comrades in Sheridan's army had left in ashes in 1864. And many of Canton's citizens bore painful wounds and harsh memories of the war. Augustus Vignos, who commanded the troop that met the Virginians at the train station, had lost his right arm at Gettysburg, and Hiram Doll, the commander of McKinley's Grand Army of the Republic post, had spent fourteen months in Confederate prisons, including six months at Andersonville.[41]

McKinley had devoted four years of his life to fighting those he once called "blood-thirsty rebels," and even if he had not been harmed by them, he had seen his comrades and friends wounded and killed. But his openness to these former enemies was also genuine. After he had greeted the Confederate veterans in Canton, he told a reporter, "This is one of the most gratifying events of my life." McKinley's thinking about the war had undergone a significant shift, toward reconciliation with the South, recognizing the former Confederates' valor in the war and reaching out to them as one soldier to another.[42]

McKinley's magnanimity toward former Confederates was not entirely new; much earlier, at a time when he was with some justice accused of waving the bloody shirt, his actions sometimes betrayed a kinder, less vengeful spirit. On Memorial Day 1875, McKinley had been a member of a committee of citizens and veterans in Canton that decorated the graves not only of Union dead but of Confederate dead as well; later he urged the state of Ohio to give proper care to the graves of the 2,260 Confederates buried at Camp Chase. In 1876, when he was a candidate for Congress, he shared the platform at a local centennial celebration with George Washington Henning, a Stark County Democrat who was well known for having been arrested and put into military prison for resisting the draft during the war. Many veterans were still bitter about men like Henning; a poet writing during the centennial year said he held no grudge against those who fought in the Confederate ranks:

> We'll clasp their hands and bury the past
>   In this glad Centennial year;
> But Northern veterans can never forget
>   The cowards who fought in the rear.

Henning's draft-resisting past and Democratic sympathies were surely known to McKinley: after the war, Henning taught school with McKinley's sister Anna and was the Democratic candidate for clerk of the Court of Common Pleas at a time when McKinley was chairman of the county's Republican Central Committee. Even so, McKinley graciously agreed to speak from the same platform with him to mark the country's centennial.

The next year, when McKinley entered Congress, he confided to an associate that his ambition was "to live long enough to see his country united in bonds of affection and brotherly love."[43]

By the 1890s, the entire country was moving toward reconciliation, and McKinley was moving with it. The bitterness of the war years was receding, and as Southerners showed an interest in McKinley's economic policies, he began to reach out to them for political support. When he spoke about the war now, it was to emphasize how it had resulted in reuniting a divided country. At the site of the Battle of Chickamauga in 1895, he asked rhetorically why the war had been fought: "What was it all for? What did it mean? . . . A reunited country makes answer. No other is needed. A union, stronger and freer than ever before." McKinley had much to gain by extending a reconciling hand to the South, but he did so sincerely; he no longer bore any grudges about the war. He might have echoed the words of one Confederate veteran: "We are all growing old and as we approach the summit of life things look different." What he did say, repeatedly, was that the reunification of the country was the deepest desire of his life.[44]

At the same time the country was moving toward reconciliation, it was moving away from a concern for the rights of black Americans, and McKinley was moving in that direction, too. Reconciliation between Northerners and Southerners came at the expense of blacks. "We have made friends with the Southerners," William Graham Sumner said. "They and we are hugging each other. . . . The negro's day is over. He is out of fashion." Little was said, North or South, about the violence toward blacks and the assaults on their rights—the legalization of disfranchisement and segregation—that were increasing in the country. McKinley's presidency coincided with what has been called the nadir of American race relations; in the 1890s an average of 111 blacks were lynched each year in the United States; in the year of McKinley's election the United States Supreme Court justified segregation with its "separate but equal" ruling in *Plessy v. Ferguson*. When McKinley was elected to the presidency—an office he might have used to help improve relations between the races—he found little support for doing so, and consequently he attempted little—much less than he might have twenty or thirty years before.[45]

Nevertheless, in his personal relations, McKinley continued to treat blacks with great respect, and a significant number of them gave him their political support. During the election of 1896, John Green spoke unreservedly for McKinley because, he said, McKinley had fought "not more for the preservation of the Union than for the liberties of the poor slave" and because of his championship of rights for blacks when he was in Congress, his stand against lynching when he was governor, and the support he showed for Green when Green was discriminated against in Cincinnati. Bishop Benjamin W. Arnett, accompanying a delegation from the African Methodist Episcopal Church to Canton during the campaign, told McKinley that "eight millions of colored people look upon you as the star of hope of their race and of this country." On behalf of all the bishops of the church, Arnett later presented McKinley with the Bible he used at his inauguration as president. Among the groups that came to Canton was the Cleveland L'Overture Rifles, "the crack colored independent military organization of the state"—four hundred strong—who showed their support for McKinley by making him an honorary member of the Rifles.[46]

McKinley reciprocated by making a brief statement about lynching in his inaugural address—"Lynchings must not be tolerated in a great and civilized country like the United States; courts, not mobs, must execute the penalties of the law"—and by appointing blacks to a variety of federal positions. He appointed John Green to the position of chief of the U.S. Stamp Agency; Blanche K. Bruce and later Judson W. Lyons became register of the treasury; and Henry P. Cheatham was appointed recorder of deeds in the District of Columbia. In the state of Georgia, McKinley appointed more blacks to responsible positions than all his predecessors combined, including positions not previously held by blacks. In 1899, 200 black Americans were employed in the Interior Department, 168 in the Government Printing Office, and 15,050 were serving in the U.S. Army. By 1900, blacks across the country were receiving more than $6 million a year in salaries and benefits from the federal government.[47]

When McKinley was inaugurated as president, the ceremonies included both recollections of the war and indications of his new emphasis on reconciliation with the South. A large body of regular army troops marched in the inaugural parade, "which recalled to old-timers in the crowd the Grand Review of 1865." Veterans of McKinley's old regiment, waving blue pennants inscribed with "Twenty-third Ohio" in gold, marched in a place of honor directly behind the president's carriage; Russell Hastings, James Botsford, John Ellen, Milton DeShong, Charles Manchester, Andrew Duncan, and William Zimmerman were among McKinley's army friends who shared the day with him. Former Confederates also marched in the parade, and the new president congratulated the country on the "fraternal spirit of the people and the manifestations of good will everywhere" in his inaugural address. "The North and South no longer divide on the old lines," he said, "but upon principles and policies," and he pledged himself to do nothing that would "arrest or disturb this growing sentiment of unity and co-operation."[48]

McKinley had spent the evening before the inauguration with the outgoing president, Grover Cleveland. The most important issue on McKinley's mind was the threatened war with Spain. He went over the steps Cleveland had taken to avert a war and expressed his determination to carry out the same policy. Cleveland said that in a conversation full of "sadness and sincerity" McKinley

> adverted to the horrors of war, and was intensely saddened by the prospect incident to the loss of life, the destruction of property, the blows dealt at the higher morality, and the terrible responsibility thrust upon him. In parting he said: "Mr. President, if I can only go out of office, at the end of my term, with the knowledge that I have done what lay in my power to avert this terrible calamity, with the success that has crowned your patience and persistence, I shall be the happiest man in the world."[49]

But the clamor for war with Spain increased. On the surface, McKinley appeared to be in tune with the martial spirit of the country. He continued to frequent military gatherings; in the first year of his presidency, he visited an encampment of the Vermont National Guard and reviewed federal troops at Lake Champlain; he attended a reunion of the Army of the Potomac at Troy, New York, a Grand Army of the Republic encampment at Buffalo, New York, and the reunion of his own regiment at Fremont, Ohio. But he had said in his inaugural address that "war should never be entered upon until every agency of peace has failed," and he was trying valiantly to arrange for home rule for Cuba and a peaceful withdrawal of Spanish troops. And he was convinced that, without pressure from the public, he could settle the matter without war.[50]

War itself no longer held any attraction for him. He told his comrades at Fremont that "the memories of the war are sweeter than service in the war." He confided to Senator William Allison that he had been full of enthusiasm when he enlisted in the army as a youth, not realizing what war was. But he "soon found out its horrors. Because of my personal recollections of the suffering of men on the field of battle, I have deprecated war, and besides, as I have grown older, I have come to understand . . . [that] it means empty houses, empty hearts and empty futures for our young men and women." Two members of his administration, Theodore Roosevelt and Leonard Wood, were among those who were eager for war. McKinley treated them with "amused tolerance," teasingly asking Wood when he came to the White House, "Well, have you and Theodore declared war yet?" But he was serious in his opposition to war. He told Wood: "I shall never get into a war until I am sure that God and man approve. I have been through one war; I have seen the dead piled up; and I do not want to see another."[51]

The pressure for war continued to mount, and although McKinley succeeded in postponing it, he found that he could not prevent it. Spain remained unbending in its attitude toward Cuba, arguing on one occasion that its reconcentration policy "was no worse than the devastation in the Civil War by Sheridan and Hunter in the Shenandoah Valley and by Sherman in Georgia." After the sinking of the *Maine*, Congress appropriated $50 million for national defense and authorized McKinley to administer the funds. Then with the finding that the *Maine* had been sunk by a mine, McKinley realized the necessity of asking Congress to authorize the use of military force to restore peace in Cuba. As war began to appear inevitable, McKinley's thoughts turned to his own military past. He asked his sister Helen to send him his commission as a brevet major and then asked a White House official to have it framed for him. Two of his Civil War associates were at his side when he signed the joint resolution of Congress declaring war with Spain: his friend Russell Hastings and Webb Hayes, who as a boy had followed him about Camp White, calling out, "Hullo Billy McKinley on a bobtail nag." McKinley particularly enjoyed having Hastings at the White House, spent a good deal of time with him, and discussed news about the war with him as it came in.[52]

Once war had been declared, McKinley took firm control of military operations in his role as commander in chief. He had spent his youth in the company of generals, had learned about war from them, and was comfortable taking command. New technology gave him immediate command, allowing him to communicate by telephone with Congress and the executive departments and by telegraph with the troops in Cuba—reaching army headquarters there in twenty minutes. A few days after the war began, he had a War Room prepared in the White House with twenty telegraph wires, military reference books, and charts and maps with "countless little flags to denote the position of this vessel or that regiment." All cipher dispatches from the field to the Departments of State, Army, and Navy were routed through the White House War Room, and copies were given to McKinley before they were delivered to the departments. And

The War Room in the White House. Painting by George Gibbs. From
Collier's Weekly. Courtesy of the Prints and Photographs Division, LC.

McKinley insisted on seeing all military orders before they were sent out.
Adjutant General of the Army Henry Corbin, Secretary of War Russell
Alger, and Secretary of the Navy John Long met with him at the White
House almost every evening—often until one, two, or three o'clock in the
morning.[53]

George B. Cortelyou, the assistant to McKinley's secretary, noted that
the president took great interest in all matters connected with the war and
seemed to be growing "more masterful day by day. . . . In all the movements of the Army and Navy the President's hand is seen. . . . He is the
strong man of the Cabinet, the dominating force." Another contemporary
called him "the man at the helm." If there had to be a war, McKinley would
take command of it and see that it was as short and decisive as possible.
It was the president who authorized the order for Commodore George
Dewey to proceed to the Philippines and "capture vessels or destroy," an
order McKinley considered "the greatest single act" of his life. His force-
ful direction of the war was also displayed when Gen. William Shafter
reported that the commander of the Spanish army in Cuba wanted his
troops to be allowed to retain their arms if they surrendered. McKinley

shaped the reply: "What you went to Santiago for was the Spanish army. If you allow it to evacuate with its arms you must meet it somewhere else. This is not war. If the Spanish commander desires to leave the city and its people, let him surrender, and we will then discuss the question as to what shall be done with them."[54]

McKinley understood that his administration's actions in wartime would be criticized. When the criticisms came, Cortelyou said that McKinley, thinking about his other war, "cited the bitter hostility to Stanton [and] Grant—that Grant was called 'The Butcher.'" McKinley always trusted the wisdom of the American people, but, as Cortelyou noted, he also recognized that the people were "hasty and unreasonable sometimes," and he led the war effort in his own way, confident of his military experience and judgment. When widespread criticisms of the War Department forced McKinley to appoint a commission to investigate the charges, he turned to veterans of the Civil War, appointing eight Union veterans and one former Confederate to serve on the commission.[55]

Having been a private soldier himself, McKinley took an interest in the welfare of individual soldiers, taking time to act on the requests for their discharges and furloughs that came to his attention. He also took great interest in the careers of his nephew James F. McKinley and Ida McKinley's nephew John D. Barber, who had enlisted in the 8th Ohio Volunteer Infantry. James was the president's ward, and when McKinley gave his permission for him to enlist, he said that "he is only 18 years old, possibly rather young for a soldier," perhaps recalling how young he had been himself when he enlisted. The veteran soldier gave James some fatherly advice: "Keep your life and your speech both clean; and be brave. Keep your nerve always; never lose your courage nor your level head. Nerve and levelheadedness are indispensable to a good soldier. Do your whole duty; obey all the orders of your superior; be kind to those who are subordinate to you." When James's sister Grace expressed her fears about her brother's going to the Philippines, McKinley told her, "One can die but once and such a death is the honor of a soldier." Another nephew of Ida's, James Barber, served as an assistant paymaster in the navy; he did die in the service—at Hong Kong of typhoid fever.[56]

The president invited his nephews and some of their "messmates" to dinner at the White House (where they all asked if they could take baths) and also visited Camp Alger, where they were stationed, three miles from Falls Church, Virginia, near the place where McKinley himself had been stationed during the Civil War. At Camp Alger, he reviewed some twelve thousand troops but spent most of his time visiting with the 8th Ohio

volunteers, "shaking hands and chatting with all the boys." He also visited
Fort Myer, and shortly after the war was over, he visited Camp Meade in
Pennsylvania, went through a hospital train at Greensburg, Pennsylvania,
and then traveled to Camp Wikoff at Montauk Point on Long Island. Poor
conditions had been reported among the returned volunteers at Camp Wikoff, and McKinley made the trip to assure himself and the country about
the situation there. In fact, the camp was a sobering sight. Nine men had
died in the thirty-six hours before McKinley arrived, and 1,415 men were
hospitalized.[57]

During the war, McKinley was besieged by people seeking government
contracts. Ike Hoover, a member of the White House staff, said the president would attempt to divert them by taking them to a window overlooking
the Potomac and "recalling the days when he himself fought through the
Civil War," pointing to the South where he had fought and telling them
"he knew only too well what war was."[58]

Military appointments consumed much of his time during the war;
in all, he made 1,032 appointments in the volunteer army. He offered positions in the army to old friends, appointing James Botsford lieutenant colonel and chief quartermaster of volunteers and Harrison Gray Otis, formerly of the 23d Ohio, brigadier general of volunteers. He also appointed
black Americans, men such as John R. Lynch and Richard R. Wright, who
served as army paymasters with the rank of major; during the war 266
blacks held commissions in the army. And he did what he could to encourage the states to commission black officers. He could take pride in his own
state of Ohio, which fielded a black battalion commanded by a black graduate of West Point, Maj. Charles Young. When McKinley received word
that the 8th Illinois Regiment was ready for service in Cuba—a black regiment with a complete roster of black officers—he declared it "the happiest moment of his life." Many black leaders had hoped for more from the
president—commissions in the regular army and positions of command in
the four black regiments authorized by Congress—but the mood of the
country kept the cautious McKinley from doing any more than he had
already done.[59]

McKinley's best-known appointments were of former Confederate
officers. Even though as a congressman he had opposed commissioning
former Confederates (those who he said had "for four years fought to destroy this Government"), as president he offered commissions to four men
who had been general officers in the Confederate army: Fitzhugh Lee and
Thomas L. Rosser of Virginia, Joseph Wheeler of Alabama, and Matthew
Calbraith Butler of South Carolina. Other prominent Southerners were

also appointed—the sons of Generals George E. Pickett, James Longstreet, and J. E. B. Stuart, for example—but the widely publicized appointments of Fitzhugh Lee and Joseph Wheeler as major generals would have been enough to endear McKinley to the South. McKinley hoped to unify the country with his appointments of Southerners, and in fact, those appointments and the enlistments of many other Southerners brought a unity the country had not seen since the end of the Civil War. Now, instead of singing "Dixie" or "Marching Through Georgia," the country was singing "He Laid Away a Suit of Gray to Wear the Union Blue," "The Blue and Gray Together," "Lincoln, Grant and Lee," and "There's No North or South Today."[60]

Not long after the war, on a visit to Georgia, McKinley made two conciliatory gestures to the South that only a Union veteran could have made and still kept his support among Northerners: he said the time had come for the North to care for the graves of Confederate as well as Union soldiers, and he wore a Confederate badge pinned on him by a Confederate veteran.

Accompanied by Maj. Gen. Joseph Wheeler, McKinley was honored at Atlanta by a parade that included six thousand infantrymen and five hundred Confederate veterans. In a speech before the Georgia legislature, McKinley praised the Southerners for their efforts in the war with Spain and celebrated the fact that "sectional lines no longer mar the map of the United States. Sectional feeling no longer holds back the love we bear each other." Then he won his audience by saying that the time had come for the North to share with the South in the care of the graves of Confederate soldiers. That statement was greeted with "a storm of applause." One of his listeners, the son of a Confederate veteran, said that "every person in the hall stood and every handkerchief went up into the air. Tears flowed down the cheeks of Confederate veterans." When McKinley's speech was over, the veterans, especially, rushed forward to shake the president's hand.[61]

At Macon, Georgia, where McKinley went to review seven regiments of federal troops—four of them black soldiers—he was met by both the 7th Cavalry and four hundred Confederate veterans, who gave him the rebel yell. As he was leaving the railroad station, a representative of the Bibb County Camp of Confederate Veterans pinned a gray ribbon on him, which had printed on it the name of the association, a picture of McKinley, and the words about the Confederate graves that McKinley had spoken in Atlanta. At the same time, someone waved the Confederate flag over his head, and another veteran said, "He can't say now that he never stood beneath the Stars and Bars." McKinley wore the ribbon during his visit, and his willingness to wear it and his suggestion about caring for the graves of Confederate soldiers were widely publicized and praised throughout the South. One woman in Georgia, who had been intensely devoted to the Confederate cause, wrote that "we are all McKinleyites now."[62]

Despite the general goodwill shown to McKinley in the South, some tensions appeared. At Montgomery, Alabama, the first capital of the Confederacy, Governor and Confederate veteran Joseph Johnston made a point of saying that "Alabama has nothing to take back of what she did in 1861." McKinley, conciliatory about much but not about the war itself, replied—to great applause—"We have nothing to take back for having kept you in the Union. We are glad you did not go out, and you are glad you stayed in."[63]

On the same southern trip, McKinley visited the Tuskegee Institute in Tuskegee, Alabama, and the Georgia Agricultural and Mechanical College at Savannah, both schools for blacks, going out of his way to make the visits to show his "interest and faith in the race." At Savannah, he told the story of the black color-bearer who died protecting the flag during the Civil War, and he praised the "splendid heroism" of the black soldiers who had fought in Cuba. Those visits might have won him more goodwill among blacks if there had not been a serious riot in Wilmington, North Carolina, shortly before, in which at least eleven blacks were killed. Booker T. Washington was convinced that McKinley's "heart was greatly burdened" by the riot, but whatever his personal feelings were, McKinley believed that he had no authority to intervene in the situation at Wilmington and he not only did nothing but also said nothing about it. Racial incidents continued to erupt in the South, and McKinley came under increasing criticism for not using the power of the government to prevent them. Reverdy C. Ransom, a prominent Chicago clergyman, and Bishop Henry M. Turner of the African Methodist Episcopal Church were among black leaders who criticized him for not at least using his office to condemn the wrongs, but apart from a brief repetition to Congress of the statement about lynching he had made in his inaugural address, he kept silent about the rising assaults on the rights of blacks. At the same time, he used the presidency as what Theodore Roosevelt called a "bully pulpit" in repeated appeals for unity between the North and the South, an endeavor that worked against rather than for the rights of black Americans.[64]

McKinley also appealed to public sentiment on behalf of the continuing war in the Philippines. He traveled extensively in 1899, often meeting troops returning from the Philippines and calling on the public to support the military effort there. In McKinley's mind, the United States had become the recognized authority in the Philippines, and the rebellion against that authority had to be ended just as the Southern rebellion had been ended by the Civil War. "There is a little rebellion in the islands over there," he liked to say, "but it will be put down as we put down all rebellions." The warfare in the Philippines was painful to him; every drop of blood shed, he said, "whether from the veins of an American soldier or a misguided Filipino, is anguish to my heart," but he still insisted that the insurrection had to be put down: "There will be no useless parley, no pause, until the insurrection is suppressed."[65]

In his travels as president, McKinley was almost constantly in the company of military men. He was often escorted by military units; he inspected troops; he attended the launching of the torpedo boat *Shubrick* at Richmond, Virginia; he visited a soldiers' home, a reunion of the Army of the Tennessee at Chicago, an encampment of the Grand Army of the Republic at Philadelphia, and a Blue and Gray Reunion at Evansville, Indiana. Even on visits to Smith College and the seaside resort at Long Branch, New Jersey, the president was met and accompanied by military escorts. Wherever he was, he made himself available to veterans and was willing to use his office to do what he could for them. One of his associates said that he invariably took an interest in "the old soldier with a cork leg who wants a job." McKinley's secretary told Russell Hastings that if Hastings knew of a "Twenty-third Regiment man who is not provided for" the president wanted to know about him. Such actions were more than a concern for his friends; McKinley thought it should be public policy to give preference in government employment to veterans as well as their widows and orphans.[66]

One of his 1899 trips took McKinley through Civil War sites in the Shenandoah Valley. Returning from a vacation at Hot Springs, Virginia, McKinley spent a day traveling slowly by rail down the valley, standing on the train's rear platform and pointing out places of interest. The local citizens greeted him warmly along the way, leading one reporter to say that "if there is any bitterness remaining over the Civil strife there was nothing in the enthusiasm shown today to indicate it." The train stopped at Harrisonburg, where McKinley spoke at the courthouse square, offering his congratulations on a reunited country. At Woodstock, McKinley was greeted by James H. Williams, who had commanded a Confederate battery at the Battle of Kernstown. "I was one of those who shot at you," he said. "I am glad I missed you, and now I am glad to shake your hand." After passing Fisher's Hill, the train reached Strasburg, where an old man called out,

"Mr. President, I expect you find it pleasanter going down the valley today than you did on another occasion."[67]

At Cedar Creek a local minister presented the president with a bayonet and some bullets picked up on the battlefield. McKinley recognized his surroundings: "This ground looks familiar," he said, "there is the old mill, too. The Sixth corps encamped along the road there, and over here Sheridan had his headquarters." The train's rear car was resting on a bridge over the creek, and McKinley said, "They drove us across this creek pell mell, and then we came back and took our old grounds." After stops at Middletown and Kernstown, McKinley arrived at Winchester. There he left the train to visit Hiram Lodge, where he had been initiated as a Mason, and the National Cemetery, where fifteen men from his regiment were among those buried. Then he went to Mount Hebron Cemetery, where the Confederate dead were buried. The local citizens noted that McKinley removed his hat and expressed his respect for the brave men buried there. Another "large and enthusiastic crowd" greeted him at Harpers Ferry before he returned to Washington.[68]

The following year, he visited Antietam for the first time since the Civil War. After attending a reunion of the Army of the Potomac at Fredericksburg, Virginia, McKinley, along with members of his cabinet and Russell Hastings, went to Antietam for the dedication of a monument to the Union and Confederate soldiers from the state of Maryland who had fought there. Both Union and Confederate veterans attended, bringing with them flags and music of both the North and the South. The speakers included former Confederate general James Longstreet and Secretary of War Elihu Root, who recounted the story of McKinley's feeding the troops during the battle. When McKinley spoke, he reflected on the difference between his two visits to Antietam: warfare the first time and "a common sentiment,—that of loyalty to the government of the United States, love for our flag and our free institutions" the second time. He said he was glad for the surrender at Appomattox—"glad we were kept together"—and he celebrated the "one glorious fact that must be gratifying to all of us— American soldiers never surrendered but to Americans!" And then he spoke about the new unity the war with Spain had brought, with Northerners and Southerners fighting together in Cuba and Puerto Rico and still fighting together in the Philippines "for the flag they love." Later, during a ride over the battlefield, McKinley said that he enjoyed the occasion "as he had scarcely enjoyed any similar occasion in his memory."[69]

Six weeks later, McKinley was in Canton to receive official notification of his nomination for a second term as president. About forty veterans of the 23d Ohio attended the notification ceremony and were seated in places of honor. McKinley spent the summer in Canton, where his home was equipped with a long distance telephone that allowed him to keep informed about the situation of the American forces he had ordered to China—on his own authority, as commander in chief—to help suppress the Boxer Rebellion.[70]

McKinley's military record was again an issue in the 1900 campaign. Thirty-five years had passed since the end of the Civil War, but the vote of veterans was still a significant factor in the election. A book published by the opposition, C. R. Mabee's *McKinley in the Witness Box*, sought political advantage by demeaning McKinley's service as a soldier. Along with cartoons ridiculing his service, a pretended interrogation of McKinley by Uncle Sam made light of his accomplishments in the army.

> U.S.—Did you ever kill a Rebel?
> McK.—No.
> U.S.—Did you ever fire a gun in an engagement?
> McK.—No, sir.
> U.S.—Did you ever carry a gun in an engagement?
> McK.—No.
> U.S.—What did you do when you went to war[?]
> McK.—I was Company Cook. . . .
> U.S.—What did you do in the latter part of 1862?
> McK.—I drove army mules in Maryland.
> U.S.—How many times were you under fire during the war?
> McK.—Twice.
> U.S.—At Antietam and where else?
> McK.—At the battle of Winchester, Va.
> U.S.—In what capacity were you acting at this battle?
> McK.—I was a messenger boy.
> U.S.—Why was it you did not continue your position as Company Cook?
> McK.—Because I was accused by my comrades of selling portions of the commissary supplies and pocketing the money.

Mabee's book hinted that McKinley had enlisted under the influence of liquor at the "Sparrow Tavern" and said that he "broke down and carried on like a baby" when he left for the front, that he deserted the army at Cedar Creek, and that his promotion to major came twelve years after the war and was given for political purposes.[71]

The veterans of the 23d Ohio spent a large portion of their 1900 reunion discussing the attacks on their comrade's military service and unanimously passed a resolution denying the charges. "From our earliest acquaintance with William McKinley as a private soldier in the spring of 1861, to the time when he attained to the rank of captain in 1865, no man can truthfully say that he ever avoided any duty, or in the remotest degree evidenced cowardice or flinched in the presence of danger. That in his personality he was always prompt, courteous, kind, and efficient."[72]

Military displays marked McKinley's second inauguration as president. Electric lights on the State, War, and Navy Building depicted the badges of the two army corps the public associated with McKinley: the six-pointed star of the Eighth Corps and the crossed gun and anchor of the Ninth. Navy warships steamed up the Potomac River for the event, with Admiral George Dewey in command. More than one thousand Civil War veterans, including members of the 23d Ohio, marched alongside the four thousand soldiers who participated in the parade. One foreign critic wrote that "four thousand fully armed soldiers escort him, and the rare pomp of the military spectacle inflames yet more the jingoism of the Americans." He referred to McKinley as "the Emperor in a dress suit." Aware of the criticisms, McKinley tried later to reassure the public. In a speech at El Paso, Texas, he asserted his belief in arbitration between nations. "We want to exhaust every peaceful means for settlement before we go to war. . . . So don't be alarmed about militarism, or imperialism." He often said that "we are not a military people. We are not dedicated to arms." Yet, as commander in chief, McKinley had overseen military governments in Cuba, Puerto Rico, and the Philippines long after the war with Spain was over, and military action continued throughout his presidency: the war in the Philippines was not ended until after his death.[73]

Some prominent black leaders had opposed McKinley in the 1900 election. Bishop Turner gave his support to William Jennings Bryan, not only because of McKinley's refusal to act against racial violence in the South but also because of what he called "the unholy war of conquest" in the Philippines, where it seemed to him that "any Negro soldier is a fool or a villain" for fighting against the dark-skinned Filipinos. McKinley strongly defended his Philippine policy in his second inaugural address—"We will not leave the destiny of the loyal millions in the islands to the disloyal thousands who are in rebellion against the United States"—but never mentioned the assaults against the lives or rights of blacks in the South. Instead, he once again sounded the theme of national unity: "We are reunited. Sectionalism has disappeared. Division on public questions can no

WHERE MCKINLEY DECIDED TO ENLIST.

MCKINLEY WAS HIS COMPANY'S COOK.

Cartoons ridiculing McKinley's military service that were published during the presidential campaign of 1900. From C.R. Mabee, *McKinley in the Witness Box*.

MCKINLEY DRIVING ARMY MULES IN MARYLAND.

MCKINLEY RUNNING AWAY FROM THE REBELS.

longer be traced by the war maps of 1861." After his second inauguration, he did not ignore black Americans but limited his public concern for them to such things as visits to black schools; on a western trip in 1901, he stopped briefly at Southern University at Baton Rouge, Louisiana, and the state normal school at Prairie View, Texas, where he spoke about education and the good performance of black soldiers in Cuba and the Philippines.[74]

At the beginning of his 1901 western trip, McKinley stopped at Lynchburg, Virginia, and made a brief speech that was greeted with laughter and applause.

> The first time I ever tried to come to Lynchburg I did not succeed. I came here with a number of other gentlemen who sought entrance, but the gates were closed. We could not open them, and you would not. And so we departed to seek another host, if not more hospitable, less formidable than the one that greeted us here. It is a happy time for me to come to Lynchburg now—the war over, no exchange of greetings with shot and shell as then, but with the friendly welcome of all the people which typifies the respect and regard and goodwill which subsist between all sections of our common country.

Although McKinley was well received on his brief stop at Lynchburg, on another occasion when he was invited to speak at Randolph-Macon Woman's College there, one resident took offense. An elderly woman, who had been at the home called Sandusky when McKinley stayed there during the assault on Lynchburg, wrote to tell him that some of the feathers the Yankees had scattered about the yard were still there and that they would be used to tar and feather him if he dared to come back.[75]

McKinley's western trip was filled with familiar activities. In most of the southern cities he passed through, he was welcomed by groups of veterans—Confederate as well as Union. In San Francisco, he asked federal officials for a position for a one-legged veteran of his old regiment, reviewed troops just returned from the Philippines, went through the wards of a military hospital, turned over the first shovelful of sod at a proposed monument commemorating Admiral Dewey's victory at Manila Bay, attended a Grand Army of the Republic reception, and participated in the launching of the battleship *Ohio*. In a speech to the Ohio Society, he praised a fellow Ohioan, "that gallant little Irishman, Phil Sheridan, who did not permit Jubal Early to rest in the summer of 1864 in the Shenandoah Valley,"

and in a speech to the Union League, he paid tribute to his secretary of
state, John Hay, "who was beside Mr. Lincoln during the four years of the
great Civil war, sustaining him, [and] has been by my side in the past four
years sustaining me."[76]

McKinley's last trip took him to the Pan-American Exposition at Buffalo, New York, in September 1901. There, too, a military atmosphere
prevailed. Federal and New York State troops were assigned to escort the
president, various military units were assembled for his review, and the
War and Navy Departments staged popular exhibits. Despite the military
atmosphere, McKinley's speech at the exposition included an eloquent endorsement of peace: "Let us ever remember that our interest is in concord,
not conflict, and that our real eminence rests in the victories of peace, not
those of war."[77]

McKinley was greeting the public under the watch of secret service
agents, exposition police, Buffalo detectives, and a corporal and ten artil-
lerymen when he was shot twice by an anarchist, Leon Czolgosz. The
veteran who had gone through four years of war unharmed was fatally
wounded at a public reception in a time of peace. While McKinley lay dying
in Buffalo, the veterans of the 23d Ohio were holding their annual reunion
in Cleveland. His comrades had hoped to have McKinley visit the reunion
and an encampment of the Grand Army of the Republic that was being
held in Cleveland at the same time, but instead they learned of the shooting and prepared a letter offering him their love and sympathy. McKinley
died on September 14, the thirty-ninth anniversary of the Battle of South
Mountain.[78]

When the undertaker had finished his work, Abner McKinley noticed
that the red, white, and blue rosette of the Loyal Legion his brother always wore was missing from his coat. A search was made, and the badge
was found in the lapel of the coat McKinley had been wearing when he was
shot. "It was removed and tenderly placed in the accustomed place on the
breast of the great man who had worn it so proudly during his life."[79]

He was surrounded in death by soldiers and sailors. They escorted him,
carried him, and guarded him, and their bands and buglers played for him,
first at Buffalo, then at Washington, and finally at Canton. For the trip to
Canton, the railroad provided an observation car with large windows that
was "flooded with light." The curious crowds along the way could see the
flag-draped casket inside, a soldier with a bayoneted rifle standing at the
head and a sailor with a drawn cutlass at the foot, as well as a guard of soldiers and sailors occupying the platforms. When the train reached Canton,

the military escort joined the five thousand soldiers of the Ohio National Guard, details from all the military branches of the federal service, and members of the various posts of the Grand Army of the Republic that had assembled for the funeral. They, in turn, were joined by thousands of McKinley's neighbors and friends who had come to pay their respects to the one they knew even when he was president as Major McKinley.[80]

The funeral service was held at the First Methodist Church, with the Reverend Charles E. Manchester officiating. Manchester, who had been McKinley's pastor for the past five years, had also served in the 23d Ohio Infantry, and during the times McKinley had been at home during his presidency, the two enjoyed a friendship that included reminiscing about their experiences in the army. On the Sunday before the funeral, Manchester spoke to his congregation about his relationship to the president. "I first knew Mr. McKinley in 1861 in the army. I saw him come and go in the discharge of his duties of camp life. I saw him the first time he wore shoulder straps and appeared with a sword as an officer of the company of which I was a member. I saw him in the heat of battle. At Antietam I saw him holding the lines and driving the mules, with supplies of food for the men." Other veterans of the 23d soon assembled in Canton, where they were joined by their old commander's sons, Webb and Birchard Hayes. When the veterans came to the funeral service, they brought the battle flags the regiment had carried through the war and took them into the church with them. A group of Confederate veterans also came for the funeral, the Gate City Guards of Atlanta, Georgia, who brought with them a Confederate battle flag draped in black for the funeral procession. One Confederate veteran, who was convinced that blacks had turned their backs on McKinley once he became reconciled with Southern whites, claimed that he saw "but one negro" in Canton during the funeral.[81]

McKinley's body was placed in a vault in Westlawn Cemetery, where it was guarded by a contingent of eighty federal soldiers housed in wooden barracks erected in the cemetery. The contingent, later reduced in number, continued to guard the vault until 1907, when a large monument built to house the bodies of William and Ida McKinley and their two children was dedicated in Canton. Alongside the four thousand soldiers who came to Canton for the dedication were the veterans of the 23d Ohio, who returned one last time to pay their respects to their comrade; the Gate City Guards also returned from Atlanta and were given places of honor with McKinley's comrades of the 23d. One of the monument's subtle features, not apparent to the casual visitor, is its location at the junction of the blade, guard, and hilt of a large sword, laid out on the grounds in memory of one who bore a sword—as an officer and as commander in chief—in two of his country's wars.[82]

After the funeral, Canton was flooded with letters of condolence. Some of the most heartfelt were from the South, attesting to the good-will McKinley had earned among former Confederates. One letter from Louisiana said that "if, once upon a time, he helped to capture us by force of arms and valor, he made the final capture, single handed by his broad-minded patriotism, his charity, his recognition of our Americanism, and his desire for the effacement of all sectional issues." The Texas Division, United Daughters of the Confederacy, said that "he remembered the graves of our Blessed Dead . . . and such consideration we can never forget." A group of Confederate veterans in Alabama said, "We recognize that we of the South have lost a true friend." One of the few dissenting voices was that of former Confederate general John McCausland, who had fought against McKinley at Cloyd's Mountain, Lexington, and Lynchburg. When he learned about McKinley's death, McCausland expressed his lingering bitterness about the war: "I'm glad of it. He was one of General Hunter's staff."[83]

As the years passed, legends grew up about McKinley's exploits in the army, stories that range from clearly false to possibly true. John Whipple King, a veteran of a New York battery, told the *Philadelphia Press* that he met McKinley during an engagement at the Boydton Plank Road during the war. King was firing a gun against the New Orleans Irish battery when McKinley came up with his orderly and showed him how to use the gun sight, saying, "Now you kin hit a pocket handkerchief at 1500 yards." Just at that moment a shell hit, almost at their feet. McKinley merely laughed, brushed the dirt off his clothes, and said, "Pretty close, wasn't it?" King said McKinley was "cool as a coo-cumber—the darndest, blamedest, coolest man I ever saw in my life." After that McKinley and his orderly rescued four abandoned cannon, turned them on the enemy, and saved the day. Unfortunately for the truth of the tale, McKinley was not present during any of the fighting at the Boydton Plank Road.[84]

A resident of Macon, Georgia, Arnold B. Hall, claimed that at the Battle of Antietam, Gen. Stonewall Jackson saved McKinley's life. One of Jackson's soldiers was preparing to shoot a young Union soldier when Jackson stopped him, saying: "I have watched that boy all day. He is too brave to be killed." The young soldier was none other than William McKinley. However, when asked about his source for the story, Hall was less than convincing. He said an old schoolmate of his had an aunt who heard the story from a "fine historian" when she was in school in Ohio. "I have never heard of the statement being denied," Hall said, "and don't believe it can be successfully disproved."[85]

Still another story could be true, even if part of it is not. A family tradition, published in 1927, told of a small troop of Union cavalrymen that stopped at a farmhouse near White Sulphur Springs, West Virginia. The householder was gone with the Southern army, but the troopers were received with kindness by the women who remained there, and when the soldiers left, the officer in charge detailed a noncommissioned officer to remain overnight to protect the family. While the soldier sat outside with his horse saddled and his arm through the bridle, a dark-haired girl in her early teens came out to ask him why he was still there. When he told her, she said "with impish delight" that it seemed funny that he had to protect them from other Northerners. As they talked, she asked if he had a sweetheart at home. He said he hoped that he did. She told him about her sweetheart and about her father, who was a prisoner of war, and how they wanted him home. Reaching out for her hand, the soldier asked, "What's your name? I want to remember you." "Mary Frances Jarrett," she said. "I am 13 years old." The girl was called inside before she learned the soldier's name, but after he left, she told her mother about the conversation, and her curious mother sought out the officer in command of the troop and learned that the young soldier was William McKinley. In truth, McKinley was never part of a cavalry troop, but he was in the vicinity of White Sulphur Springs during the war, and the girl's story claims so little that it may well be true.[86]

Those stories, true or false, were told by people who remembered McKinley as a participant in the Civil War, but in time, most people forgot that he had been a soldier and remembered only the paunchy president, clad in a frock coat, wearing a carnation, talking about the tariff, and hiding his cigar from the photographer, the politician that Joe Cannon said held his ear so close to the ground that it was full of grasshoppers, the man Theodore Roosevelt said had no more backbone than a chocolate éclair. But if anyone had asked Rutherford Hayes or George Crook or Philip Sheridan about the man they knew on the battlefield at Opequon and Cedar Creek, they would have reminded the questioner that, before anything else, he was a soldier.

ABBREVIATIONS

LC   Library of Congress, Washington, D.C.

LHS   Lenox Historical Society, Lenox Township, Ashtabula County, Ohio

NA   National Archives, Washington, D.C.

OHS   Ohio Historical Society, Columbus, Ohio

OR   *The War of the Rebellion: A Compilation of the Official Records of the Union and Confederate Armies*

OVI   Ohio Volunteer Infantry

RBH   Rutherford Birchard Hayes (1822–93)

RBHPC   [Library of the] Rutherford B. Hayes Presidential Center, Fremont, Ohio

RG   Record Group (of documents in the National Archives, Washington, D.C.)

RRLMM   Ramsayer Research Library, McKinley Museum, Canton, Ohio

USAMHI   U.S. Army Military History Institute, Carlisle Barracks, Pennsylvania

WM   William McKinley (1843–1901)

WRHS   Western Reserve Historical Society, Cleveland, Ohio

NOTES

PREFACE

1. *The Autobiography of William Allen White* (New York: Macmillan, 1946), 251, 335.

2. Ibid., 292, 332, 335. White made similar remarks in his *Masks in a Pageant* (New York: Macmillan, 1929).

3. Russell Hastings, "Genealogy and Autobiography," chap. 7, pp. 17–18, "A Staff Officer's Recollection of the Battle of Opequan," 35, and [Cyrus S.] Roberts to Russell Hastings, Mar. 20, 1865, all in Russell Hastings Papers, RBHPC; *Canton Repository,* Oct. 20, 1901.

4. Deaths in the 23d Regiment and comparisons with other regiments are from William F. Fox, *Regimental Losses in the American Civil War, 1861–1865* (Albany, N.Y.: Albany Publishing, 1889), 122–423.

5. *Speeches and Addresses of William McKinley from His Election to Congress to the Present Time* (New York: D. Appleton, 1893), 365.

1. PRIVATE

1. James M. McPherson, *For Cause and Comrades* (New York: Oxford Univ. Press, 1997), 16.

2. *Mahoning Sentinel,* Apr. 24, 1861; *Mahoning Register,* May 2, 9, 1861; *Canton Repository,* June 25, 1891; Diary of Daniel May, Apr. 22, June 1, 2, 5, 1861, WHRS.

3. *Mahoning Register,* May 30, June 13, 1861; *Mahoning Sentinel,* June 12, 1861; May Diary, June 6, 1861.

4. "President William McKinley," *Ohio Archaeological and Historical Publications* 10 (1902): 233; *Canton Repository,* Feb. 27, 1898; *Niles Daily News,* Oct. 5, 1917; Samuel Leland Powers, *Portraits of a Half Century* (Boston: Little, Brown, 1925), 164.

5. "President William McKinley," 233; *Canton Repository,* Feb. 27, 1898, May 25, 1900; *Speeches and Addresses of William McKinley* (1893), 359.

6. May Diary, June 11, 1861; *Mahoning Register,* June 20, 1861; Diary of John W. Cracraft, June 12–13, 1861, in Roy Bird Cook Papers, West Virginia and Regional History Collection, West Virginia University Libraries, Morgantown, W.Va.

7. *Canton Repository,* Aug. 20, 1896; Louis Le Grand, *The Military Hand-Book, and Soldier's Manual of Information* (New York: Beadle, 1861), 30; Cracraft Diary, June 13, 1861; *Mahoning Register,* June 20, 1861. Robinson's recollection of the muster is in *New York Tribune,* June 28, 1896. McKinley's height is given in the Descriptive Book, Companies A–F, 23d OVI, RG 94, NA, his weight in Andrew J. Duncan, "A Sketch of the Life of William McKinley," in WM Papers, WRHS.

8. *Niles Daily Times,* Jan. 29, 1943. McKinley became a member of the Sons of the American Revolution on the basis of his great-grandfather David McKinley's military service. See his application for membership, national number 2406, Ohio state number 206, at the National Society of the Sons of the American Revolution, Louisville, Ky.

9. Harriet Taylor Upton, *History of the Western Reserve,* 3 vols. (Chicago: Lewis, 1910), 1:210; Duncan, "Sketch"; Henry B. Russell, *The Lives of William McKinley and Garret A. Hobart* (Hartford, Conn.: A. D. Worthington, 1896), 50; Jane Elliott Snow, *The Life of William McKinley* (Cleveland: Gardner Printing, 1908), 24–26; Charles H. Grosvenor, *William McKinley: His Life and Work* (Washington, D.C.: Continental Assembly, 1901), 176; *Philadelphia Inquirer,* Dec. 5, 1897.

10. Duncan, "Sketch"; *Canton Repository,* Aug. 27, 1891; *Mahoning Valley Vindicator,* Mar. 17, 1876; *Cleveland Leader,* Nov. 1, 1896; Russell, *Lives of William McKinley and Garret A. Hobart,* 55; Grosvenor, *William McKinley,* 177; Eliza Allen Rice to WM, May 23, 1898, roll 61, WM Papers, LC.

11. Don Marshall Larrabee, "William McKinley's College Days at Allegheny," *Alleghenian* 5 (Mar. 1940): 2–3, 12; D. M. Larrabee to Philip M. Benjamin, Apr. 29, 1957, "Boyhood" file, WM Papers, RRLMM; Ernest Ashton Smith, *Allegheny—a Century of Education, 1815–1915* (Meadville, Pa.: Allegheny College History Co., 1916), 446–48; Allegheny College *Campus* 12, new ser. (June 30, 1895) and 13 (Nov. 11, 1896). 1859 seems the most likely date for his enrollment at the college, even though a plaque there and the Office of Alumni Affairs permanent record card say 1860.

12. Henry Steele Morrison, "President McKinley's Boyhood," *New Voice,* June 10, 1899, scrapbook, p. 169, roll 96, WM Papers, LC; Duncan, "Sketch."

13. May Diary, Mar. 24, 1860; Duncan, "Sketch"; *Cleveland Leader,* Aug. 25, 1895; Robert P. Porter, *Life of William McKinley, Soldier, Lawyer, Statesman,* 4th ed. (Cleveland: N. G. Hamilton, 1896), 47; Invitation to Debate at the Athenian Literary Society, Poland, Ohio, Mar. 22, 1861, from the Builders of Youngstown Collection, file "Poland 1801, 2A," and *Youngstown Vindicator,* Mar. 27, 1938 (clipping), both in the Mahoning Valley Historical Society, 648 Wick Avenue, Youngstown, Ohio, 44502.

14. Mahlon J. Stutz to WM, Mar. 9, 1899, roll 66, WM Papers, LC; *Canton Repository,* Dec. 16, 1897; Charles S. Olcott, *The Life of William McKinley,* 2 vols. (Boston: Houghton Mifflin, 1916), 1:6; Interview with Nancy McKinley in WM Scrapbook 147, p. 33, WRHS; Margaret Leech, *In the Days of McKinley* (New York: Harper & Brothers, 1959), 113.

15. May Diary, Aug. 28, 1859; L. Allen Viehmeyer, *Fruits of the Vine: A History of the Methodist Congregation in Poland, Ohio* (Poland, Ohio: N.p., 1984), 17–18; *Epworth Outlook* (Cleveland, Ohio) 1 (Sept. 4, 1897), with Ward Beecher Pickard to WM, Sept. 4,

1897, roll 59, WM Papers, LC; *The Life of William McKinley* (New York: P. F. Collier & Son, 1901), 11, 14; J. L. Campbell, *Our Martyred President: A Memorial Sermon on the Assassination of President William McKinley* (New York: A. G. Sherwood, [1901?]), 11; Russell, *Lives of William McKinley and Garret A. Hobart*, 55–56. McKinley's baptism may have taken place on April 13, 1856, when Aaron Morton baptized twenty-one people. See May Diary for that date.

16. *Canton Repository*, Aug. 9, 1900; G. W. Townsend, *Memorial Life of William McKinley* (N.p.: D. Z. Howell, 1901), 86.

17. J. N. Fradenburgh, *History of Erie Conference*, 2 vols. (Oil City, Pa.: Derrick, 1907), 2:265–67; May Diary, Aug. 31, 1856, Oct. 8, 1857, Dec. 21, 1859, Nov. 6, 1860; E. T. Heald, typescript biography of WM, vol. 1, p. 84, RRLMM; Biographical sketch of Andrew J. Duncan with his "Sketch of the Life of William McKinley" in WM Papers, WRHS.

18. Grosvenor, *William McKinley*, 178; May Diary, June 12, 13, 1856; Marshall Everett, *Complete Life of William McKinley and Story of His Assassination* (N.p.: Marshall Everett, 1901), 127.

19. Grotius Giddings was promoted to major and transferred to the 14th U.S. Infantry on July 23, 1861.

20. Stephen W. Sears, ed., *For Country, Cause and Leader: The Civil War Journal of Charles B. Haydon* (New York: Ticknor & Fields, 1993), 19–20; *Lorain County News*, June 19, 1861.

21. Charles Richard Williams, ed., *Diary and Letters of Rutherford Birchard Hayes, Nineteenth President of the United States*, 5 vols. (Columbus: Ohio State Archaeological and Historical Society, 1922–26), 2:26–27, 35, 60; Andrew J. Duncan to "Dear Sister," June 9, 1861, in WM Papers, WRHS; Russell Hastings, "Genealogy and Autobiography," chap. 7, p. 16, Hastings Papers; *Mahoning Register*, June 13, 1861; *Cleveland Leader*, Sept. 19, 1895.

22. H. R. Brinkerhoff, *Some Army Reminiscences* (N.p.: Excelsior Press, 1889), 17; *Ashtabula Sentinel*, June 10, 1861; *Cleveland Weekly Herald*, June 8, 15, 1861; Andrew J. Duncan to "Dear Sister," June 9, 1861, in WM Papers, WRHS. Camp Chase is described in Robert W. McCormick, "About Six Acres of Land: Camp Chase, Civil War Prison," *Timeline* 11 (Oct. 1994): 34–43.

23. Edward Stratemeyer, *American Boys' Life of William McKinley* (Boston: Lothrop, Lee & Shepard, 1901), 38; Cracraft Diary, June 30, July 1, 1861; *Mahoning Register*, June 27, July 6, 1861; Diary of WM, June 30, July 3, 6, 10, 1861, in H. Wayne Morgan, ed., "A Civil War Diary of William McKinley," *Ohio Historical Quarterly* 69 (July 1960): 272–90.

24. WM to Anna McKinley, June 16, 1861, item 35 in Joseph Rubinfine, American Historical Autographs, List 79 (1984).

25. Ibid.; W. W. Lyle, *Lights and Shadows of Army Life*. . . (Cincinnati: R. W. Carroll, 1865), 129; WM Diary, June 16, 23, July 9, 1861.

26. *Mahoning Register*, July 6, 1861; WM Diary, July 4, 5, 7, 1861; *Lorain County News*, July 17, 1861; *Mahoning Sentinel*, July 17, 1861.

27. *Mahoning Sentinel*, June 26, 1861; Hastings, "Genealogy and Autobiography," chap. 7, pp. 18–19; *Mahoning Register*, June 27, July 6, 1861.

28. *OR*, ser. 1, vol. 51, 1:333; *Canton Repository*, Mar. 23, 1877. See also Harry L. Coles, *Ohio Forms an Army* (Columbus: Ohio State University Press, 1962).

29. *Columbus (Ohio) Daily Capital City Fact,* July 15, 1861; *Mahoning Register,* July 25, Aug. 1, 1861.

30. Diary of Andrew J. Duncan, July 23, 24, 1861, Schoff Civil War Collection, William L. Clements Library, University of Michigan, Ann Arbor, Mich.; WM, "Personal Recollections of Rutherford B. Hayes," *Chautauquan* 17 (Apr. 1893): 42–44; *Speeches and Addresses of William McKinley* (1893), 642–43. See also Charles Richard Williams, *Life of Rutherford Birchard Hayes, Nineteenth President of the United States,* 2 vols. (Boston: Houghton Mifflin, 1914), 1:126, n. 1.

31. *Cleveland Leader,* Aug. 25, 1895; *Columbus (Ohio) Daily Capital City Fact,* July 24, 1861; *Elyria Independent Democrat,* July 31, 1861.

32. Duncan Diary, July 24, 1861.

33. Hastings, "Genealogy and Autobiography," chap. 7, pp. 19–20; *Speeches and Addresses of William McKinley* (1893), 642–43; WM, "Personal Recollections of Rutherford B. Hayes," 42; Ohio Wesleyan *College Transcript,* June 21, 1893.

34. Hastings, "Genealogy and Autobiography," chap. 8, p. 2; *Mahoning Register,* Aug. 1, 1861; Duncan Diary, July 22, 24–26, 1861; Benjamin L. Askue Jr. to "Dear Companion," July 29, 1861, Benjamin L. Askue Jr. Letters, LHS; Williams, ed., *Diary and Letters of Hayes,* 2:44–46.

35. T. Harry Williams, *Hayes of the Twenty-third: The Civil War Volunteer Officer* (New York: Knopf, 1965), 60–61; Edward T. Downer, "Ohio Troops in the Field," *Civil War History* 3 (Sept. 1957): 257; *OR,* ser. 1, vol. 2:762–63.

36. *Lorain County News,* Aug. 7, 1861; James I. Robertson Jr., *Tenting Tonight* (Alexandria, Va.: Time-Life Books, 1984), 72; Emil Rosenblatt and Ruth Rosenblatt, eds., *Hard Marching Every Day: The Civil War Letters of Private Wilbur Fisk, 1861–1865* (Lawrence: Univ. Press of Kansas, 1992), 112, 358; Special Orders Nos. 16, 26, 29, and 32, July and Aug. 1861, Regimental Order and Circular Book, 23d OVI, RG 94, NA.

37. *Canton Repository,* Aug. 20, 1896.

38. Olcott, *Life of William McKinley,* 1:29; Roy B. Cook, "William McKinley: The Soldier in West Virginia," *West Virginia Review* 1 (Mar. 1924): 18; Williams, ed., *Diary and Letters of Hayes,* 2:45, 52.

39. *Mahoning Register,* Aug. 8, 15, Sept. 19, 1861; *Elyria Independent Democrat,* Aug. 14, 1861; Cook, "William McKinley," 18–19.

40. Cook, "William McKinley," 18; Olcott, *Life of William McKinley,* 1:29–32. The incident recorded in Olcott is also related in *Mahoning Register,* Aug. 22, 1861.

41. *Lorain County News,* Aug. 7, 1861; *Cleveland Plain Dealer,* Aug. 5, 1861; *Elyria Independent Democrat,* Aug. 21, 1861; *Ashland Times,* Aug. 29, 1861; *Painesville Telegraph,* Aug. 15, 1861.

42. Duncan Diary, Aug. 5–14, 1861; Williams, ed., *Diary and Letters of Hayes,* 2:63.

43. Williams, ed., *Diary and Letters of Hayes,* 2:66; Cracraft Diary, Aug. 15, 1861; WM Diary, Aug. 15, 16, 1861.

44. *Mahoning Register,* Sept. 5, 1861; *Mahoning Sentinel,* Sept. 10, 1861; Duncan Diary, Aug. 17, 1861; WM Diary, Aug. 18, 1861; Cracraft Diary, Aug. 17, 1861.

45. *Mahoning Sentinel,* Aug. 14, 1861.

46. *Mahoning Register,* Sept. 5, 1861; Duncan Diary, Aug. 20, 21, 1861; Cracraft Diary, Aug. 20, 1861.

47. Duncan Diary, Aug. 24, 1861; Cracraft Diary, Aug. 24, 1861; WM Diary, Aug. 24, 26, 1861.

48. Williams, ed., *Diary and Letters of Hayes*, 2:76–83; Duncan Diary, Aug. 29, 31, Sept. 1, 1861; WM Diary, Aug. 27, 29, 30, 1861; Cracraft Diary, Aug. 27, 31, 1861.

49. Local tradition also suggests that McKinley may have fathered a child in Braxton County. The *Braxton Democrat-Central* of Feb. 6, 1998, reported a family tradition that McKinley sired a son named Moman Rhea by one of Dr. Rhea's slaves. The 1910 U.S. Census returns for Braxton County, W.Va., however, which lists Momen Rhea, mulatto, gives his age as fifty-five, which means that he was born about 1855, six years before McKinley arrived in the county. In the 1900 census, where he is listed as Charles P. M. Rhea, his birthdate is given as June 1853. A resemblance of Moman Rhea to McKinley, combined with a knowledge of McKinley's military service in Braxton County, is probably the basis for the tale.

50. WM Diary, Sept. 3–7, 1861; Cracraft Diary, Sept. 9, 1861.

51. *Cleveland Weekly Herald*, Sept. 28, 1861; *Canton Repository*, Mar. 6, 1896.

52. *Mahoning Register*, Sept. 26, 1861; *Canton Repository*, Mar. 6, 1896, which identifies Hayes's law partner as "Rogers"; WM, "Personal Recollections of Rutherford B. Hayes," 43; WM Diary, Sept. 10, 1861. On the Battle of Carnifex Ferry, see Williams, *Hayes of the Twenty-third*, 82–87; *OR*, ser. 1, vol. 5:128–65; and Terry Lowry, *September Blood: The Battle of Carnifex Ferry* (Charleston, W.Va.: Pictorial Histories, 1985).

53. WM Diary, Sept. 11, 1861; Duncan Diary, Sept. 11, 14, 1861; *Speeches and Addresses of William McKinley* (1893), p. 643.

54. WM Diary, June 15, Sept. 13, 1861; Duncan Diary, Sept. 13, 1861; R. H. Titherington, "A Brief Outline of McKinley's Career," *Munsey's Magazine* 26 (Nov. 1901): 168; *Canton Repository*, Jan. 29, 1928.

55. *Youngstown Daily Vindicator*, Oct. 7, 1898; James L. Botsford compiled military service record, NA; Williams, ed., *Diary and Letters of Hayes*, 2:202; *Cleveland Leader*, June 17, 1894.

56. WM Diary, Sept. 17, Nov. 1, 1861; WM to Annie McKinley, Oct. 27, 1861, *The Collector: A Magazine for Autograph and Historical Collectors* 920 (1987): 13.

57. The events at Sewell Mountain are described in Tim McKinney, *Robert E. Lee at Sewell Mountain: The West Virginia Campaign* (Charleston, W.Va.: Pictorial Histories Publishing Co., 1990).

58. *Painesville Telegraph*, Apr. 3, 1862.

59. *Ashland Union*, Dec. 11, 1861; Roy P. Basler, ed., *The Collected Works of Abraham Lincoln*, 9 vols. (New Brunswick, N.J.: Rutgers University Press, 1953), 5:50.

60. Williams, ed., *Diary and Letters of Hayes*, 2:145–48, 159, 163, 173–76, 178, 188; *Mahoning Register*, Nov. 14, 28, 1861; *Ashtabula Sentinel*, Dec. 11, 1861; Brinkerhoff, *Some Army Reminiscences*, 39; *Painesville Telegraph*, Apr. 3, 1862.

61. *Lorain County News*, Oct. 23, 1861; Brinkerhoff, *Some Army Reminiscences*, 39–41; *Elyria Independent Democrat*, Dec. 18, 1861; *Cleveland Weekly Herald*, Dec. 28, 1861.

62. Olcott, *Life of William McKinley*, 1:33; Williams, ed., *Diary and Letters of Hayes*, 2:166; Andrew J. Duncan to "Dear Sister," Feb. 14, 1862, in WM Papers, WRHS; Porter, *Life of William McKinley*, 109; WM Diary, Nov. 3, 1861.

63. Williams, ed., *Diary and Letters of Hayes*, 2:170–71, 180, 205, 207–9, 213; *Cleveland Morning Leader*, Jan. 9, 1862; *Cleveland Weekly Herald*, Jan. 25, 1862; *Ashland Union*, Mar. 5, 1862; *Ashtabula Sentinel*, Mar. 5, 1862; Richard O. Curry and F. Gerald Ham, eds., "The Bushwhackers' War: Insurgency and Counter-Insurgency in West

Virginia," *Civil War History* 10 (Dec. 1964): 423; *Elyria Independent Democrat*, May 7, 1862; *Ashland Times*, Feb. 20, 1862.

64. Martin F. Schmitt, ed., *General George Crook: His Autobiography* (Norman: Univ. of Oklahoma Press, 1960), 86–88; William H. Dunham, fragment of letter written Jan. 1862, William H. Dunham Letters, Civil War Misc. Collection, USAMHI; Lester L. Kempfer, *The Salem Light Guard: Company G, 36th Regiment Ohio Volunteer Infantry, Marietta, Ohio, 1861–5* (Chicago: Adams Press, 1973), 40–41.

65. Lyle, *Lights and Shadows of Army Life*, 86; William H. Dunham to "Dear H," May 11, 1862, in Dunham Letters; Diary of M. L. Sheets, Oct. 30, 1862, *Civil War Times Illustrated* Collection, USAMHI; *Lorain County News*, Nov. 19, 1862; *Cleveland Weekly Herald*, Nov. 15, 1862. Another account says that the person decapitated with a scythe was a fourteen-year-old officer's cook; see *National Tribune* (Washington, D.C.), Jan. 9, 1902.

66. Benjamin L. Askue Jr. to "Dear Wife," Apr. 7, 1862, Askue Letters; *Cleveland Weekly Herald*, Feb. 15, 1862; Robert B. Cornwell letter of Feb. 28, 1862, Robert B. Cornwell Letters, Harrisburg Civil War Round Table Collection, USAMHI.

2. COMMISSARY SERGEANT

1. *Mahoning Register*, Mar. 27, 1862.

2. *Official Roster of the Soldiers of the State of Ohio in the War of the Rebellion, 1861–1866*, 12 vols. (Cincinnati: Ohio Valley Pub. & Mfg. Co., 1886–95), 3:72; General Orders No. 10, Apr. 15, 1862, Regimental Order and Circular Book, 23d OVI, RG 94, NA. The commissary sergeant of the 8th Ohio is pictured wearing these chevrons in Franklin Sawyer, *A Military History of the 8th Regiment Ohio Volunteer Infantry* (1881, rpt. Huntington, W.Va.: Blue Acorn Press, 1994), following 128.

3. *Mahoning Register*, Mar. 27, 1862; General Orders No. 10, Apr. 15, 1862, Regimental Order and Circular Book, 23d OVI, RG 94, NA.

4. James Parly Coburn to "Dear Folks at Home," Jan. 18, 1863, and Coburn to [?], Feb. 22, 1863, James Parly Coburn Papers, USAMHI.

5. James Parly Coburn to "Dear ones at home," Feb. 26, 1863, ibid. Desiccated, or dried, vegetables were not well received; the soldiers called them "desecrated" vegetables.

6. Warren Lee Goss, *Jed: A Boy's Adventures in the Army of '61–'65* (New York: Thomas Y. Crowell, 1889), 91; James Parly Coburn to "Dear Parents," Sept. 29, 1863, Coburn Papers.

7. *Canton Repository*, Aug. 20, 1896. For the position of commissary sergeant, see also Albion W. Tourgée, *The Story of a Thousand* (Buffalo: S. McGerald & Son, 1896), 333–46, and the diary of Commissary Sergeant William T. Patterson, OHS. Also useful are Mildred Throne, ed., "A Commissary in the Union Army: Letters of C. C. Carpenter," *Iowa Journal of History* 53 (Jan. 1955): 59–88, and Frank L. Byrne, ed., *The View from Headquarters: Civil War Letters of Harvey Reid* (Madison: State Historical Society of Wisconsin, 1965).

8. Williams, *Hayes of the Twenty-third*, 104–6; Lyle, *Lights and Shadows of Army Life*, 95.

9. *Cleveland Weekly Herald,* May 10, 1862; Williams, ed., *Diary and Letters of Hayes,* 2:238–42, 245–46; *Lorain County News,* May 21, 1862; E. Parker Scammon, "West Virginia, and Some Incidents of the Civil War," *Catholic World* 57 (July 1893): 508–10; *OR,* ser. 1, vol. 12, 1:449. Reports on casualties at Clark's Hollow differ.

10. *OR,* ser. 1, vol. 12, 1:450; *Cleveland Weekly Herald,* May 17, 1862; Benjamin L. Askue Jr. to "Dear Companion," April 24–May 3, 1862, Askue Letters; Harrison W. Strayley II, *Memoirs of Old Princeton* (Bluefield, W.Va.: Telegraph Commercial Printing Co., n.d.), 25–26; William Sanders, *Early Princeton and the Episcopal Church* (Parsons, W.Va.: McClain, 1993), 27–28. Strayley, p. 85, gives Mrs. McNutt's name as Ellen. The McNutt house is still standing at the corner of North Walker Street and Honaker Avenue in Princeton.

11. Williams, ed., *Diary and Letters of Hayes,* 2:248, 250.

12. *OR,* ser. 1, vol. 12, 3:127–28; Diary of John S. Ellen, May 7–13, 1862, WRHS; Williams, ed., *Diary and Letters of Hayes,* 2:257–58, 262–70; Williams, *Hayes of the Twenty-third,* 111–15; *Lorain County News,* June 11, 1862; *Cleveland Leader,* May 29, 1862; *Cleveland Weekly Herald,* June 7, 1862; Diary of Alexander Wight, May 11, 1862, RBHPC; Elizabeth Cometti, ed., "Major Cunningham's Journal, 1862," *West Virginia History* 34 (Jan. 1973): 198. Pearisburg was also called Giles Court House.

13. *Cleveland Weekly Herald,* July 19, 1862; Murat Halstead, *The Illustrious Life of William McKinley Our Martyred President* (N.p.: Murat Halstead, 1901), 116; Wight Diary, May 19, 1862.

14. Brinkerhoff, *Some Army Reminiscences,* 67; Andrew J. Duncan to "Dear Father Mother and Family," June 16, 1862, WM Papers, WRHS; Williams, ed., *Diary and Letters of Hayes,* 2:287, 289, 292, 301, 304–5, 307; Benjamin Askue Jr. [no salutation], June 1–3, 1862, Askue Letters; Alexander Wight to "Dear Brother," July 10, 1862, Wight Letters; *Ashland Times,* Aug. 21, 1862; Lyle, *Lights and Shadows of Army Life,* 96. Companies A and B had earlier been issued Enfield rifles, which they retained.

15. *OR,* ser. 1, vol. 12, 3:451, 457, 551, 555, 560–61, 567, 570; Jacob Dolson Cox, *Military Reminiscences of the Civil War,* 2 vols. (New York: Charles Scribner's Sons, 1900), 1:222–25.

16. *Cleveland Weekly Herald,* Aug. 30, 1862; *OR,* ser. 1, vol. 12, 3:577, 629; Halstead, *Illustrious Life,* 116; Williams, *Life of Hayes,* 1:188 and n. 1; Evelyn Abraham Benson, comp., *With the Army of West Virginia, 1861–1864: Reminiscences and Letters of Lt. James Abraham, Pennsylvania Dragoons, Company A, First Regiment, Virginia Cavalry* (Lancaster, Pa.: N.p., 1974), 15–16; Sheets Diary, Aug. 18, 1862.

17. Ellen Diary, Aug. 18, 20, 1862; Brinkerhoff, *Reminiscences,* 74–75; *Cleveland Weekly Herald,* Aug. 30, 1862; Williams, ed., *Diary and Letters of Hayes,* 2:329; Festus P. Summers, *The Baltimore and Ohio in the Civil War* (New York: G. P. Putnam's Sons, 1939), 165; *Elyria Independent Democrat,* Sept. 17, 1862; [Joshua H.] Horton and [?] Teverbaugh, *A History of the Eleventh Regiment (Ohio Volunteer Infantry)...* (Dayton, Ohio: W. J. Shuey, 1866), 64.

18. Alexander Wight to "Dear Brother," Aug. 25, 1862, Wight Letters; *Cleveland Weekly Herald,* Sept. 6, 1862; Andrew J. Duncan to "Dear Father and Mother," Aug. 25, 1862, WM Papers, WRHS.

19. Andrew J. Duncan to "Dear Father and Mother," Aug. 27, 30, 1862, WM Papers, WRHS; Williams, ed., *Diary and Letters of Hayes,* 2:332.

20. Williams, ed., *Diary and Letters of Hayes,* 2:337.

21. Cox, *Military Reminiscences,* 1:264; Williams, ed., *Diary and Letters of Hayes,* 2:350–51; *Ashtabula Sentinel,* Sept. 24, 1862; Typewritten extracts of Diary of John T. Booth, pp. 5–6, John T. Booth Papers, OHS.

22. For the Battle of South Mountain, see Frank J. Welcher, *The Union Army, 1861–1865: Organization and Operations,* 2 vols. (Bloomington: Indiana Univ. Press, 1989–93), 1:768–78; Warren W. Hassler Jr., "The Battle of South Mountain," *Maryland Historical Magazine* 52 (Mar. 1957): 39–64; and John Michael Priest, *Before Antietam: The Battle for South Mountain* (New York: Oxford Univ. Press, 1992).

23. *Speeches and Addresses of William McKinley* (1893), 643–44. What McKinley called "Burnside's Corps," the Ninth Corps, was then commanded by Gen. Jesse Reno.

24. *Mahoning Sentinel,* Oct. 8, 1862; Cecil D. Eby Jr., ed., *A Virginia Yankee in the Civil War: The Diaries of David Hunter Strother* (Chapel Hill: Univ. of North Carolina Press, 1961), 107–8; Benjamin L. Askue Jr. to "Dear Companion and Friends," Sept. 20, 1862, Askue Letters.

25. *OR,* ser. 1, vol. 19, 1:184–87; Halstead, *Illustrious Life,* 116; *Cleveland Leader,* Oct. 1, 15, 1862; *Address of Gen. E. P. Scammon . . . Lakeside, Ohio, Aug. 22, 1888,* in RBH Papers, RBHPC.

26. Basler, ed., *Collected Works of Abraham Lincoln,* 5:426; Cox, *Military Reminiscences,* 1:297; *OR,* ser. 1, vol. 19, 1:418–19.

27. *OR,* ser. 1, vol. 19, 1:198, 423–27, 466–68; Halstead, *Illustrious Life,* 117; Benson, comp., *With the Army of West Virginia,* 19, 90. For the Battle of Antietam, see Welcher, *Union Army,* 1:778–88, and Stephen W. Sears, *Landscape Turned Red: The Battle of Antietam* (New York: Ticknor and Fields, 1983).

28. The account of McKinley taking food onto the battlefield during the Battle of Antietam is taken from the following accounts: Russell Hastings to "Mr. President," Dec. 23, 1896, and John A. Harvey to C. B. Lower, Jan. 18, 1897, in M 670 CB 65 (with 1680 V.S. 83), RG 94, NA; W. H. Zimmerman to Grover Cleveland, Dec. 14, 1896, William T. Crump to "Mr. President," Jan. 15, 1897, and Cyrus B. Lower to "the President of the United States," Jan. 15, 1897, in 1680 V.S. 83, RG 94, NA; James Botsford in D. Cunningham and W. W. Miller, *Report of the Ohio Antietam Battlefield Commission* (Springfield, Ohio: Springfield Publishing, 1904), 26; Charles E. Manchester in *Niles Daily News,* Oct. 5, 1917; and Harrison Gray Otis in *Cleveland Leader,* Apr. 11, 1897. The accounts differ in details, particularly on the time of the incident and whether horses or mules pulled the wagon.

29. John A. Harvey to C. B. Lower, Jan. 18, 1897. James Botsford said that McKinley also loaded a second wagon, but the team was disabled; see Cunningham and Miller, *Report of the Ohio Antietam Battlefield Commission,* 26.

30. Russell Hastings to "Mr. President," Dec. 23, 1896; *Life of William McKinley,* 27; John W. Russell, "McKinley at Antietam," *Munsey's Magazine* 40 (Mar. 1909): 788.

31. James M. Comly to RBH, Oct. 5, 1862, and J. T. Webb to RBH, Oct. 5, 1862, roll 11, frames 623 and 627–28, RBH Papers. The correspondence about the Congressional Medal of Honor is in 1680 V.S. 83 (and accompanying M 670 CB 65), RG 94, NA. See also C. B. Lower to RBH, Jan. 13, 1891, roll 153, frames 632–33, RBH Papers, and [Geo?] W. Davis to WM, June 29, 1897, and accompanying memorandum, roll 2, WM Papers, LC. For the monument, see Cunningham and Miller, *Report of the Ohio Antietam Battlefield Commission,* 19, 22, 24, 27–28.

32. Robert Goldthwaite Carter, *Four Brothers in Blue*... (1913; rpt. Austin: Univ. of Texas Press, 1978), 115–16; *Mahoning Sentinel*, Oct. 8, 1862; Cox, *Military Reminiscences*, 1:227–28, 349.

33. *Ashtabula Sentinel*, Oct. 22, 1862; Lyle, *Lights and Shadows of Army Life*, 177.

34. Alexander Wight to "Dear Brother," Oct. 5, 1862, Wight Letters; Brinkerhoff, *Reminiscences*, 110–12; "Record of the Twenty-third Regiment," Oct. 1, 1862, roll 1, frame 378, James M. Comly Papers, OHS; Whitelaw Reid, *Ohio in the War*, 2 vols. (Cincinnati: Moore, Wilstach & Baldwin, 1868), 2:161.

35. *Abraham Lincoln: An Address by William McKinley of Ohio Before the Marquette Club, Chicago, Feb. 12, 1896* (N.p: N.p., 1896), 24–25; *New York Sun*, May 31, 1900, scrapbook, p. 132, roll 96, WM Papers, LC.

36. Basler, ed., *Collected Works of Abraham Lincoln*, 4:437. McKinley quoted Lincoln's words in his 1896 address, *Abraham Lincoln*, 4–5.

37. Robert B. Wilson, "A Historical Sketch of the Kanawha Division...," 29 (with Robert B. Wilson to M. A. Hanna, July 28, 1896), roll 57, WM Papers, LC; *OR*, ser. 1, vol. 12, 3:560–61, 629; Stan Cohen, *The Civil War in West Virginia: A Pictorial History* (Charleston: Pictorial Histories, 1976), 85–86.

38. Brinkerhoff, *Reminiscences*, 113–19; Booth Diary, Oct. 8, 1862; Horton and Teverbaugh, *History of the Eleventh Regiment*, 79; *Cleveland Weekly Herald*, Oct. 25, 1862; *Ashtabula Sentinel*, Oct. 29, 1862; Lyle, *Lights and Shadows of Army Life*, 181–87; Halstead, *Illustrious Life*, 117.

39. *Cleveland Weekly Herald*, Oct. 25, Nov. 15, 1862; *Mahoning Register*, Dec. 4, 1862; *Ashtabula Sentinel*, Dec. 3, 1862; *OR*, ser. 1, vol. 19, 2:530; Cohen, *Civil War in West Virginia*, 62.

40. *Ashtabula Sentinel*, Nov. 12, 1862; Special Orders No. 55, Nov. 9, 1862, 23d OVI, WM compiled military service record, NA (listed as Special Orders No. 54, Nov. 13, 1862, in Regimental Order and Circular Book, 23d OVI, RG 94, NA).

41. *Ashland Press*, Sept. 18, 1901.

42. RBH speech at Lakeside, Ohio, July 30, 1891, typewritten copy on roll 296, frames 690–92, and WM to RBH, July 2, 1888, roll 140, frames 318–21, RBH Papers.

43. *Ashland Press*, Sept. 18, 1901; Hastings, "Genealogy and Autobiography," chap. 9, p. 10.

44. May Diary, Nov. 19, 1862; Olcott, *Life of William McKinley*, 1:38.

45. *Official Roster of the Soldiers of the State of Ohio*, 3:98–102; May Diary, Aug. 21, Sept. 11, 28, Oct. 1, 6, 1862; *Cleveland Leader*, Sept. 24, 1862; *Mahoning Register*, Oct. 24, Dec. 5, 1861, Mar. 20, Apr. 17, 1862, Jan. 8, 1863.

46. *Mahoning Register*, Nov. 27, 1862; "Directions for Enlisting and Organizing Volunteer Forces in Ohio [1862]," roll 21, Ohio Governors' Papers, OHS; *Cleveland Leader*, Sept. 14, 1902; Special Orders No. 55, Nov. 9, 1862, 23d OVI, WM compiled military service record, NA; Williams, ed., *Diary and Letters of Hayes*, 2:374.

47. Williams, ed., *Diary and Letters of Hayes*, 2:374.

3. QUARTERMASTER

1. *Canton Repository*, Aug. 20, 1896; *Canton Weekly Repository*, July 2, 1891; Stratemeyer, *American Boys' Life of William McKinley*, 54, 59–61. Even though he wrote

for boys, Stratemeyer's interviews with veterans provide valuable recollections of McKinley.

2. General Orders No. 42, Dec. 29, 1862, and Special Orders No. 3, Jan. 4, 1863, Regimental Order and Circular Book, 23d OVI, RG 94, NA; Williams, ed., *Diary and Letters of Hayes,* 2:366, 375, 380; *Mahoning Register,* Jan. 8, Feb. 5, 1863; *Lorain County News,* Jan. 7, 1863; *Cleveland Weekly Herald,* Jan. 3, 1863; *Holmes County Republican,* Jan. 15, 1863; *Painesville Telegraph,* Jan. 29, 1863. McKinley's contribution to the monument is noted on an unnumbered frame of roll 273, RBH Papers.

3. *Cleveland Weekly Herald,* Jan. 24, 1863; Williams, *Hayes of the Twenty-third,* 144–46; WM compiled military service record, NA. Officers "acting" in a position had the position's responsibilities without its pay. See William Thompson Lusk, *War Letters of William Thompson Lusk, Captain, Assistant Adjutant-General, United States Volunteers, 1861–1863, Afterward M.D., LL.D.* (New York: Privately printed, 1911), 200–201; and Josiah Marshall Favill, *The Diary of a Young Officer Serving with the Armies of the United States During the War of the Rebellion* (Chicago: R. R. Donnelley & Sons, 1909), 264.

4. Ellen Diary, Dec. 3, 1862, Feb. 23, 28, 1863.

5. The description of McKinley's duties as quartermaster is drawn from his quartermaster papers in WM Papers, WRHS, and materials in RG 393, NA, especially those in the quartermaster letter book kept by McKinley (vol. 108 W.Va.).

6. "Abstract of forage issued at Camp White . . . in the month ending on the 31st of January 1864 by Lt. William McKinley, Jr.," and WM endorsement on J. S. Ellen report, Oct. 1, 1863, both in WM Papers, WRHS; WM to Capt. Vincent Phelps, Oct. 26, 1863, and WM to Lt. Col. Enochs, Mar. 18, 1864, vol. 108 W.Va., RG 393, NA. A few of McKinley's quartermaster letters concern ordnance matters.

7. WM to John Ellen, Apr. 3, 1864, vol. 108 W.Va., RG 393, NA; Charles H. Brown to William McKinley Jr., Aug. 19, 1869, WM Papers, WRHS; William S. Lincoln, *Life with the Thirty-fourth Massachusetts Infantry in the War of the Rebellion* (Worcester: Noyes, Snow, 1879), 222. The quartermaster papers in the WM Papers, WRHS, appear to be the ones returned to McKinley in 1869.

8. "Roll of non-commissioned officers and privates employed on extra duty . . . at Camp White . . . during the month of February 1864 by Lt. William McKinley, Jr.," WM Papers, WRHS; *OR,* ser. 1, vol. 25, 2:159–60; *Lorain County News,* Jan. 7, 1863.

9. "Abstract of stationery issued at Camp White," to Lt. William McKinley Jr., July 1863, and a similar report for June 1864, WM Papers, WRHS.

10. Special Orders No. 23, First Brigade, District of Kanawha, Apr. 16, 1863, in WM Papers, WRHS; Special Orders No. 1, Jan. 2, 1863, Regimental Order and Circular Book, 23d OVI, RG 94, NA; Francis A. Lord, *They Fought for the Union* (Harrisburg, Pa.: Stackpole, 1960), 114; Porter, *Life of William McKinley,* 110.

11. WM to Sarah McKinley, Mar. 8, 1863, in the collection of H. Wayne Morgan, Norman, OK; Special Orders No. 1, Jan. 12, 1863, Entry 1190 (No. 138 W.Va.), RG 393, NA; Stratemeyer, *American Boys' Life of William McKinley,* 53, 61–62; David L. McCall to Curator, n.d., and Thomas J. Culbertson to McCall, Oct. 5, 1994, RBHPC; James P. McIlrath to David Tod, Feb. 25, 1863, Letter book of 23d OVI, RG 94, NA; WM compiled military service record, NA. The promotion was to date from February 7, 1863.

NOTES TO PAGES 52–57

12. *Lorain County News,* Apr. 15, 1863; *Cleveland Weekly Herald,* Feb. 28, 1863; "Record of the Twenty-third Regiment," Jan. 24, 1863, roll 1, frame 387, Comly Papers; Williams, ed., *Diary and Letters of Hayes,* 2:392; *Mahoning Register,* Mar. 26, 1863; *Holmes County Republican,* Mar. 12, 1863.

13. Brinkerhoff, *Some Army Reminiscences,* 33–34; Williams, ed., *Diary and Letters of Hayes,* 2:391–92.

14. Williams, ed., *Diary and Letters of Hayes,* 2:385–87, 390, 392, 394; "Record of the Twenty-third Regiment," Jan. 24, 1863, roll 1, frame 387, Comly Papers.

15. Williams, ed., *Diary and Letters of Hayes,* 2:395–96; *Cleveland Weekly Herald,* Mar. 28, 1863; *Holmes County Republican,* Apr. 2, 1863.

16. *Gallipolis Journal,* Apr. 23, 1863; *Cleveland Weekly Herald,* Apr. 4, 1863; *Ashtabula Sentinel,* Apr. 8, 1863.

17. Williams, ed., *Diary and Letters of Hayes,* 2:396, 409; Special Orders No. 45, June 22, 1863, Entry 1190 (No. 138 W.Va.), RG 393, NA; Andrew J. Duncan to "Dear Father and Mother," Apr. 11, 1863, WM Papers, WRHS; *Holmes County Republican,* Apr. 16, 1863.

18. Lawrence Wilson, *Itinerary of the Seventh Ohio Volunteer Infantry, 1861–1864* (New York: Neale, 1907), 94; *Lorain County News,* May 6, 1863; J. E. D. Ward, *Twelfth Ohio Volunteer Inf[antry]* (Ripley, Ohio: N.p., 1864), 45–47; speech of John A. Duncan, Jan. 28, 1949, in Duncan items (E711.6 Z), WRHS; Richard Andre, Stan Cohen, and Bill Wintz, *Bullets and Steel: The Fight for the Great Kanawha Valley, 1861–1865* (Charleston, W.Va.: Pictorial Histories, 1995), 133; *Charleston Daily Mail,* Oct. 27, 1940 (clipping courtesy of Richard A. Andre of Charleston, W.Va.); Williams, ed., *Diary and Letters of Hayes,* 2:398, 406, 409, 413–14.

19. Williams, ed., *Diary and Letters of Hayes,* 2:416–19; *Lorain County News,* Aug. 19, 1863.

20. Manning F. Force's Reminiscences of RBH, roll 298, frames 504–5, RBH Papers; "Record of the Twenty-third Regiment," July 16–22, 1863, roll 1, frames 390–94, Comly Papers; *OR,* ser. 1, vol. 23, 1:13–14, 677–79, 778, 808; *Lorain County News,* Aug. 19, 1863; *Cleveland Leader,* Dec. 19, 1890; Halstead, *Illustrious Life,* 117. For Morgan's raid, see John S. Still, "Blitzkrieg, 1863: Morgan's Raid and Rout," *Civil War History* 3 (Sept. 1957): 291–306.

21. Diary of James M. Comly, July 24, 1863, roll 1, Comly Papers; Special Orders No. 53, July 26, 1863, Entry 1190 (No. 138 W.Va.), RG 393, NA; Lucy Webb Hayes to RBH, Aug. 2, 1863 (saying "a note from Lt. McKinley he passed through"), roll 11, frame 823, RBH Papers; May Diary, July 30, Aug. 2, 1863.

22. May Diary, July 26, 1863; *National Tribune* (Washington, D.C.), July 25, 1901, Feb. 6, 1902; Joseph G. Butler Jr., *History of Youngstown and the Mahoning Valley, Ohio* (Chicago: American Historical Society, 1921), 818–20; *Canton Repository,* Feb. 26, 1893.

23. Benjamin L. Askue Jr. to "Dear Companion," Aug. 16, 30, 1863, Askue Letters; Diary of Andrew Stiarwalt, 8–9, in Hastings Papers.

24. *Holmes County Republican,* Sept. 3, Oct. 15, Nov. 5, 1863; Benjamin L. Askue Jr. to "Dear Friends," Sept. 20, 1863, Askue Letters.

25. Hastings, "Genealogy and Autobiography," chap. 9, p. 11, chap. 10, pp. 13–14, and chap. 11, p. 1.

26. Ibid., chap. 10, p. 2; James L. Botsford to RBH, Oct. 7, 1863, roll 11, frame 892, RBH Papers.

27. Ellen Diary, Nov. 19, 1863; Benjamin L. Askue Jr. to "Dear Companion & Friends," Aug. 25, 1863, Askue Letters; History of the 23d Regiment, roll 271, frame 246, RBH Papers.

28. *Mahoning Register,* Aug. 27, 1863; *Cleveland Weekly Herald,* June 27, 1863; *Bucyrus Weekly Journal,* Sept. 4, 1863.

29. Williams, ed., *Diary and Letters of Hayes,* 2:440–41; Diary of John Mc-Nulty Clugston, Oct. 13, 1863, RBHPC; *Canton Repository,* Oct. 31, 1895, Aug. 5, 1900; James L. Vallandigham to "Bro. White," Jan. 26, 1899, in clipping dated Feb. 2, 1899, pp. 144–45 of scrapbook, roll 96, WM Papers, LC; *Cleveland Leader,* Dec. 13, 1897.

30. J. J. Sutton, *History of the Second Regiment West Virginia Cavalry Volunteers, During the War of the Rebellion* (Portsmouth, Ohio: N.p., 1892), 105; Lord, *They Fought for the Union,* 12–14; General Orders No. 191, June 25, 1863, *General Orders Affecting the Volunteer Force, 1863* (Washington, D.C.: GPO, 1864); Halstead, *Illustrious Life,* 118; Williams, ed., *Diary and Letters of Hayes,* 2:450, n.

31. Williams, ed., *Diary and Letters of Hayes,* 2:445; *Canton Repository,* Oct. 6, 1876.

32. Duncan, "Sketch," WM Papers, WRHS; *Cleveland Leader,* Nov. 18, 1900. McKinley had smoked before he was close to Hayes; see Morgan, ed., "Civil War Diary of William McKinley," 278–79. *The American President,* by Philip Kunhardt Jr., Philip P. Kunhardt III, and Peter W. Kunhardt (New York: Riverhead Books, 1999) includes a prewar picture of McKinley with a cigar in his mouth (page 314), which suggests that he at least sampled cigars before the war.

33. Mrs. Joseph E. Barrett, "Memories of the Civil War," p. 5, RBHPC; Williams, ed., *Diary and Letters of Hayes,* 2:393, 5:461, 464; *Cleveland Leader,* Mar. 24, 1890.

34. Hastings, "Genealogy and Autobiography," chap. 9, p. 10; *Boston Sunday Globe,* Sept. 8, 1901, clipping in McKinley Scrapbooks (MIC 143), OHS. A slightly different version of the story of McKinley and the veteran is told in Stratemeyer, *American Boys' Life of William McKinley,* 195–96.

35. Williams, ed., *Diary and Letters of Hayes,* 5:228 and illustration facing p. 206; Benjamin L. Askue Jr. to "Dear Companion in Life's Journey," Mar. 8 (continued on Mar. 12), 1864, Askue Letters.

36. *Youngstown Evening Register and Tribune,* Nov. 4, 1876.

37. Unidentified clipping titled "William McKinley Courted Ida Saxton with All the Ardor of Young Swain" in "Ida Saxton McKinley" File, WM Papers, RRLMM; *Canton Repository,* Jan. 29, 1928; Lucy Webb Hayes to RBH, Sept. 7, 1863, roll 11, RBH Papers. McKinley is described in Descriptive Book, Cos. A–F, 23d OVI, RG 94, NA, John A. Porter to Waldo C. Moore, Dec. 9, 1897, roll 23, WM Papers, LC, and Charles R. Miller, "William McKinley, the Lawyer," *Ohio Law Reporter* 14 (1917): 197.

38. Williams, ed., *Diary and Letters of Hayes,* 2:438; Barrett, "Memories of the Civil War," 1, 5; WM to RBH and Mrs. Hayes, Dec. 12, 1870, roll 20, frame 272, RBH Papers. The poem "Casabianca" by Felicia Dorothea Hemans was first published in America in 1826. Rutherford Hayes was twenty years older than McKinley; Lucy Hayes was eleven years older.

39. Williams, ed., *Diary and Letters of Hayes,* 2:447; *Holmes County Republican,* Jan. 7, 1864; *Lorain County News,* Feb. 18, 1863; Throne, ed., "A Commissary in the Union Army," 83.

40. "Abstract of stationery issued in the field," month ending May 31, 1864, WM Papers, WRHS.

41. *Holmes County Republican*, Jan. 7, 1864; Ellen Diary, Dec. 8–17, 1863; *OR*, ser. 1, vol. 29, 1:920–25, 939–40, and 2:550–52; Ward, *Twelfth Ohio Volunteer Inf[antry]*, 70; "Record of the Twenty-third Regiment," Dec. 17, 1863, roll 1, frames 397–99, Comly Papers.

42. Williams, ed., *Diary and Letters of Hayes*, 2:449–50. For McKinley's assignments on Hayes's staff, see "Descriptive List of the Twenty-third OVI," roll 272, frames 475–76, RBH Papers. The picture of McKinley taken on his twenty-first birthday was published in the *Cleveland Leader*, Nov. 18, 1900.

43. May Diary, Sept. 26, Oct. 13, 19, 1863, Feb. 7, 14, 27, 28, Mar. 3, 6, 1864; *Niles Daily Times*, Jan. 29, 1943; Andrew J. Duncan to "Dear Brother," Mar. 26, 1864, WM Papers, WRHS; *Official Roster*, 9:222, 437; Fradenburgh, *History of Erie Conference*, 2:266–67; unidentified newspaper clipping about Osborne family in "WM Biography" File, WM Papers, RRLMM; Joseph A. Osborn[e] compiled military service record, NA.

44. *OR*, ser. 1, vol. 33:109–12, 557, 740, 765–66, 945; Williams, *Hayes of the Twenty-third*, 166–67.

45. Hastings, "Genealogy and Autobiography," chap. 11, p. 3; four orders signed by McKinley and dated Apr. 19, 1864, Entry 1184 (Vol. 139 W.Va.), RG 393, NA; Cox, *Military Reminiscences*, 1:81–82; *Lorain County News*, June 15, 1864; "Descriptive List of the Twenty-third OVI," roll 272, frames 475–76, RBH Papers, RBHPC.

46. Hastings, "Genealogy and Autobiography," chap. 11, pp. 3–4; "Record of the Twenty-third Regiment," Apr. 28–30, 1864, roll 1, frames 403, 473, Comly Papers; T. M. Turner to RBH, June 28, 1889, roll 146, frames 161–62, RBH Papers. E. C. Arthur wrote a series of articles on the "Dublin Raid" for the *Ohio Soldier* in 1889. Copies are included on roll 271, RBH Papers.

47. *Speeches and Addresses of William McKinley* (1893), 644–45.

48. Stratemeyer, *American Boys' Life of William McKinley*, 62–63.

49. *Ashtabula Sentinel*, June 22, 1864; Hastings, "Genealogy and Autobiography," chap. 11, p. 9; Halstead, *Illustrious Life*, 117; *Speeches and Addresses of William McKinley* (1893), 645.

50. *OR*, ser. 1, vol. 37, 1:10–15; Williams, *Hayes of the Twenty-third*, 177–78; C. A. Sperry to RBH, Nov. 20, 1889, RBH Papers; Howard Rollins McManus, *The Battle of Cloyds Mountain: The Virginia and Tennessee Railroad Raid, April 29–May 19, 1864* (Lynchburg, Va.: H. E. Howard, 1989), 81. See also Milton W. Humphries, "The Battle at Cloyd's Farm," *Confederate Veteran* 17 (Dec. 1909): 598–99, W. P. Robinson, "The Battle of Cloyd's Farm," *Confederate Veteran* 33 (Mar. 1925): 97–100, and James I. Robertson Jr., "Cloyd's Mountain," in Frances H. Kennedy, ed., *The Civil War Battlefield Guide* (Boston: Houghton Mifflin, 1990), 200–202.

51. Williams, *Hayes of the Twenty-third*, 178–85; Benjamin L. Askue Jr. to "Ever Dear Companion and Friends," May 22, 1864, Askue Letters.

52. Reid, *Ohio in the War*, 2:163; Clugston Diary, May 11, 12, 1864; Halstead, *Illustrious Life*, 117; *OR*, ser. 1, vol. 37, 1:12; *Ashtabula Sentinel*, June 22, 1864; internet: www.mtnlakehotel.com; Hastings, "Genealogy and Autobiography," chap. 11, pp. 15–16.

53. *Mahoning Register*, June 2, 1864; Williams, *Hayes of the Twenty-third*, 185–87; Clugston Diary, May 15, 21, 1864, RBHPC; Hastings, "Genealogy and Autobiography," chap. 11, p. 17; *Lorain County News*, June 15, 1864; Williams, ed., *Diary and Letters of Hayes*, 2:461–62; *Ashtabula Sentinel*, June 22, 1864.

54. Williams, *Hayes of the Twenty-third,* 183; Williams, *Life of Hayes,* 1:221, n. 2; Robert B. Wilson, "A Historical Sketch of the Kanawha Division," 62–64, 68, 69–70 (with Robert B. Wilson to M. A. Hanna, July 28, 1896), roll 57, WM Papers, LC; Reid, *Ohio in the War,* 2:163; Stratemeyer, *American Boys' Life of William McKinley,* 67–68.

55. *OR,* ser. 1, vol. 37, 1:492, 507, 535–36, 548, 598; Philip H. Sheridan, *Personal Memoirs of P. H. Sheridan,* 2 vols. (New York: Charles L. Webster, 1888), 1:415–16 n.; Williams, ed., *Diary and Letters of Hayes,* 2:469–71; *Mahoning Register,* July 7, 1864; Benjamin L. Askue Jr. [no salutation], June 1, 2, 3, 8, 1864, Askue Letters; Cracraft Diary, June 2, 1864.

56. Williams, ed., *Diary and Letters of Hayes,* 2:473; *Cleveland Morning Leader,* July 4, 1864. The 12th Ohio Infantry, which also lost men who did not reenlist, was consolidated with the 23d on July 2, 1864.

57. Sutton, *History of the Second Regiment,* 125–27; Benson, comp., *With the Army of West Virginia,* 47–48, 50; General Orders No. 39, Department of West Virginia, June 9, 1864, Entry 5699 (vol. 20 W.Va.), RG 393, NA; J. Scott Moore, "General Hunter's Raid," *Southern Historical Society Papers* 27 (1899): 183–85, 187–88; Eby, ed., *Virginia Yankee,* 259; William C. Walker, *History of the Eighteenth Regiment Conn. Volunteers in the War for the Union* (Norwich, Conn.: The Committee, 1885), 251.

58. Williams, *Life of Hayes,* 1:223; Edward A. Miller Jr., *Lincoln's Abolitionist General: The Biography of David Hunter* (Columbia: Univ. of South Carolina Press, 1997), 122–23; Francis H. Smith, *The Virginia Military Institute, Its Building and Rebuilding* (Lynchburg: J. P. Bell, 1912), 205; Lincoln, *Life with the Thirty-fourth Massachusetts Infantry,* 306–7; Charles G. Halpine [Pvt. Miles O'Reilly], *Baked Meats of the Funeral* (New York: Carleton, 1866), 309–11, 319; Williams, ed., *Diary and Letters of Hayes,* 2:473–74, 478–79; E. E. Ewing, *Bugles and Bells; Or, Stories Told Again. Including the Story of the Ninety-first Ohio Volunteer Infantry. Reunion Poems and Social Tributes* (Cincinnati: Curts & Jennings, 1899), 35; Emmett W. MacCorkle, "George Washington: Prisoner of War," *Civil War Times Illustrated* 23 (Mar. 1984): 30–35.

59. Eby, *Virginia Yankee,* 253, 257–58; H. A. Du Pont, *The Campaign of 1864 in the Valley of Virginia and the Expedition to Lynchburg* (New York: National Americana Society, 1925), 68–69.

60. Halpine, *Baked Meats,* 322, 324–25, 339–41; Williams, *Hayes of the Twenty-third,* 195–96; Charles H. Lynch, *The Civil War Diary, 1862–1865, of Charles H. Lynch, 18th Conn. Vol's* (Hartford, Conn.: Case, Lockwood & Brainard, 1915), 74–79.

61. Lynch, *Civil War Diary,* 79–80; Williams, *Hayes of the Twenty-third,* 196–98; Halpine, *Baked Meats,* 344–46; Eby, *Virginia Yankee,* 264; "When Hutter's House Was Hunter's House" and "The Battle of Lynchburg," *Iron Worker* 10 (Summer 1947): 1–6. Hutter's house, Sandusky, is still standing in Lynchburg.

62. Halstead, *Illustrious Life,* 118. Col. Isaac H. Duval, who commanded the 9th West Virginia Infantry, later commanded a division in Crook's Army of the Kanawha.

63. Thomas F. Wildes, *Record of the One Hundred and Sixteenth Regiment Ohio Infantry Volunteers in the War of the Rebellion* (Sandusky, Ohio: I. F. Mack & Bro., 1884), 112; Halpine, *Baked Meats,* 364; William B. Stark, "The Great Skedaddle," *Atlantic Monthly* 162 (July 1938): 86–94; Du Pont, *Campaign of 1864,* 90–91; *Mahoning Register,* July 14, 1864; Patterson Diary, June 22–27, 1864; William G. Watson Memoirs (MS 037), 31, Virginia Military Institute Archives, Lexington, Va.; Eby, *Virginia Yankee,*

273; *Speeches and Addresses of William McKinley* (1893), 645; Hastings, "Genealogy and Autobiography," chap. 12, pp. 18–19, Hastings Papers, RBHPC.

64. Stark, "Great Skedaddle," 90, 92; Watson Memoirs, 26–28; Lincoln, *Life with the Thirty-fourth Massachusetts*, 324; Du Pont, *Campaign of 1864*, 91.

65. Halstead, *Illustrious Life*, 118.

66. Undated and unidentified clipping titled "Hayes's War Story" in scrapbook, pp. 143–44, roll 98, WM Papers, LC.

67. Ewing, *Bugles and Bells*, 126; Williams, ed., *Diary and Letters of Hayes*, 2:480; Welcher, *Union Army*, 1:190–91, 207–9.

68. Welcher, *Union Army*, 1:209–10; Wildes, *Record of the One Hundred and Sixteenth Regiment*, 124; Walker, *History of the Eighteenth Regiment*, 276–80; Lynch, *Civil War Diary*, 95; Hastings, "Genealogy and Autobiography," chap. 13, pp. 3–10; Williams, *Hayes of the Twenty-third*, 204–16; *Ashtabula Sentinel*, Aug. 17, 1864; *Speeches and Addresses of William McKinley* (1893), 645; *OR*, ser. 1, vol. 46, 1:26–27.

69. *OR*, ser. 1, vol. 37, 1:311–12; Porter, *Life of William McKinley*, 87–94; *Gallipolis Journal*, Aug. 11, 1864; Ewing, *Bugles and Bells*, 127; *Cleveland Weekly Herald*, Aug. 13, 1864. This was the second battle at Kernstown. An earlier battle had been fought there on March 23, 1862.

70. *Life of William McKinley*, 95–96.

71. Ibid., 96–97.

72. Ibid., 98; Hastings, "Genealogy and Autobiography," chap. 13, p. 17.

73. *Ashtabula Sentinel*, Aug. 17, 1864; *Gallipolis Journal*, Aug. 11, 1864; *Cleveland Weekly Herald*, Aug. 13, 1864; Porter, *Life of William McKinley*, 98–101.

74. Summers, *Baltimore and Ohio*, 123–25; Lynch, *Civil War Diary*, 106; *OR*, ser. 1, vol. 37, 1:288–90, 311–12. For the Battle of Kernstown, see also Joseph W. A. Whitehorne, "Second Kernstown," in Kennedy, ed., *Civil War Battlefield Guide*, 239–42.

75. Stratemeyer, *American Boys' Life of William McKinley*, 83; James M. Comly to B. R. Cowen, July 16, 1864, 23d OVI letterbook, RG 94, NA; Williams, ed., *Diary and Letters of Hayes*, 2:486.

4. ADJUTANT

1. Edward Stratemeyer, *American Boys' Life of William McKinley* (Boston: Lothrop, Lee & Shepard, 1901), 75; RBH speech at Lakeside, Ohio, July 30, 1891, roll 296, frames 690–92, RBH Papers; Williams, ed., *Diary and Letters of Hayes*, 2:492.

2. RBH to "My Dear Son," Aug. 4, 1864, roll 169, frames 537–38, RBH Papers; unidentified clipping dated Dec. 16, [1900], scrapbooks, p. 180, roll 95, WM Papers, LC.

3. Williams, *Hayes of the Twenty-third*, 233.

4. WM to James F. McKinley, Apr. 13, 1899, roll 18, WM Papers, LC.

5. Ambrose Bierce, *Tales of Soldiers and Civilians by Ambrose Bierce* (New York: Heritage Press, 1943), 40; *McKinley Memorial Addresses* (Cleveland: Tippecanoe Club Co., 1913), 26.

6. Lusk, *War Letters*, 170; Russell Hastings, "A Staff Officer's Recollection of the Battle of Opequan," p. 1, Hastings Papers; RBH speech at Marietta, Ohio, Sept. 7, 1877, roll 291, frame 743, RBH Papers; Benjamin L. Askue Jr. to "Ever Dear Companion

and Friends," May 22, 1864, Askue Letters; Williams, ed., *Diary and Letters of Hayes*, 3:25–26.

7. Lynch, *Civil War Diary*, 106–10; John William De Forest, *A Volunteer's Adventures: A Union Captain's Record of the Civil War* (New Haven: Yale Univ. Press, 1946), 163.

8. *Cleveland Leader*, Aug. 7, 1888; *OR*, ser. 1, vol. 46, 1:27–28; Welcher, *Union Army*, 1:210–11, 293; Williams, ed., *Diary and Letters of Hayes*, 2:498. Crook's army was often called, incorrectly, the Eighth Corps.

9. Eby, *Virginia Yankee*, 286; Robert I. Alotta, *Civil War Justice: Union Army Executions Under Lincoln* (Shippensburg, Pa.: White Mane, 1989), 121, 196–97, 206; Williams, ed., *Diary and Letters of Hayes*, 3:337, 347–51. The proceedings of the court-martial are on roll 11, frames 1056–67, RBH Papers.

10. *Mahoning Register*, Sept. 8, 1864; Lincoln, *Life with the Thirty-fourth Mass. Infantry*, 341–42; Lynch, *Civil War Diary*, 110–11; Comly Diary, Aug. 4–5, 1864, roll 1, frame 547, Comly Papers; *Youngstown Evening Register and Tribune*, Aug. 29, 1876.

11. *OR*, ser. 1, vol. 43, 1:40–45, 81, 360, 405; Halstead, *Illustrious Life*, 119; *Life of William McKinley*, 33; Hastings, "A Staff Officer's Recollection," 5–6.

12. James E. Taylor, *With Sheridan Up the Shenandoah Valley in 1864: Leaves from a Special Artist's Sketchbook and Diary*. Western Reserve Historical Society Publication 173 (Dayton, Ohio: Morningside House, 1989), 264, 281, n. 26; Williams, ed., *Diary and Letters of Hayes*, 2:502–3.

13. *Proceedings of the Tenth Reunion of the Society of the Army of West Virginia . . .* (Portsmouth, Ohio: Portsmouth Printing, 1887), 99; *Holmes County Republican*, Sept. 22, 1864; *Mahoning Register*, Sept. 22, 1864; *OR*, ser. 1, vol. 43, 1:405; Halstead, *Illustrious Life*, 119; *Life of William McKinley*, 36.

14. *Life of William McKinley*, 36; Williams, ed., *Diary and Letters of Hayes*, 2:534.

15. *Life of William McKinley*, 36; *Cleveland Leader*, Dec. 5, 1897; Stratemeyer, *American Boys' Life of William McKinley*, 84–85; Russell, *Lives of William McKinley and Garret A. Hobart*, 109.

16. De Forest, *Volunteer's Adventures*, 166, 170–71; Sheridan, *Personal Memoirs*, 1:500. McKinley's letters and orders for this period are in Records of the Department of West Virginia, vol. 2, W.Va., RG 393, NA. See also *OR*, ser. 1, vol. 43, 2:59, 91.

17. *OR*, ser. 1, vol. 46, 1:28–29.

18. Sheridan, *Personal Memoirs*, 2:13–17; Hastings, "A Staff Officer's Recollection," 1–18. Hastings incorrectly states that McKinley was still serving on Hayes's staff during this battle.

19. *Canton Repository*, Feb. 6, 1896; *Life of William McKinley*, 34; Porter, *Life of William McKinley*, 104–6.

20. Hastings, "A Staff Officer's Recollection," 12–13, 19–26; Schmitt, ed., *General George Crook*, 126–27; Du Pont, *Campaign of 1864*, 120–21.

21. Hastings, "A Staff Officer's Recollection," 27–35; Halstead, *Illustrious Life*, 119; *Cleveland Leader*, Mar. 6, 1897; Williams, ed., *Diary and Letters of Hayes*, 2:508–11; Williams, *Life of Hayes*, 1:242–43; Jeffry D. Wert, *Custer: The Controversial Life of George Armstrong Custer* (New York: Simon & Schuster, 1996), 182–83.

22. Hastings, "A Staff Officer's Recollection," 36–59; Basler, ed., *Collected Works of Abraham Lincoln*, 8:13; Williams, *Hayes of the Twenty-third*, 264, n. 4; Richard R. Duncan, ed., *Alexander Neil and the Last Shenandoah Valley Campaign: Letters of an*

Army Surgeon to His Family, 1864 (Shippensburg, Pa.: White Mane, 1996), 67; Taylor, *With Sheridan Up the Shenandoah Valley,* 388; unidentified clipping [*Globe?*] about Hastings, Mar. 11, 1897, scrapbooks, roll 95, WM Papers, LC.

23. *Ashtabula Sentinel,* Oct. 12, 1864; *Mahoning Register,* Oct. 13, 1864; Du Pont, *Campaign of 1864,* 133–38; *Speeches and Addresses of William McKinley* (1893), 646; Halstead, *Illustrious Life,* 120; *OR,* ser. 1, vol. 43, 1:363–64, and 2:153. See also Jeffry Wert, "First Fair Chance," *Civil War Times Illustrated* 18 (Aug. 1979): 4–9, 40–45.

24. Taylor, *With Sheridan Up the Shenandoah Valley,* 419–20.

25. Herman J. Viola, ed., *The Memoirs of Charles Henry Veil: A Soldier's Recollections of the Civil War and the Arizona Territory* (New York: Orion Books, 1993), 47–49, 185; Jeffry D. Wert, *Mosby's Rangers* (New York: Simon & Schuster, 1990), 197, 211–19, 232, 244–50; John S. Mosby, "Retaliation: The Execution of Seven Prisoners by Col. John S. Mosby," *Southern Historical Society Papers* 27 (1899): 314–22; Taylor, *With Sheridan Up the Shenandoah Valley,* 290; *OR,* ser. 1, vol. 43, 2:566.

26. *OR,* ser. 1, vol. 43, 2:308; Wert, *Mosby's Rangers,* 232; Taylor, *With Sheridan Up the Shenandoah Valley,* 429–34, 438–39, 462; Fred. C. Newhall, *With General Sheridan in Lee's Last Campaign* (Philadelphia: J. B. Lippincott, 1866), 26. Other accounts assert that the men who killed Meigs were Confederate cavalrymen; see Thomas A. Lewis, *The Guns of Cedar Creek* (New York: Dell, 1988), 65.

27. *OR,* ser. 1, vol. 43, 1:43, 2:202; Jeffry D. Wert, *From Winchester to Cedar Creek: The Shenandoah Campaign of 1864* (New York: Simon & Schuster, 1987), 144, 158.

28. *OR,* ser. 1, vol. 43, 1:49–50, 2:307–8; Comly Diary, Sept. 30, Oct. 8, 1864; Taylor, *With Sheridan Up the Shenandoah Valley,* 441, 444; Wert, *From Winchester to Cedar Creek,* 158–60.

29. Taylor, *With Sheridan Up the Shenandoah Valley,* 459–60; Williams, ed., *Diary and Letters of Hayes,* 2:524–25; Halstead, *Illustrious Life,* 120.

30. Sutton, *History of the Second Regiment West Virginia Cavalry Volunteers,* 174–75; Taylor, *With Sheridan Up the Shenandoah Valley,* 488–91; Edward W. Emerson, *Life and Letters of Charles Russell Lowell* (Boston: Houghton Mifflin, 1907), 476.

31. Williams, *Hayes of the Twenty-third,* 303–6.

32. George A. Forsyth, *Thrilling Days in Army Life* (1900; rpt. Lincoln: Univ. of Nebraska Press, 1994), 125–68; James M. Comly in *Cincinnati Enquirer,* Jan. 11, 1885, clipping on roll 3, frames 119–20, Comly Papers. Some of the soldiers claimed that the greater part of the Union army was not demoralized and had formed their lines before Sheridan returned; see *National Tribune* (Washington, D.C.), Nov. 21, Dec. 5, 1901.

33. Richard Marius, ed., *The Columbia Book of Civil War Poetry* (New York: Columbia Univ. Press, 1994), 184–86. Herman Melville wrote a lesser-known poem called "Sheridan at Cedar Creek," ibid., 187–89.

34. Sheridan, *Personal Memoirs,* 2:80–82; Taylor, *With Sheridan Up the Shenandoah Valley,* 498, 501, 508; Halstead, *Illustrious Life,* 123; *National Tribune* (Washington, D.C.), Dec. 1, 1910; *Cleveland Leader and Morning Herald,* Aug. 7, 1888; Porter, *Life of William McKinley,* 107–8; *Canton Repository,* May 25, 1901. Although Sheridan called him "Major McKinley," he was a captain at the time of Sheridan's ride.

35. Unidentified clipping dated Dec. 16, [1900], scrapbooks, p. 180, roll 95, WM Papers, LC.

36. Taylor, *With Sheridan Up the Shenandoah Valley,* 524–44.

37. Favill, *Diary of a Young Officer,* 156; *OR,* ser. 1, vol. 43, 2:473.

38. *OR*, ser. 1, vol. 43, 2:470–71.

39. *Gallipolis Journal*, Oct. 28, 1864; Williams, ed., *Diary and Letters of Hayes*, 2:524, 526, 535–36; Williams, *Life of Hayes*, 1:263–64; *Canton Repository*, July 3, 1900. Taylor, *With Sheridan Up the Shenandoah Valley*, 546–48, has a drawing of the election (reproduced here) that includes McKinley; an earlier version of the drawing published in *Frank Leslie's Illustrated Newspaper*, Dec. 3, 1864, did not include him.

40. *OR*, ser. 1, vol. 43, 2:573; Taylor, *With Sheridan Up the Shenandoah Valley*, 574; Williams, ed., *Diary and Letters of Hayes*, 2:533, 535, 537–38, 543–44.

41. Williams, ed., *Diary and Letters of Hayes*, 2:547–49; Taylor, *With Sheridan Up the Shenandoah Valley*, 591.

42. Williams, ed., *Diary and Letters of Hayes*, 2:545, 550, 552; *OR*, ser. 1, vol. 43, 2:802, 813; Welcher, *Union Army*, 1:193, 296; Taylor, *With Sheridan Up the Shenandoah Valley*, 591; Hastings, "Genealogy and Autobiography," chap. 15, pp. 30–31.

43. *OR*, ser. 1, vol. 43, 2:800, 804, 833, 841; General Orders No. 1, Jan. 2, 1865, and No. 2, Jan. 3, 1865, Department of West Virginia, vol. 21, W.Va., RG 393, NA.

44. *OR*, ser. 1, vol. 46, 2:108; Benjamin L. Askue Jr. [no salutation], Jan. 18, 1865, Askue Letters; Stratemeyer, *American Boys' Life of William McKinley*, 103–6.

45. Williams, ed., *Diary and Letters of Hayes*, 2:554, 557–59; Diary of RBH, Feb. 16, 1865, roll 2, and J. M. Comly to RBH, Jan. 28, 1865, roll 12, frame 140, (as well as printed invitations on roll 12, frames 136 and 153–54), RBH Papers.

46. [Cyrus S.] Roberts to Russell Hastings, Mar. 20, 1865, Hastings Papers.

47. Jesse C. M'Neill, "Capture of Generals Kelly and Crook," *Confederate Veteran* 14 (Sept. 1906): 410–13; J. W. Duffey, "Capture of Generals Crook and Kelly," *Confederate Veteran* 33 (Nov. 1925): 420–23, 437; Schmitt, *General George Crook*, 303–5; *OR*, ser. 1, vol. 46, 1:468–72, 2:620–28, 665; RBH to U. S. Grant and RBH to Lucy Webb Hayes, Feb. 21, 1865, roll 169, frames 872–77, RBH Papers. Some sources place Kelley at the Barnum House instead of the St. Nicholas Hotel.

48. Williams, ed., *Diary and Letters of Hayes*, 2:561; "Marion Gordon Willis," *Confederate Veteran* 38 (Sept. 1930): 356–57; Anna McKinley to WM, Mar. 14, 1865, WM Papers, WRHS.

49. *OR*, ser. 1, vol. 46, 2:623–24; *National Cyclopaedia of American Biography*, 63 vols. (New York: James T. White, 1898–1984), 21:205.

50. *OR*, ser. 1, vol. 46, 2:704, 706–7, 713, 724–25.

51. General Orders No. 36, Feb. 28, 1865, and No. 40, Mar. 8, 1865, Department of West Virginia, vol. 21, W.Va., RG 393, NA; *OR*, ser. 1, vol. 46, 1:525, 2:777, 820, 863.

52. RBH to Lucy Webb Hayes, Mar. 12, 1865, roll 169, frames 914–15, RBH Papers; *OR*, ser. 1, vol. 46, 2:863, 893; General Orders No. 41, Mar. 20, 1865, and No. 42, Mar. 22, 1865, Department of West Virginia, vol. 21, W.Va., RG 393, NA.

53. Favill, *Diary of a Young Officer*, 223; David T. Hedrick and Gordon Barry Davis Jr., *I'm Surrounded by Methodists... Diary of John H.W. Stuckenberg, Chaplain of the 145th Pennsylvania Volunteer Infantry* (Gettysburg, Pa.: Thomas, 1995), 30–31. See also David M. Jordan, *Winfield Scott Hancock: A Soldier's Life* (Bloomington: Indiana Univ. Press, 1988), 37, 57–58.

54. *OR*, ser. 1, vol. 46, 3:167; Welcher, *Union Army*, 1:297; Robert P. Kennedy to Brig. Gen. Morgan, Apr. 5, 6, 1865, Department of West Virginia, vol. 3, W.Va., RG 393, NA; Special Orders No. 78, Apr. 6, 1865, Department of West Virginia, vol. 21, W.Va., RG 393, NA.

55. Ezra J. Warner, *Generals in Blue: Lives of the Union Commanders* (Baton Rouge: Louisiana State Univ. Press, 1964), 73; Jack D. Welsh, *Medical Histories of Union Generals* (Kent, Ohio: Kent State Univ. Press, 1996), 58–60; Francis A. Walker, *History of the Second Army Corps in the Army of the Potomac* (New York: Charles Scribner's Sons, 1886), 480; John Y. Simon, ed., *The Papers of Ulysses S. Grant*, 22 vols. to date (Carbondale: Southern Illinois Univ. Press, 1967–98), 14:191; William Kepler, *History of the Three Months' and Three Years' Service . . . of the Fourth Regiment Ohio Volunteer Infantry . . .* (1886, rpt. Huntington, W.Va.: Blue Acorn Press, 1992), 173; Halstead, *Illustrious Life*, 121.

56. General Orders No. 1, Apr. 6, 1865, Fourth Provisional Division, Army of the Shenandoah, Old Book 37, RG 393, NA; Lord, *They Fought for the Union*, 111; Cox, *Military Reminiscences*, 2:296; Cornelius Cadle, "An Adjutant's Recollections," in W. H. Chamberlin et al., eds., *Sketches of War History, 1861–65, Papers Prepared for the Commandery of the State of Ohio, Military Order of the Loyal Legion of the United States*, 6 vols. (Cincinnati: Robert Clarke, 1888–1903): 5:384–401; Favill, *Diary of a Young Officer*, 57, 59–60; George Haven Putnam, *Memories of My Youth, 1844–1865* (New York: G. P. Putnam's Sons, 1914), 288–94; James Boyle, "William McKinley as I Knew Him," *The Week: A Journal of Fundamental Democracy* 10 (Jan. 23, 1915): 14.

57. William Hanchett, *Irish: Charles G. Halpine in Civil War America* (Syracuse: Syracuse Univ. Press, 1970), 62; Favill, *Diary of a Young Officer*, 57.

58. Robert P. Kennedy to George W. Harrison, Apr. 5, 1865, Department of West Virginia, vol. 3, W.Va., RG 393, NA; WM to George W. Harrison, Apr. 5, 1865, Department of West Virginia, vol. 4, W.Va., RG 393, NA; General Orders No. 102, Apr. 25, 1863, *General Orders Affecting the Volunteer Force;* John Holland Diary, Apr. 9, 10, 1865, Collection R405, Western Historical Manuscript Collection, University of Missouri–Rolla; General Orders No. 2, Apr. 10, 1865, Fourth Provisional Division, Army of the Shenandoah, Old Book 37, RG 393, NA; E. T. Heald, typescript biography of WM, vol. 1, 5:182, RRLMM.

59. McKinley orders, Apr. 27, 29, 1865, Fourth Provisional Division, Orderly Book, with Duncan Diary; General Orders No. 3, Apr. 20, 1865, No. 5, Apr. 21, 1865, and No. 6, Apr. 22, 1865, Fourth Provisional Division, Army of the Shenandoah, Old Book 37, RG 393, NA.

60. Benjamin L. Askue Jr. to "Dear Flavia," Apr. 18, 1865, Askue Letters; J. T. Webb to RBH, May 3, 1865, roll 12, frame 236, RBH Papers; Welcher, *Union Army*, 1:8; General Orders No. 1, May 10, 1865, Old Book 38, Hancock's First Army Corps, RG 393, NA.

61. McKinley's instructions for the march to Camp Stoneman, dated May 2, 1865, are in Old Book 41, Hancock's First Army Corps, RG 393, NA.

62. Horatio C. King, "How McKinley Became a Mason," *Grand Lodge Bulletin, Grand Lodge of Iowa, A.F. & A.M.* 30 (Jan. 1929): 7–8.

63. William Moseley Brown, *Freemasonry in Winchester, Virginia, 1768–1948* (Staunton, Va.: McClure, 1949), 96–102, 104, 115, 118; *Winchester Evening Star*, Sept. 7, 25, 1901.

64. Holland Diary, May 4–8, 1865.

65. Lord, *They Fought for the Union*, 63–64, 187; *OR*, ser. 1, vol. 42, 3:728, and ser. 3, vol. 4:970–71, 1088–89, 1283; *Holmes County Republican*, Mar. 16, 1865;

Jordan, *Winfield Scott Hancock*, 169–74; Frederick H. Dyer, *A Compendium of the War of the Rebellion*, 3 vols. (New York: Thomas Yoseloff, 1959), 1:245, 2:1717–18; Welcher, *Union Army*, 1:312; *New York Times*, June 7, 1865; Holland Diary, May 22, 1865.

66. *OR*, ser. 1, vol. 46, 3:1193; Holland Diary, May 25, 1865; *Canton Weekly Repository*, June 4, 1891.

67. Holland Diary, June 6, 1865; *New York Times*, June 7, 1865.

68. David McKinney letter, June 16, [1865], David McKinney Papers, *Civil War Times Illustrated* Collection, USAMHI; General Orders No. 6, June 13, 1865, and No. 11, July 12, 1865, Hancock's First Army Corps, vol. 15/38, RG 393, NA; Holland Diary, June 15, 1865; Special Orders No. 121, June 19, 1865, First Division, First Army Corps, WM compiled military service record, NA; May Diary, July 5, 1865; Notation: "Poland Ohio June 23 1865 William McKinley Jr." in orderly book, with Duncan Diary.

69. WM oath of office, July 11, 1865, and WM to L. Thomas, July 12, 1865, 1680 V.S. 83, RG 94, NA; "Statement of the Military Service of Brevet Major William McKinley, Jr.," roll 2, WM Papers, LC; Adjutant General's Registry of Brevet Commissions Issued and Distributed, RG 94, NA; *Niles Daily News*, Oct. 5, 1917.

70. Martin R. Connolly to Hattie Burleigh, June 7, 1865, Hattie Burleigh Collection, USAMHI; Ephraim G. Wagley Memoir, July 7, 1865, Civil War Miscellaneous Collection, USAMHI; Holland Diary, July 7, 1865; *Daily National Republican* (Washington, D.C.), July 7, 17, 1865; General Orders No. 10, July 17, 1865, and No. 13, July 14, 1865, and notice of Carroll's and McKinley's end of assignment (in vol. 9), Records of Hancock's First Army Corps, RG 393, NA; *New York Times*, July 18, 1865.

71. WM to L. Thomas (with endorsements), July 19, 1865, 1680 V.S. 83, RG 94, NA; AAG to WM, July 27, 1865, Records of Hancock's First Army Corps, vol. 6, RG 393, NA; Russell, *Lives of William McKinley and Garret A. Hobart*, 126–28.

72. Record of Board of Examination, July 29, 1865, Records of Hancock's First Army Corps, vol. 13, RG 393, NA; C. W. Foster to WM, July 29, 1865, WM compiled military service record, NA.

73. *Cleveland Leader*, Aug. 25, 1895, Aug. 22, 1897. G. W. Townsend credited McKinley's sister Anna with dissuading him from accepting the commission; see his *Memorial Life of William McKinley*, 38–39.

74. *Speeches and Addresses of William McKinley* (1893), 360.

75. *Canton Repository*, Aug. 13, 1891; *Literary Digest* 13 (Aug. 8, 1896): 452.

5. VETERAN

1. *Mahoning Register*, Aug. 17, 31, 1865; May Diary, Aug. 18, 1865; G. B. Cortelyou to Roswell Douglass Blandy, Sept. 16, 1897, roll 21, WM Papers, LC; *Cleveland Leader*, Aug. 25, 1895.

2. WM to Russell Hastings, Aug. 28, 1865, Hastings Papers; *Mahoning Register*, Nov. 9, 1865.

3. Edward Thornton Heald, *The William McKinley Story* ([Canton, Ohio]: Stark County Historical Society, 1964), 11–12; Olcott, *Life of William McKinley*, 1:57–58;

New York Tribune, Sept. 26, 1901; WM to Adjutant General, U.S.A., Nov. 12, 1866, 1680 V.S. 83, RG 94, NA; Henry Rood, comp. and ed., *Memories of the White House: The Home Life of Our Presidents from Lincoln to Roosevelt, Being Personal Recollections of Colonel W. H. Crook* (Boston: Little, Brown, 1911), 236; form letter about medals from B. R. Cowen, June 1, 1866, roll 12, frame 436, RBH Papers.

4. Heald, *William McKinley Story*, 12–14; Olcott, *Life of William McKinley*, 1:58; Russell, *Lives of William McKinley and Garret A. Hobart*, 132; Eugene V. Smalley, "William McKinley—A Study of His Character and Career," *Review of Reviews* 14 (July 1896): 37–38; *Pittsburgh Times*, Sept. 7, 1901, in WM Scrapbooks (MIC 143), OHS; Alexander K. McClure and Charles Morris, *The Authentic Life of William McKinley Our Third Martyr President* (N.p.: W. E. Scull, 1901), 102–4; undated manuscript speech by WM beginning "The issues between the contending parties," in container 1, folder 2, WM Papers, WRHS. From its contents, this speech appears to be from the fall of 1867.

5. Charles Thomas Hickok, *The Negro in Ohio, 1802–1870* (1896, rpt. New York: AMS Press, 1975), 72–73; Frank U. Quillin, *The Color Line in Ohio: A History of Race Prejudice in a Typical Northern State* (1913, rpt. New York: Negro Univ. Press, 1969), 97–99; *Memorial Proceedings on Occasion of the Death of Hon. William McKinley* (N.p.: Stark County Bar Association, n.d.), 19.

6. Undated manuscript speech by WM beginning "The issues between the contending parties," in container 1, folder 2, WM Papers, WRHS; Quillin, *Color Line in Ohio*, 98, 100.

7. *Canton Repository*, Mar. 30, 1965; undated manuscript speech by WM beginning "The campaign before us," container 1, folder 2, WM Papers, WRHS.

8. Undated manuscript speech by WM beginning "The campaign before us."

9. *Canton Repository*, Oct. 6, 1871; undated manuscript speech by WM beginning "My countrymen," container 1, folder 2, WM Papers, WRHS.

10. *Canton Repository*, Aug. 18, 25, 1876; *Stark County Democrat*, Sept. 28, Oct. 5, 1876, Sept. 26, 1878; *Ohio Patriot*, Sept. 14, 21, 1876; *Mahoning Valley Vindicator*, Oct. 6, 1876; Heald, typescript biography of WM, vol. 2, 12:35. McKinley is called the "Little Tin Major" in an unidentified clipping in the "Addresses, Lectures, Speeches, Tariff" file, WM Papers, RRLMM.

11. H. Wayne Morgan, *William McKinley and His America* (Syracuse: Syracuse Univ. Press, 1963), 52; D. R. Hunter to RBH, June 18, 1876, roll 38, frame 665, RBH Papers; Williams, ed., *Diary and Letters of Hayes*, 2:173–74, 431; Special Orders No. 34, July 4, 1862, and General Orders No. 26, Apr. 30, 1863, and No. 52, Sept. 11, 1863, Regimental Order and Circular Book, 23d OVI, RG 94, NA.

12. *Youngstown Vindicator*, Aug. 25, Sept. 8, 15, 1876; Williams, ed., *Diary and Letters of Hayes*, 3:337, 347–51; clipping from *Columbus Dispatch*, Aug. 25, 1876, roll 2, frame 151, Comly Papers; *Stark County Democrat*, Sept. 7, 21, 1876.

13. *Cleveland Leader*, Sept. 15, Nov. 6, 1876.

14. Heald, *William McKinley Story*, 25, 32, 34, 37–38, 43; Ari Hoogenboom, *Rutherford B. Hayes: Warrior and President* (Lawrence: Univ. Press of Kansas, 1995), 295; Henry S. Belden III, comp., *Grand Tour of Ida Saxton McKinley and Sister Mary Saxton Barber, 1869* (Canton, Ohio: Reserve, 1985), foreword, pp. 7–9; Rood, comp., *Memories of the White House*, 237; Hastings, "Genealogy and Autobiography," chap. 16, p. 4.

In June 1878, Hastings married Rutherford Hayes's niece Emily Platt. In January 1879, Russell and Emily Hastings moved to Bermuda.

15. *Annual Report of the Board of Visitors to the United States Military Academy . . . 1880* (Washington, D.C.: GPO, 1880); "Report of the Congressional Board of Visitors to the West Point Academy for 1880," Senate Misc. Doc. No. 18, 46th Cong., 3d sess., 12.

16. John F. Marszalek, *Assault at West Point: The Court-Martial of Johnson Whittaker* (New York: Macmillan, 1972), 134, 155–57; "Report of the Congressional Board of Visitors to the West Point Academy for 1880," 7, 9–13. See Marszalek for a full account of the Whittaker case.

In 1893, President Grover Cleveland appointed McKinley—then serving as governor of Ohio—to the U.S. Naval Academy's Board of Visitors, but McKinley declined that appointment. (Extract from the "Proceedings of the Board of Visitors to the U.S. Naval Academy 1893," provided by the Archives of the U.S. Naval Academy, Apr. 5, 1995.)

17. *Speeches and Addresses of William McKinley* (1893), 52, 58, 170–71, 517.

18. Ibid., 181–82.

19. Williams, ed., *Diary and Letters of Hayes*, 4:236; *Speeches and Addresses of William McKinley* (1893), 227–29; Olcott, *Life of William McKinley*, 1:214–24.

20. *Speeches and Addresses of William McKinley* (1893), 179, 192, 217; clipping from *Cleveland Leader*, Sept. 30, 1896, in WM biographical file, RBHPC.

21. Halstead, *Illustrious Life*, 115–21; Williams, ed., *Diary and Letters of Hayes*, 5:440; clipping from the *Fremont Daily News* with Webb C. Hayes to WM, Apr. 6, 1897, roll 58, WM Papers, LC; printed invitation to the Canton reunion, dated July 6, 1880, in container 2, folder 5, WM Papers, WRHS; Harry James Brown and Frederick D. Williams, eds., *The Diary of James A. Garfield*, 4 vols. (East Lansing: Michigan State Univ. Press, 1973), 4:448 (n. 249), 449; *Canton Repository*, Sept. 2, 1880; Heald, typescript biography of WM, vol. 2, 13:25.

22. *Cleveland Leader*, May 31, 1877, July 5, 1896; inscription on the Soldiers' Monument, Riverside Cemetery, Poland, Ohio; *Canton Repository*, Aug. 13, 21, 1891.

23. *Speeches and Addresses of William McKinley* (1893), 358–67.

24. Joseph P. Smith, comp., *McKinley, the People's Choice, The Congratulations of the Country, The Calls of Delegations at Canton, The Addresses by Them. His Eloquent and Effective Responses. Full Text of Each Speech or Address Made by Him from June 18 to August 1, 1896* (Canton: Repository Press, 1896), 39; William T. Kuhns, *Memories of Old Canton and My Personal Recollections of William McKinley* (Canton: Privately printed, 1937), 55–56.

25. *Cleveland Leader*, Sept. 11, 1891, Oct. 28, 1894.

26. *Cleveland Leader*, Sept. 8, 1891; *Canton Repository*, Sept. 8, 1891.

27. *Canton Repository*, July 2 (weekly), Aug. 15, 27, 1891.

28. Hoogenboom, *Rutherford B. Hayes*, 502. Hayes's speech is on roll 296, frames 690–92, RBH Papers.

29. *Cleveland Leader*, Jan. 11, 1892; *Canton Repository*, Jan. 14, Oct. 23, 1892; *Youngstown Daily Vindicator*, Oct. 7, 1898. McKinley's military staff is listed in *Annual Report of the Secretary of State to the Governor of the State of Ohio, for the Year Ending November 15, 1892* (Norwalk, Ohio: Laning, 1893), 17.

30. *Canton Repository*, Feb. 6, 1892, Nov. 17, 1895.

31. *Canton Repository*, Apr. 14, 1892; John A. Logan, *The Great Conspiracy: Its Origin and History* (New York: A. R. Hart, 1886), 501–2, n.

32. Williams, *Life of Hayes*, 2:405.

33. *Cleveland Leader*, Jan. 8, 1894; *Canton Repository* (weekly) Jan. 4, 11, 18, 1894, and (daily) Jan. 9, Apr. 19, 1894; Frank B. Gessner, "William McKinley," *McClure's Magazine* 2 (Dec. 1893): 22; Russell, *Lives of McKinley and Hobart*, 63–65.

34. Porter, *Life of William McKinley*, 400; Charles A. Peckham, "The Ohio National Guard and Its Police Duties, 1894," *Ohio History* 83 (Winter 1974): 51.

35. Peckham, "Ohio National Guard," 57–59; *Canton Repository*, Nov. 21, 22, 1894; Porter, *Life of William McKinley*, 403–4.

36. Peckham, "Ohio National Guard," 59–67; John Waksmundski, "Governor McKinley and the Workingman," *Historian* 38 (Aug. 1976): 636–43; *Canton Repository*, June 9, 10, 12, 1894; Leech, *In the Days of McKinley*, 54–55; Porter, *Life of William McKinley*, 402.

37. Cunningham and Miller, *Report of the Ohio Antietam Battlefield Commission*, 15–16; WM remarks at Pacific Grove, Calif., May 11, 1901, roll 84, WM Papers, LC; *Canton Repository*, May 17, 1896, May 25, 1900; Herbert Croly, *Marcus Alonzo Hanna: His Life and Work* (New York: Macmillan, 1912), 44–46.

38. *Canton Repository*, May 21, 1896; *Harper's Weekly*, Aug. 29, 1896; pamphlet published by the National Headquarters of the Union Veterans' Patriotic League, New York City, Aug. 8, 1896, in "Spanish-American War" file, WM Papers, RRLMM; *Cleveland Leader*, Oct. 17, 20, 1896.

39. WM to S. J. McCready, Sept. 5, 1896, roll 17, WM Papers, LC; *Canton Repository*, Sept. 17, 1896.

40. Smith, *McKinley, the People's Choice*, 48; *Canton Repository*, Aug. 20, 1896; *Cleveland Leader*, Sept. 3, 1897.

41. *Canton Repository*, Aug. 2, Oct. 11, 1896; *Cleveland Leader*, Oct. 10, 1896; *New York Tribune*, Oct. 10, 1896; William Henry Perrin, ed., *History of Stark County with an Outline Sketch of Ohio* (Chicago: Baskin & Battey, 1881), 639–40, 840.

42. *Mahoning Register*, Sept. 5, 1861; *Pittsburgh Times*, Sept. 7, 1901, clipping in WM scrapbooks (MIC 143), OHS.

43. *Canton Repository*, Aug. 19, 1868, May 28, 1875, Aug. 25, Sept. 1, 1876; *Confederate Veteran* 10 (July 1902): 292, 294; S. W. Fordyce in *Confederate Veteran* 19 (May 1911): 244; *Youngstown Evening Register and Tribune*, Sept. 14, 1876.

44. *Cleveland Leader*, Sept. 19, 1895; D. H. Russell to Ida S. McKinley, Sept. 25, 1901, letters of condolence, WM Papers, WRHS. On the theme of reunion, see Nina Silber, *The Romance of Reunion: Northerners and the South, 1865–1900* (Chapel Hill: Univ. of North Carolina Press, 1993).

45. Albert Galloway Keller and Maurice R. Davie, eds., *Essays of William Graham Sumner*, 2 vols. (New Haven: Yale Univ. Press, 1934), 2:297; National Association for the Advancement of Colored People, *Thirty Years of Lynching in the United States, 1889–1918* (New York: NAACP, 1919), 29. See also Rayford W. Logan, *The Betrayal of the Negro from Rutherford B. Hayes to Woodrow Wilson*, new ed. (New York: Collier Books, 1965).

46. *Cleveland Leader*, Feb. 28, Sept. 29, 1896, Mar. 3, 1897; E. T. Heald, typescript biography of WM, vol. 6, 23:82–84.

47. *Inaugural Addresses of the Presidents of the United States,* House Doc. 218, 87th Cong., 1st sess., 173; *Cleveland Leader,* Aug. 28, 1900; Clarence A. Bacote, "Negro Officeholders in Georgia Under President McKinley," *Journal of Negro History* 44 (July 1959): 234; *Our Colored Citizens,* 1900 campaign pamphlet, OHS.

48. Leech, *In the Days of McKinley,* 119; *Cleveland Leader,* Mar. 5–6, 1897; *Canton Repository,* Jan. 24, 1897; *Inaugural Addresses,* 176–77.

49. George F. Parker, *Recollections of Grover Cleveland* (New York: Century, 1911), 249–50.

50. *Cleveland Leader,* Aug. 21, 26, Sept. 3, 1897; John A. Porter to H. S. Clement, Aug. 12, 1897, and John A. Porter to Jacob Kline, Aug. 23, 1897, roll 21, WM Papers, LC; *Harper's Weekly,* Aug. 21, 1897; *Inaugural Addresses,* 175; Henry S. Pritchett, "Some Recollections of President McKinley and the Cuban Intervention," *North American Review* 189 (Mar. 1909): 399–401; *New York Times,* Sept. 1, 1912.

51. *Speeches and Addresses of William McKinley from March 1, 1897, to May 30, 1900* (New York: Doubleday & McClure, 1900), 42–43; *Canton Repository,* Apr. 10, 1898; Hermann Hagedorn, *Leonard Wood: A Biography,* 2 vols. (New York: Harper & Brothers, 1931), 1:141.

52. Gerald F. Linderman, *The Mirror of War: American Society and the Spanish-American War* (Ann Arbor: Univ. of Michigan Press, 1974), 130–31; WM to Helen McKinley, Feb. 5, 1898, roll 17, and receipt from W. H. Cooper for framing the commission, Feb. 14, 1898 [also with May 1, 1898, date], roll 61, WM Papers, LC; Rood, comp., *Memories of the White House,* 254; typed copy of an undated item beginning "Inkstand, Pen and Penholder," from Webb C. Hayes in Subject File H-K, and Diary of George Bruce Cortelyou, Apr. 23–26, May 3, 1898, George Bruce Cortelyou Papers, LC.

53. *Cleveland Leader,* Sept. 21, 1898, Apr. 20, 1902; *Canton Repository,* June 3, 1900, July 1, 1901; Pritchett, "Some Recollections," 397–99; Cortelyou Diary, Apr. 22, May 3, June 17, 1898; William Eleroy Curtis, "President McKinley and the War," *Chautauquan* 28 (Oct. 1898): 50–51; Lewis L. Gould, *The Spanish-American War and President McKinley* (Lawrence: Univ. Press of Kansas, 1982), 55–59; William Seale, *The President's House: A History,* 2 vols. (Washington, D.C.: White House Historical Association, 1986), 2:630–33; Irwin Hood (Ike) Hoover, *Forty-two Years in the White House* (Boston: Houghton Mifflin, 1934), 24.

54. Cortelyou Diary, May 3, June 8, 17, 1898; A. B. Nettleton, "The Man at the Helm," *American Monthly Review of Reviews* 18 (Oct. 1898): 405–14; Theodore Roosevelt, *The Rough Riders and Men of Action* (New York: Charles Scribner's Sons, 1926), 240; Leech, *In the Days of McKinley,* 191–92, 233–34, 266, 270; *Cleveland Leader,* July 9, 1901, Apr. 20, 1902; Curtis, "President McKinley and the War," 50.

55. Cortelyou Diary, Aug. 23, 1898; Leech, *In the Days of McKinley,* 315.

56. J. A. Porter to H. C. Corbin, Sept. 9, 1898, and G. B. Cortelyou to H. C. Corbin, Sept. 12, 15, 1898, roll 33, WM to C. V. Hard, June 23, 1898, roll 18, and WM to James F. McKinley Nov. 1, 1899, roll 42, WM Papers, LC; Cortelyou Diary, Jan. 1, 1900; *Canton Repository,* Nov. 15, 1900.

57. *Canton Repository,* May 29, Sept. 1, 1898; Heald, typescript biography of WM, vol. 8, 27:83; Cortelyou Diary, Sept. 20, 1898; *Cleveland Leader,* Aug. 28, 31, Sept. 4, 1898; unidentified clipping, Sept. 6, 1898, roll 62, WM Papers, LC.

58. Hoover, *Forty-two Years in the White House*, 24–25.

59. Leech, *In the Days of McKinley*, 234–36; *Youngstown Daily Vindicator*, Oct. 7, 1898; John A. Porter to Wm. J. McIntyre, June 10, 1898, roll 30, WM Papers, LC; *Cleveland Leader*, Aug. 28, 1900; Willard B. Gatewood Jr., "Ohio's Negro Battalion in the Spanish-American War," *Northwest Ohio Quarterly* 45 (Spring 1973): 55–66; Willard B. Gatewood Jr., *Black Americans and the White Man's Burden, 1898–1903* (Urbana: Univ. of Illinois Press, 1975), 88–91, 94–95, 112–14, 119.

60. Olcott, *Life of William McKinley*, 1:219; Ezra J. Warner, *Generals in Gray: Lives of Confederate Commanders* (Baton Rouge: Louisiana State Univ. Press, 1959), 40–41, 178–79, 264–65, 332–33; *Cleveland Leader*, May 17, June 10, 1898. McKinley also appointed former Confederate general Simon B. Buckner to the Board of Visitors to the U.S. Military Academy; see the board's report for 1898.

61. *Cleveland Leader*, Dec. 16, 1898; *Speeches and Addresses of William McKinley* (1900), 158–59; H. H. Kohlsaat, *From McKinley to Harding: Personal Recollections of Our Presidents* (New York: Charles Scribner's Sons, 1923), 24–26. One result of McKinley's proposal to care for the graves of Confederate soldiers was the establishment of a "New Confederate Section" at Arlington National Cemetery; see "Confederate Dead," *Southern Historical Society Papers* 29 (1901): 354–55.

62. John Gingerich, "The Badge That McKinley Wore," *Keynoter* 91 (Spring 1991): 4–8; *New York Tribune*, Dec. 20, 1898, Jan. 15, 1899; J. K. Ohl to George B. Cortelyou, Dec. 22, 1898, roll 5, WM Papers, LC. As a Republican veteran, McKinley might also have been able to return captured Confederate flags to the Southern states, something that the Democratic Grover Cleveland attempted but failed to do. By the time McKinley was in office, a national encampment of the Grand Army of the Republic argued that it was time to return the flags, but McKinley, on the advice of Secretary of War Elihu Root that congressional action was necessary before the flags could be returned, made no attempt to return them. See John M. Taylor, "Grover Cleveland and the Rebel Banners," *Civil War Times Illustrated* 32 (Sept.–Oct. 1993): 22–24; GAR resolution with item by Theodore F. Lang, Oct. 1899, roll 69, and Elihu Root to the President, Apr. 10, 1900, roll 9, WM Papers, LC.

63. John S. Kountz to WM, Dec. 19, 1898, roll 64, WM Papers, LC; *Speeches and Addresses of William McKinley* (1900), 171.

64. Louis R. Harlan et al., eds., *The Booker T. Washington Papers*, 14 vols. (Urbana: Univ. of Illinois Press, 1972–89), 1:127–34, 376–81; *Speeches and Addresses of William McKinley* (1900), 176–78; *Cleveland Leader*, Nov. 12, 13, 1898; Richard B. Sherman, *The Republican Party and Black America: From McKinley to Hoover, 1896–1933* (Charlottesville: Univ. Press of Virginia, 1973), 12–14; R. C. Ransom to John E. Green, June 27, 1899, roll 7, and "The Sun," July 2, 1899, p. 121, roll 94, WM Papers, LC; *Canton Repository*, Dec. 6, 1899; Gatewood, *Black Americans and the White Man's Burden*, 115–16.

65. *Canton Repository*, Oct. 19, 1899; *Speeches and Addresses of William McKinley* (1900), 193, 216. See also WM to Henry Cabot Lodge, Sept. 8, 1900, pp. 22–37, roll 49, WM Papers, LC.

66. Heald, typescript biography of WM, vol. 10, 29:170–D; Myron T. Herrick to WM, July 1, 1897, roll 2, WM to John Sherman, Apr. 12, 1897, roll 17, George B. Cortelyou to Russell Hastings, Dec. 19, 1899, roll 44, and WM to Henry Cabot Lodge, Sept. 8, 1900, roll 49, WM Papers, LC.

67. *Canton Repository,* May 21, 1899.

68. Ibid.; T. H. Savage to WM, June 12, 26, 1899, roll 7, WM Papers, LC; *Winchester Evening Star,* Sept. 7, 1901.

69. *Canton Repository,* May 25, 1900; John W. Schildt, "State Monument Dedicated May 30, 1900," *Maryland Cracker Barrel,* June 1989, 8–9; Hastings, "Genealogy and Autobiography," chap. 17, p. 15; clipping from *New York Sun,* May 31, 1900, scrapbook, p. 132, roll 96, *Program of Ceremonies at the Dedication of the Maryland Soldier's Monument, Antietam, May 30, 1900,* roll 72, and Elihu Root speech, May 30, 1900, roll 83, WM Papers, LC; *Speeches and Addresses of William McKinley* (1900), 369–70.

70. *Canton Repository,* July 12–13, 1900; Heald, typescript biography of WM, vol. 11, 30:260, 266–67.

71. C. R. Mabee, *McKinley in the Witness Box* (Cleveland: Century, 1900), 10–11, 15–23, 160, 188–90.

72. *Cleveland Leader,* Aug. 31, 1900.

73. *Cleveland Leader,* Mar. 1, 1901; Joseph J. Brittain to David J. Hill, Mar. 20, 1901, roll 15, WM's remarks at El Paso, Tex., May 6, 1901, roll 84, and WM's remarks at Huntsville, Ala., Apr. 30, 1901, roll 84, WM Papers, LC. George Crook's army was often called, incorrectly, the Eighth Corps.

74. Stephen Ward Angell, *Bishop Henry McNeal Turner and African-American Religion in the South* (Knoxville: Univ. of Tennessee Press, 1992), 236; Bacote, "Negro Officeholders in Georgia," 237; *Inaugural Addresses,* 179; *Canton Repository,* May 2, 5, 1901.

75. *New York Tribune,* Apr. 30, 1901; Robert D. Meade to Watt P. Marchman, Dec. 5, 1947, WM biographical file, RBHPC.

76. *Canton Repository,* May 18, 24–25, 1901.

77. *Canton Repository,* June 23, Aug. 25, Sept. 2, 1901; Halstead, *Illustrious Life,* 227.

78. Heald, typescript biography of WM, vol. 12, 33:1; *Canton Repository,* Sept. 11, 1901.

79. *Peoria (Illinois) Star,* Sept. 17, 1901, clipping in WM scrapbooks, no. 126, vol. 3, WRHS.

80. Unidentified clipping dated Sept. 17 [1901], courtesy of Beth Cupp, Burton, Ohio; unidentified clipping dated Sept. 18 [1901], "Funeral" file, WM Papers, RRLMM.

81. *Canton Repository,* Sept. 16, 19, 22, 1901; Townsend, *Memorial Life of William McKinley,* 373; *Cleveland Leader,* Sept. 20, 21, 1901; "Late President McKinley," *Confederate Veteran* 9 (Sept. 1901): 395.

82. *Canton Repository,* Oct. 27, 1901, Sept. 14, 1902; *Stark County Democrat,* May 28, 1907; unidentified clipping dated either Sept. 14 or 19, 1907, in "Banquets" file and unidentified clipping dated Sept. 30, 1907, in "McKinley National Memorial Dedication" file, WM Papers, RRLMM; Frederic S. Hartzel, *The Nation's Memorial to William McKinley Erected at Canton, Ohio,* 2d ed. (Canton: McKinley National Memorial Association, 1929), 60; *Canton Free Press,* Aug. 16, 1992.

83. J. W. Minnich to Geo. B. Cortelyou, n.d., letter from Texas Division, United Daughters of the Confederacy, Sept. 18, 1901, and resolution from Camp Lomax, United Confederate Veteran Camp No. 151, Montgomery, Ala., Sept. 19, 1901, all in letters of condolence, WM Papers, WRHS; Shirley Donnelly, "General 'Tiger John' McCausland: The Man Who Burned Chambersburg," *West Virginia History* 23 (Jan.

1962): 141. See too the many tributes to McKinley from Southern leaders quoted in Grosvenor, *William McKinley*.

84. *Canton Repository*, Jan. 20, 1901.

85. William C. Chase, *Story of Stonewall Jackson* (Atlanta, Ga.: D. E. Luther, 1901), unnumbered pp. 7 (of intro.), 537–38; *New York Times*, Feb. 1, 1925, sec. 7, p. 12.

86. Dale Payne and Bob Beckelheimer, comps., *Tales and Trails from the Fayette [W.Va.] Tribune* (N.p.: n.p., 1991), 70–71. This reference is courtesy of Robert S. Conte.

BIBLIOGRAPHY

PRIMARY SOURCES

Manuscripts

William L. Clements Library, University of Michigan, Ann Arbor
    Schoff Civil War Collection
        Andrew J. Duncan Diary and [William McKinley] Orderly Book
Rutherford B. Hayes Presidential Center, Fremont, Ohio
    Mrs. Joseph E. Barrett. "Memories of the Civil War."
    John McNulty Clugston Diary
    Michael Deady Diary
    Russell Hastings Papers
    Lucy Webb Hayes Correspondence
    Rutherford B. Hayes Papers
    William McKinley Biographical File
    Joseph T. Webb Correspondence
    Alexander Wight Diary and Letters
Lenox Historical Society, Lenox Township, Ashtabula County, Ohio
    Benjamin L. Askue Jr. Letters
Library of Congress, Washington, D.C.
    George Bruce Cortelyou Papers
    William McKinley Papers
Mahoning Valley Historical Society, Youngstown, Ohio
    William McKinley Folder
    Poland Box 1801, #2A, Builders of Youngstown Collection
    Poland Schools File
University of Missouri–Rolla
    Western Historical Manuscript Collection
        John Holland Diary, 1865

H. Wayne Morgan Collection, Norman, Oklahoma
    Letter, William McKinley to Sarah McKinley, March 8, 1863
National Archives, Washington, D.C.
    Records of the Adjutant General's Office, RG 94
    Records of the U.S. Army Continental Commands, RG 393
Ohio Historical Society, Columbus
    Adjutant General, Civil War, Personnel Records
    John T. Booth Papers
    James M. Comly Papers
    William McKinley Civil War Diary
    William McKinley Scrapbooks
    Ohio Governors' Papers
    William T. Patterson Diary
Ramsayer Research Library, McKinley Museum of History, Science and
Industry, Canton, Ohio
    E. T. Heald Typescript Biography of William McKinley
    William McKinley Papers
U.S. Army Military History Institute, Carlisle Barracks, Pennsylvania
    Timothy R. Brookes Collection
        Isaac T. Williams Letters
    Hattie Burleigh Collection
        Martin R. Connolly Letters
    Civil War Misc. Collection
        Henry C. Campbell Memoir
        William H. Dunham Letters
        J. R. Test Letters
        Ephraim G. Wagley Memoir
        Ezra L. Walker Diary
        John W. Weed Memoir
    Civil War Times Illustrated Collection
        David McKinney Papers
        Jesse Middaugh Letters
        Isaac C. Nelson Diary
        William Noblitt Letter
        Edward E. Schweitzer Diary
        M. L. Sheets Diary
    James Parly Coburn Papers
    George Crook Papers
    Harrisburg Civil War Round Table Collection
        Robert B. Cornwell Letters
Virginia Military Institute Archives, Lexington, Virginia
    Joseph W. Crowther Diary
    William G. Watson Memoirs

Western Reserve Historical Society, Cleveland, Ohio
    John S. Ellen Diary
    William McKinley Papers
    William McKinley Scrapbooks
    Daniel May Diaries
West Virginia University Libraries, Morgantown
    West Virginia and Regional History Collection
        Roy Bird Cook Papers
            John W. Cracraft Diary

Ohio Newspapers

Ashland Times
Ashland Union
Ashtabula Sentinel (Jefferson)
Bellefontaine Republican
Bucyrus Weekly Journal
Canton Repository
Cleveland Weekly Herald
Cleveland Leader
Cleveland Plain Dealer
Daily Capital City Fact (Columbus)
Daily Ohio State Journal (Columbus)
Elyria Independent Democrat
Gallipolis Journal
Holmes County Republican (Millersburg)
Lorain County News (Wellington)
Mahoning Herald (Canfield)
Mahoning Register (Youngstown)
Mahoning Sentinel (Youngstown)
Mahoning Valley Vindicator (Youngstown)
Niles Daily News
Ohio Patriot (New Lisbon)
Painesville Telegraph
Stark County Democrat (Canton)
Youngstown Evening Register and Tribune

SECONDARY SOURCES

Books and Articles

Andre, Richard, Stan Cohen, and Bill Wintz. *Bullets and Steel: The Fight for the Great Kanawha Valley, 1861–1865.* Charleston, W.Va.: Pictorial Histories, 1995.

Barbour, Charlotte A. "Quartermastering for the 2nd Colorado Volunteers." *Colorado Magazine* 38 (Oct. 1961): 301–6.

Beck, Brandon H., and Charles S. Grunder. *Three Battles of Winchester: A History and Guided Tour*. Berryville, Va.: Country Publishers, 1988.

Benson, Evelyn Abraham, comp. *With the Army of West Virginia, 1861–1864: Reminiscences and Letters of Lt. James Abraham, Pennsylvania Dragoons, Company A, First Regiment, Virginia Cavalry*. Lancaster, Pa.: N.p., 1974.

Billings, John D. *Hardtack and Coffee: Or the Unwritten Story of Army Life*. 1889. Reprint. Gettysburg, Pa.: *Civil War Times Illustrated*, 1974.

Bowman, Forest J. "Capture of Generals Crook and Kelley." *Civil War Times Illustrated* 7 (Feb. 1969): 28–37.

Bradford, James C., ed. *Crucible of Empire: The Spanish-American War and Its Aftermath*. Annapolis, Md.: Naval Institute Press, 1993.

Brinkerhoff, H. R. *Some Army Reminiscences*. N.p.: Excelsior Press, 1889.

Byrne, Frank L., ed. *The View from Headquarters: Civil War Letters of Harvey Reid*. Madison: State Historical Society of Wisconsin, 1965.

Cohen, Stan. *The Civil War in West Virginia: A Pictorial History*. Charleston, W.Va.: Pictorial Histories, 1976.

———. *A Pictorial Guide to West Virginia's Civil War Sites*. Charleston, W.Va.: Pictorial Histories, 1990.

Coles, Harry L. *Ohio Forms an Army*. Columbus: Ohio State University Press, 1962.

Cook, Roy B. "William McKinley: The Soldier in West Virginia." *West Virginia Review* 1 (Mar. 1924): 18–19.

Cox, Jacob Dolson. *Military Reminiscences of the Civil War*. 2 vols. New York: Charles Scribner's Sons, 1900.

Cunningham, D., and W. W. Miller. *Report of the Ohio Antietam Battlefield Commission*. Springfield, Ohio: Springfield Publishing, 1904.

Curry, Richard O., and F. Gerald Ham, eds. "The Bushwhackers' War: Insurgency and Counter-Insurgency in West Virginia." *Civil War History* 10 (Dec. 1964): 416–33.

Curtis, William Eleroy. "President McKinley and the War." *Chautauquan* 28 (Oct. 1898): 49–53.

Dawson, Joseph G. III, ed. *Commanders in Chief: Presidential Leadership in Modern Wars*. Lawrence: University Press of Kansas, 1993.

De Forest, John William. *A Volunteer's Adventures: A Union Captain's Record of the Civil War*. New Haven: Yale University Press, 1946.

Donnelly, Clarence Shirley. *The Battle of Carnifex Ferry*. Fayetteville, W.Va.: State Sentinel, 1950.

Duffey, J. W. *Two Generals Kidnapped*. 4th ed. Moorefield, W.Va.: Moorefield Examiner, 1944.

Duncan, Richard R. *Lee's Endangered Left: The Civil War in Western Virginia Spring of 1864*. Baton Rouge: Louisiana State University Press, 1998.

———, ed. *Alexander Neil and the Last Shenandoah Valley Campaign: Letters of an Army Surgeon to His Family, 1864.* Shippensburg, Pa.: White Mane, 1996.

Du Pont, H. A. *The Campaign of 1864 in the Valley of Virginia and the Expedition to Lynchburg.* New York: National Americana Society, 1925.

Eby, Cecil D. Jr., ed. *A Virginia Yankee in the Civil War: The Diaries of David Hunter Strother.* Chapel Hill: University of North Carolina Press, 1961.

Everett, Marshall. *Complete Life of William McKinley and Story of His Assassination.* N.p.: Marshall Everett, 1901.

Ewing, E. E. *Bugles and Bells; Or, Stories Told Again. Including the Story of the Ninety-First Ohio Volunteer Infantry. Reunion Poems and Social Tributes.* Cincinnati: Curts & Jennings, 1899.

Favill, Josiah Marshall. *The Diary of a Young Officer Serving with the Armies of the United States During the War of the Rebellion.* Chicago: R. R. Donnelley, 1909.

Fay, John B. *The Capture of Maj. Genl's Crook and Kelley: An Adventure of the Civil War.* Copied from the *Cumberland Alleghenian* of Mar. 30, 1893.

Forsyth, George A. *Thrilling Days in Army Life.* 1900. Reprint. Lincoln: University of Nebraska Press, 1994.

Frassanito, William A. *Antietam: The Photographic Legacy of America's Bloodiest Day.* New York: Charles Scribner's Sons, 1978.

Gallagher, Gary W., ed. *Struggle for the Shenandoah: Essays on the 1864 Valley Campaign.* Kent, Ohio: Kent State University Press, 1991.

Gatewood, Willard B. Jr. *Black Americans and the White Man's Burden, 1898–1903.* Urbana: University of Illinois Press, 1975.

Geer, Emily Apt. *First Lady: The Life of Lucy Webb Hayes.* Kent, Ohio: Kent State University Press and Rutherford B. Hayes Presidential Center, 1984.

Gould, Lewis L. *The Presidency of William McKinley.* Lawrence: Regents Press of Kansas, 1980.

———. *The Spanish-American War and President McKinley.* Lawrence: University Press of Kansas, 1982.

Grosvenor, Charles H. *William McKinley: His Life and Work.* Washington, D.C.: Continental Assembly, 1901.

Halpine, Charles G. [Private Miles O'Reilly]. *Baked Meats of the Funeral.* New York: Carleton, 1866.

Halstead, Murat. *The Illustrious Life of William McKinley Our Martyred President.* N.p.: Murat Halstead, 1901.

Hanchett, William. *Irish: Charles G. Halpine in Civil War America.* Syracuse: Syracuse University Press, 1970.

Hassler, Warren W. Jr. "The Battle of South Mountain." *Maryland Historical Magazine* 52 (Mar. 1957): 39–64.

Heald, Edward Thornton. *The William McKinley Story.* [Canton, Ohio]: Stark County Historical Society, 1964.

Hewitt, William. *History of the Twelfth West Virginia Volunteer Infantry....* N.p.: Twelfth West Virginia Infantry Association, 1892.

Hirshson, Stanley P. *Farewell to the Bloody Shirt: Northern Republicans and the Southern Negro, 1877–1893.* Bloomington: Indiana University Press, 1962.

Hoogenboom, Ari. *Rutherford B. Hayes: Warrior and President.* Lawrence: University Press of Kansas, 1995.

Horton, [Joshua H.], and [?] Teverbaugh. *A History of the Eleventh Regiment, (Ohio Volunteer Infantry)....* Dayton, Ohio: W. J. Shuey, 1866.

Humphreys, Milton W. *A History of the Lynchburg Campaign.* Charlottesville, Va.: Michie, 1924.

Johnson, Patricia Givens. *The United States Army Invades the New River Valley May 1864.* Christiansburg, Va.: Walpa, 1986.

Kempfer, Lester L. *The Salem Light Guard: Company G, 36th Regiment Ohio Volunteer Infantry, Marietta, Ohio, 1861–5.* Chicago: Adams Press, 1973.

Keyes, C. M. *The Military History of the 123d Regiment Ohio Volunteer Infantry.* Sandusky, Ohio: Register Steam Press, 1874.

Le Duc, William G. *Recollections of a Civil War Quartermaster: The Autobiography of William G. Le Duc.* St. Paul, Minn.: North Central, 1963.

Leech, Margaret. *In the Days of McKinley.* New York: Harper and Brothers, 1959.

Lewis, Thomas A. *The Guns of Cedar Creek.* New York: Dell, 1988.

Lewis, Thomas A., and the editors of Time-Life Books. *The Shenandoah in Flames: The Valley Campaign of 1864.* Alexandria, Va.: Time-Life Books, 1987.

The Life of William McKinley. New York: P. F. Collier & Son, 1901.

Lincoln, William S. *Life with the Thirty-fourth Massachusetts Infantry in the War of the Rebellion.* Worcester: Noyes, Snow, 1879.

Linderman, Gerald F. *The Mirror of War: American Society and the Spanish-American War.* Ann Arbor: University of Michigan Press, 1974.

Logan, Rayford W. *The Betrayal of the Negro from Rutherford B. Hayes to Woodrow Wilson.* New ed. New York: Collier Books, 1965.

Lord, Francis A. *They Fought for the Union.* Harrisburg, Pa.: Stackpole, 1960.

Lowry, Terry. *September Blood: The Battle of Carnifex Ferry.* Charleston, W.Va.: Pictorial Histories, 1985.

Lusk, William Thompson. *War Letters of William Thompson Lusk, Captain, Assistant Adjutant-General, United States Volunteers, 1861–1863, Afterward M.D., LL.D.* New York: Privately printed, 1911.

Lyle, W. W. *Lights and Shadows of Army Life....* Cincinnati: R. W. Carroll, 1865.

Lynch, Charles H. *The Civil War Diary, 1862–1865, of Charles H. Lynch, 18th Conn. Vol's.* Hartford, Conn.: Case, Lockwood & Brainard, 1915.

Mabee, C. R. *McKinley in the Witness Box.* Cleveland: Century, 1900.

McClure, Alexander K., and Charles Morris. *The Authentic Life of William McKinley Our Third Martyr President.* N.p.: W. E. Scull, 1901.

McConnell, Stuart. *Glorious Contentment: The Grand Army of the Republic, 1865–1900.* Chapel Hill: University of North Carolina Press, 1992.

McElroy, Richard L. *William McKinley and Our America: A Pictorial History.* Canton, Ohio: Stark County Historical Society, 1996.

McKinley, William. *Abraham Lincoln: An Address by William McKinley of Ohio Before the Marquette Club, Chicago, Feb. 12, 1896.* N.p.: N.p., 1896.

McKinley, William Jr. "Personal Recollections of Rutherford B. Hayes." *Chautauquan* 17 (Apr. 1893): 42–44.

McKinney, Tim. *The Civil War in Fayette County, West Virginia.* Charleston, W.Va.: Pictorial Histories, 1988.

———. *Robert E. Lee at Sewell Mountain: The West Virginia Campaign.* Charleston, W.Va.: Pictorial Histories, 1990.

McManus, Howard Rollins. *The Battle of Cloyds Mountain: The Virginia and Tennessee Railroad Raid, April 29–May 19, 1864.* Lynchburg, Va.: H.E. Howard, 1989.

Miller, Edward A. Jr. *Lincoln's Abolitionist General: The Biography of David Hunter.* Columbia: University of South Carolina Press, 1997.

Moore, J. Scott. "General Hunter's Raid." *Southern Historical Society Papers* 27 (1899): 179–91.

Morgan, H. Wayne. *America's Road to Empire: The War with Spain and Overseas Expansion.* New York: Wiley, 1965.

———. *William McKinley and His America.* Syracuse: Syracuse University Press, 1963.

———, ed. "A Civil War Diary of William McKinley." *Ohio Historical Quarterly* 69 (July 1960): 272–90.

Nettleton, A. B. "The Man at the Helm." *American Monthly Review of Reviews* 18 (Oct. 1898): 405–14.

Official Roster of the Soldiers of the State of Ohio in the War of the Rebellion, 1861–1866. 12 vols. Cincinnati: Ohio Valley Publishing and Manufacturing, 1886–95.

Olcott, Charles S. *The Life of William McKinley.* 2 vols. Boston: Houghton Mifflin, 1916.

Phillips, Edward H. *The Shenandoah Valley in 1864: An Episode in the History of Warfare.* Charleston, S.C.: Citadel, 1965.

Porter, Robert P. *Life of William McKinley, Soldier, Lawyer, Statesman. With Biographical Sketch of Garret A. Hobart.* 4th ed. Cleveland: N.G. Hamilton, 1896.

"President McKinley in War Times." *McClure's Magazine* 11 (July 1898): 209–24.

"President William McKinley." *Ohio Archaeological and Historical Publications* 10 (1902): 232–35.

Priest, John Michael. *Before Antietam: The Battle for South Mountain.* New York: Oxford University Press, 1992.

Pritchett, Henry S. "Some Recollections of President McKinley and the Cuban Intervention." *North American Review* 189 (Mar. 1909): 397–403.

Putnam, George Haven. *Memories of My Youth, 1844–1865.* New York: G. P. Putnam's Sons, 1914.

Reid, Whitelaw. *Ohio in the War.* 2 vols. Cincinnati: Moore, Wilstach & Baldwin, 1868.

Risch, Erna. *Quartermaster Support of the Army: A History of the Corps, 1775–1939.* Washington, D.C.: Quartermaster Historian's Office, Office of the Quartermaster General, 1962.

Rood, Henry, comp. *Memories of the White House: The Home Life of Our Presidents from Lincoln to Roosevelt, Being Personal Recollections of Colonel W. H. Crook.* Boston: Little, Brown, 1911.

Rowe, Willis S. *Boyhood Homes of William McKinley.* N.p.: Willis S. Rowe, 1903.

Russell, Henry B. *The Lives of William McKinley and Garret A. Hobart.* Hartford, Conn.: A. D. Worthington, 1896.

Russell, John W. "McKinley at Antietam." *Munsey's Magazine* 40 (Mar. 1909): 787–88.

Saunier, Joseph A. *A History of the Forty-seventh Regiment Ohio Veteran Volunteer Infantry.* Hillsboro, Ohio: Lyle, [1903].

Sawrey, Robert D. *Dubious Victory: The Reconstruction Debate in Ohio.* Lexington: University Press of Kentucky, 1992.

Scammon, E. Parker. "West Virginia, and Some Incidents of the Civil War." *Catholic World* 57 (July 1893): 505–10.

Schmitt, Martin F., ed. *General George Crook: His Autobiography.* Norman: University of Oklahoma Press, 1960.

Sears, Stephen W. *Landscape Turned Red: The Battle of Antietam.* New York: Ticknor and Fields, 1983.

Sheridan, Philip H. *Personal Memoirs of P. H. Sheridan.* 2 vols. New York: Charles L. Webster, 1888.

Sherman, Richard B. *The Republican Party and Black America: From McKinley to Hoover, 1896–1933.* Charlottesville: University Press of Virginia, 1973.

Silber, Nina. *The Romance of Reunion: Northerners and the South, 1865–1900.* Chapel Hill: University of North Carolina Press, 1993.

Sinkler, George. *The Racial Attitudes of American Presidents: From Abraham Lincoln to Theodore Roosevelt.* Garden City, N.Y.: Doubleday, 1971.

Speeches and Addresses of William McKinley from His Election to Congress to the Present Time. New York: D. Appleton, 1893.

Speeches and Addresses of William McKinley from March 1, 1897, to May 30, 1900. New York: Doubleday & McClure, 1900.

Stark, William B. "The Great Skedaddle." *Atlantic Monthly* 162 (July 1938): 86–94.

Stegmaier, Mark Joseph. "The Kidnapping of Generals Crook and Kelley by the McNeill Rangers." *West Virginia History* 29 (Oct. 1967): 13–47.

Stratemeyer, Edward. *American Boys' Life of William McKinley.* Boston: Lothrop, Lee & Shepard, 1901.

Stutler, Boyd B. *West Virginia in the Civil War.* Charleston, W.Va.: Education Foundation, 1963.

Summers, Festus P. *The Baltimore and Ohio in the Civil War.* New York: G. P. Putnam's Sons, 1939.

Sutton, J. J. *History of the Second Regiment West Virginia Cavalry Volunteers, During the War of the Rebellion.* Portsmouth, Ohio: N.p., 1892.

Taylor, James E. *With Sheridan Up the Shenandoah Valley in 1864: Leaves from a Special Artist's Sketchbook and Diary.* Western Reserve Historical Society Publication 173. Dayton, Ohio: Morningside House, 1989.

Throne, Mildred, ed. "A Commissary in the Union Army: Letters of C. C. Carpenter." *Iowa Journal of History* 53 (Jan. 1955): 59–88.

Titherington, R. H. "A Brief Outline of McKinley's Career." *Munsey's Magazine* 26 (Nov. 1901): 161–73.

Townsend, G. W. *Memorial Life of William McKinley.* N.p.: D. Z. Howell, 1901.

Walker, Gary C. *The War in Southwest Virginia, 1861–1865.* 3d ed., rev. Roanoke, Va.: A & W Enterprise, 1985.

Walker, William C. *History of the Eighteenth Regiment Conn. Volunteers in the War for the Union.* Norwich, Conn.: The Committee, 1885.

The War of the Rebellion: A Compilation of the Official Records of the Union and Confederate Armies. 128 vols. Washington, D.C.: U.S. Government Printing Office, 1880–1901.

Ward, J. E. D. *Twelfth Ohio Volunteer Inf[antry].* Ripley, Ohio: N.p., 1864.

Welcher, Frank J. *The Union Army, 1861–1865: Organization and Operations.* 2 vols. Bloomington: Indiana University Press, 1989–93.

Wert, Jeffry D. *From Winchester to Cedar Creek: The Shenandoah Campaign of 1864.* New York: Simon & Schuster, 1987.

————. *Mosby's Rangers.* New York: Simon & Schuster, 1990.

White, William Allen. *The Autobiography of William Allen White.* New York: Macmillan, 1946.

Wildes, Thomas F. *Record of the One Hundred and Sixteenth Regiment Ohio Infantry Volunteers in the War of the Rebellion.* Sandusky, Ohio: I. F. Mack & Bro., 1884.

Williams, Charles Richard. *The Life of Rutherford Birchard Hayes, Nineteenth President of the United States.* 2 vols. Boston: Houghton Mifflin, 1914.

————, ed. *Diary and Letters of Rutherford Birchard Hayes, Nineteenth President of the United States.* 5 vols. Columbus: Ohio State Archaeological and Historical Society, 1922–26.

Williams, T. Harry. *Hayes of the Twenty-third: The Civil War Volunteer Officer.* New York: Knopf, 1965.

Williams, T. Harry, and Stephen E. Ambrose. "The 23d Ohio." *Civil War Times Illustrated* 3 (May 1964): 22–25.

Wood, Richard E. "The South and Reunion, 1898." *Historian* 31 (May 1969): 415–30.

Woodford, Stewart L. *Life and Speeches of William McKinley.* New York: J. S. Ogilvie, 1896.

Woodward, C. Vann. *The Strange Career of Jim Crow.* 3d ed., rev. New York: Oxford University Press, 1974.

INDEX

Roberts, Cyrus, 94
Robinson, John C., Gen., 4, 122
Robinson, John, Pvt., 19
Robinson, Sarah, 54
Roosevelt, Theodore, 128, 133, 144
Root, Elihu, 135
Rosecrans, William S., Brig. Gen., 9, 14, 16, 21, 22, 23, 43, 115
Rosser, Thomas L., 131

Salem (Ohio), 55
Scammon, E. Parker, Gen., 24, 31, 48, 54, 56, 115; at Antietam, 39; ban on newspaper correspondence, 19; capture of, 62–63; as disciplinarian, 9, 16, 19, 38, 57; and Lewisburg march, 61; at South Mountain, 38
Scott, Nathan B., 91
Seymour, Horatio, 109
Shafter, William, Gen., 129
Sharpsburg (Maryland), 38, 43
Sheridan, Philip, Gen., 79, 80, 81, 95, 103, 115, 123, 140; at Cedar Creek, 87–90, 89; command of, 78; destruction in Shenandoah Valley, 86; at Fisher's Hill, 84–85; and Masonry, 100; at Opequon, 82, 83–84; and partisan attacks, 85–86; voting in election of 1864, 91, 92
"Sheridan's Ride" (Read), 88, 108
Sherman, William T., Gen., 63, 81, 93, 116
Sickles, Daniel E., Gen., 122, 123
Sigel, Franz, Gen., 63, 66, 122
Slaves: antislavery movement, 7–8; fugitive, 24, 34, 61, 66, 69
Smith, Joseph, 8
Soldiers and Sailors Reunion, 116
Spanish-American War, 77, 127–31, 129, 133–34, 135, 140
Sparrow House, 3, 62
Spotsylvania battlefield, 104
Stamp, von, Lieutenant, 102
Stanton, Edwin M., 87, 108, 130
Stark County Democrat, 111
Stevenson, John D., Brig. Gen., 95, 96
Strother, David, 68
Stuart, J. E. B., Gen., 43, 132
Supplies: food rations, 28–30, 32, 38–41; missing, 51–52; quartermaster's role

in, 50–51, 61; transport of, 16, 25, 30, 61, 63; uniforms, 11–12; weapons, 12–14

Tactics (Casey), 52
Tailof, Ivan, Maj., 102
Taylor, James E., 85, 86, 88, 89, 90, 93
Telegraphic dispatches, 26–27
Thoburn, Joseph, Col., 82, 83, 87
Thomas, George H., Gen., 93
Thurman, Allen G., 109
Tiady, Andy, Pvt., 19
Tod, David, Gov., 44, 52, 118, 119
Tolles, Cornelius W., 86
Tredegar Iron Works, 68
Turner, Henry M., 133, 137
Tuskegee Institute, 133

Uncle Tom's Cabin (Stowe), 8
Underground Railroad, 7
U.S. Military Academy, 112–13

Vallandigham, Clement, 57–58, 109
Vallandigham, Clement (Rev.), 58
Vermont National Guard, 127
Veterans: in Antietam monument dedication, 135; black, 109, 116–17; at funeral service, 142; Grand Army of the Republic encampments, 119, 121, 127, 134, 141; in inaugural parade, 126; pensions for, 116; posthumous tribute to Hayes, 119; preferences to, 134; in presidential campaigns, 121–24, 135–36; reunions of, 107–8, 112, 115–16, 121, 127, 134, 135, See also Confederate veterans
Virginia Military Institute, 67, 68
Virginia and Tennessee Railroad, 31, 61, 63, 65

Wade, Benjamin, 8
Wadsworth, Lydia, 6
Waite, Morrison R., 115
War Room, 128, 129
Washington, Booker T., 133
Washington, D. C., 100, 112, 121; Early's advance on, 71; Grand Review in, 101; Ohio 23d Infantry in, 34
Webb, Joseph T., 41, 48, 54, 99

MAJOR McKINLEY

was designed by Will Underwood; composed in Monotype Fournier on an Apple Quadra system
using QuarkXPress by the BookPage, Inc.; printed by sheet-fed offset lithography on 50-pound
Turin Book natural vellum stock (an acid-free, totally chlorine-free paper), notch bound in signatures
with paper covers printed in three colors on 12-point stock finished with matte film lamination by
Thomson-Shore, Inc.; and published by The Kent State University Press, Kent, Ohio 44242.